The Fisherman's Ocean

The Fisherman's Ocean

David A. Ross, Ph.D.

STACKPOLE
BOOKS

Published by
STACKPOLE BOOKS
5067 Ritter Road
Mechanicsburg, PA 17055
www.stackpolebooks.com

Printed in the United States

10 9 8 7 6 5

First edition

Cover photo from Woods Hole Oceanographic Institution
Cover design by Caroline M. Stover

Library of Congress Cataloging-in-Publication Data

Ross, David A., 1936–
    The fisherman's ocean / David A. Ross.—1st ed.
      p.   cm.
    Includes bibliographic references (p.).
    ISBN 0-8117-2771-8 (pbk.)
      1. Saltwater fishing. 2. Fishery oceanography. 3. Marine
fishes. I. Title.

SH457 .R68 2000
799.1'6—dc21
                                        00-035785

ISBN 978-0-8117-2771-6

Contents

PART III Ocean Fishing

Appendices

Preface

I have been both an oceanographer and a fisherman for more than thirty-five years, but it took me quite a while before I learned the value of combining my profession and hobby. About a decade ago on my birthday my wife, Edith, arranged a fly-fishing trip for me with my good friend Dennis Sabo. It was to be my first time fly fishing and I remember the experience as if it happened yesterday.

Dennis was a superb charter fisherman working out of Falmouth on Cape Cod, Massachusetts. He had an uncanny ability to find striped bass, even at a time when few were around, and he was one of the first charter captains in the area to encourage fly and light-tackle fishing on his boat. Dennis also was a scientist, a marine biologist who taught at the Massachusetts Maritime Academy.

I anticipated starting my trip with Dennis at 4 A.M., his usual departure time for trips to the well-known Wasque Rip off Martha's Vineyard, a few miles from Cape Cod. But instead he said that we would leave at 10 A.M., a startling time, since almost everyone on Cape Cod starts to fish very early in the morning. Nevertheless, we got into his 26-foot boat, *Peptide*, and traveled about an hour or so to a beautiful long rip near Nantucket Island that I'd never seen before. We were the only boat in the area. Finding fish in August can be difficult in this part of New England, and I was not very optimistic.

We stopped short of the rip, and Dennis gave me a fly-casting lesson with my new 8/9 weight Fenwick rod, Martin reel, and floating line. It only took me about fifteen minutes to become an "accomplished" caster, able to toss a Deceiver-like fly twenty feet or so about fifty percent of the time. Dennis said the bluefish would show in a few minutes. I thought he was blowing smoke, but within a few minutes his words came true. Hungry 6- to 8- pound bluefish came roaring down the rip in full view and crashed into my fly, regardless of the awful presentation. I had non-stop action for about an hour and a half. Finally I told Dennis that I wanted to stop, even though the fish were still biting, simply because I thought it could not get any better and this is how I wanted to remember my first day fly fishing. That remains one of my best fishing days ever.

How did Dennis know that the fish would show at this place and at this time? Well, Dennis fished almost every day and studied the water, the tides and currents, was aware of bottom structure, and knew something about the biology of fish. I also know something about the ocean, and after listening to him explain why he thought the bluefish were there, I realized how a knowledge of the ocean, its fish, and specific environments could help one find and catch fish.

Dennis and I fished and talked many times after that day and we decided to write up some of our ideas on these subjects. We started many outlines but never seemed to get further, and Dennis died a short time later.

I kept thinking about marine science and fishing, but I wasn't really motivated to write until another experience gave me the encouragement I needed to get started. On Saturday, June 24, 1995, I went to Martha's Vineyard to fish in the annual striped bass fly-fishing tournament. This is a fun catch-and-release event where "off-island" people, like me, are matched with island locals to fish from the shore for striped bass from 7 P.M. to 1 A.M. Plaques are given to the teams that catch and release the most fish, the largest fish, and so forth, and there is a raffle for larger prizes.

I was paired with Ralph Carrieri Jr., a computer jock who knows the island fairly well, and we took off for a place called Lambert's Cove. We fished in a broad open area, casting into a beautiful sunset. That year about two hundred people had entered the tournament and around forty of them were also fishing Lambert's Cove. A few went farther down the coast and fished off a rocky point that jutted out into Vineyard Sound. As best I can remember, very few fish were caught in the cove before it got dark, and the one I caught—about 28-inches—may have been the biggest. It gave me a wonderful fight as it raced back and forth along the beach. Ralph and I later went to other places, but that was the only fish we caught that night. The next morning, we learned that the guys who fished the rocky point did very well, but that most others only got one or two fish.

That afternoon I returned by ferry to my home in Falmouth on Cape Cod and decided to fish that night in a favorite estuary, Bournes Pond. I started about the same time as the night before at a favorite spot near the inlet where, with an incoming tide, I can slowly drift and work a fly along the edge of a current. The tides are tricky in this estuary, and the time of maximum current here is very different than it is just a few hundred feet away in the open ocean. Then, however, I didn't really appreciate the importance of this difference.

I quickly started to catch stripers and decided to keep count. Within two hours I had caught and released fifty-three stripers, mostly 20 inches or so, all on the same fly and in the same place. Early in the count I was excited, but by the time I quit (and the fish were still biting) I was actually getting depressed. I was thinking, "Are fish like stripers so dumb that they can be so easily caught?" One possible answer was: No, I was just in the right place at the right time and doing the right thing. But if I was so smart or good, why had I only gotten one strike and one fish in six hours of hard fishing a few miles away the previous night? The possibility that fish, or at least stripers, really are dumb was not very appealing, as it questioned the value of fishing as a challenging sport. Finding the correct answer turned me back to thinking about writing this book.

The question about fish intelligence is important to me. As a professional oceanographer at Woods Hole Oceanographic Institution, I should know the answers to questions like this or at least where to find them. This may sound like a simple task—find the right scientific book or article, read it, and you should be able to outfish anybody on the water. Well there are no such books or articles. In ichthyology books, game fish like stripers, tarpon, bonefish, and marlin do not get special treatment among the 20,000 or more species covered, and they may not even be specifically mentioned. Fish scientists often focus on smaller species that can be studied in an aquarium. Anglers, on the other hand, seek big, fast, strong fish, which are hard to study in a laboratory or in their natural environment, the ocean.

Nevertheless, I did find some useful material about fish and started to combine it with basic marine science. At about the same time, I began writing a column on marine science for fly fishers in *Saltwater Fly Fishing* magazine, and I seriously began to explore the question of how marine science could help one find and catch fish.

Fishing is not a science, and if it were, it probably wouldn't be as much fun. Scientists seek to know what cause produces what effect. We strive to find logic, patterns, and predictability in the phenomena we study. These goals, of course, are not unique to scientists. Most people look to establish such patterns in their everyday life, and we expect to find such patterns in other creatures. Our pets, for example, often follow fairly consistent patterns in feeding, sleeping, and other activities. But many times we don't know what causes these patterns, and this is often the case with fish.

Fish are widely diversified animals. Factors that control or influence their behavior include food, reproduction, season, temperature, sunlight and darkness, and tides, to name a few. The precise effects of these factors on specific species are often unknown to scientists. Studies of animals and their reactions to various stimuli and changes in environment are often hard to conduct with scientific precision. This is especially true with marine fish, because their environment cannot be duplicated or even closely simulated in a laboratory. One cannot be sure that the results of a laboratory study will accurately predict what will happen in the ocean.

Furthermore, fish are complex animals whose behavior may be influenced by factors we cannot detect or that are beyond our present understanding. There is still much to be learned about the various chemical, physical, and biological processes that occur in the ocean and how they affect fish. Finally, there is always a risk in extrapolating the results of an experiment or observation on one species of fish to another species. Different species often behave very differently in response to similar experiences.

In fact, much about fishing lacks obvious scientific answers. There are no scientific rules or equations that can guarantee that you will catch fish. Luck, insight or intuition, imagination, and determination are needed to be successful. However, considerable progress has been made in understanding how fish operate and survive in the ocean, and marine science may help you locate fish or indicate the best time to go fishing. It's good that we don't have all the answers; if we did, fishing would not be as much fun or such a challenge.

In writing and researching this book, I talked to many fishermen and learned much from them. I was encouraged that when I discussed science, most were interested. It is clear that from both the scientific and fishing viewpoints, there is much to learn about fish. I anticipate that future observations by fishermen will lead to new concepts or areas of study for marine scientists.

I wrote this book with two main objectives. The first was to describe the scientific information and marine processes most important to fishermen. My goal was to provide insight about fish behavior and the marine environment that can help anglers find fish. A key principle for successful fishing is simply to fish where the fish are. Having expensive boats and gear does not outweigh being in the right spot at the right time. Consider that Saturday night on Martha's Vineyard. Using a little scientific insight, I would have fished out on the point, rather than in the open part of the cove. Likewise, I also now know why I did so well in my local estuary on the following night, and much more importantly, that most fish are not dumb.

My second objective in writing was that by describing and explaining some of what happens in the ocean and some of the interesting things about fish, I might help make your time on the water more interesting, more pleasant, and more safe, even if you don't see or catch a single fish. You will enjoy fishing more if you know something about your quarry and understand what is happening below the water's surface. Although this book is written mainly for fly fishers, the ideas and information can be used in any type of angling.

Will you catch more fish after reading this book? I can't guarantee it. But I feel sure you will better understand the ocean and more fully enjoy your fishing.

David A. Ross
Scientist Emeritus
Woods Hole Oceanographic Institution

Acknowledgments

Many people I have either fished with or talked to have educated me as to various aspects of fishing. These individuals have been generous with their time and insight and I really appreciate it. They include: Ken Abrames, Bob Alexander, Peter Alves, Al Anderson, Dick Arthur, Jim Babb, Richard Benson, Tony Biski, Larry Backman, Joe Blaze, Michael Bothner, Gene Bourque, Ray Capobianco, Michael Champ, Dean Clark, Art Crago, George Christman, Stan Daggett, David Duane, Tom Garland, John Giacon, George Heimerdinger, John Holdren, Bill Hough, Doug Jowett, David R. Klausmeyer, Sam Levin, Richard Limeburner, Phillip Lobel, Nick Lyons (who also suggested the title for this book), Jim Macdonald, Ron Murphy, Dave Peros, Larry Pratt, Dave Reid, Terrence M. Rioux, George V. Roberts, Jr., Page Rogers, Tom Rosenbauer, Rich Rusznak, Steve Shiraka, Joe Smith, Ray Stachelek, Tony Stetzko, Terry Tessein, Brian Tucholke, and Jim Young. I have also learned much from the writings of some of the pioneers in the field of saltwater fly fishing, such as Lefty Kreh, Lou Tabory, and Mark Sosin. I especially want to thank Prof. Bill Krueger, a fishing companion and eminent ichthyologist who reviewed Chapters 6, 7, and 8.

I have also been fortunate to discuss many aspects of marine science and fishing with my colleagues in the Woods Hole science community, several of whom are mentioned above. I would especially like to thank the Woods Hole Oceanographic Insitution, which provided me with office space and support for graphics and other needs.

I would like to acknowledge Judith M. Schnell, vice president and editorial director, and Jon Rounds, associate editor, both of Stackpole Books. Judith made the decision to publish this somewhat different type of fishing book and offered encouragement and insight throughout its development and production. Jon worked with me on many of the details that go into a book's production. He has been most helpful.

I would especially like to thank four people. The first is the late Captain Dennis Sabo, who introduced me to the sport of saltwater fly fishing and whom I have mentioned earlier in the preface. The second is Joe Healy, editor of *Saltwater Fly Fishing*. Joe, in addition to his excellent editorial work on my articles in SFF, has always encouraged me to write this book. He also reviewed and edited the entire manuscript, and I am very pleased with the way he improved all aspects of the text. Joe also is fun to fish with. The third person is Richard Pittenger, a retired admiral, former Oceanographer of the Navy, and most important to me, a loyal fishing companion. I have learned much from him about the ocean, fishing, and fishermen. He also reviewed several chapters. Finally I would like to thank my wife Edith, who has tolerated my using most of our house to write this book. Edith is my main fishing companion, although she rarely actually fishes but mainly maneuvers the boat and helps find fish. She is better at both these things than I am. I clearly am blessed.

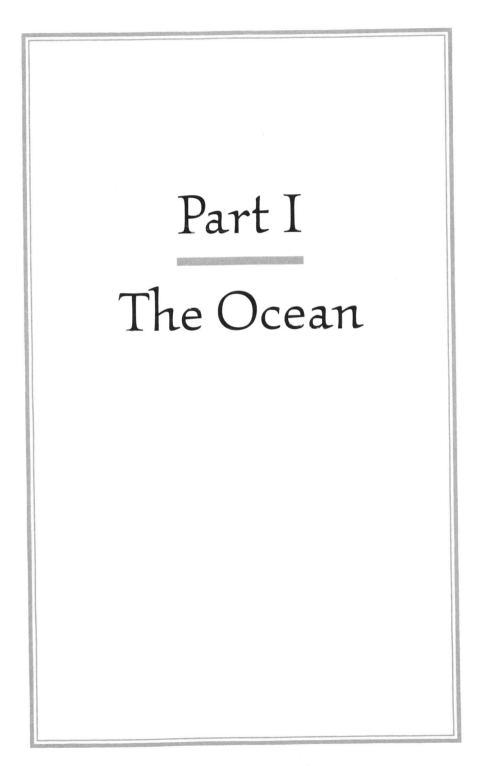

Part I

The Ocean

Chapter 1

The Marine Environment

THE DIMENSIONS OF THE OCEAN

The ocean is immense, really immense. Fully 71 percent of the surface area of our planet is covered by water. The shoreline, the physical boundary between ocean and land, is estimated to have a worldwide length of about 250,000 miles. If we divided these 250,000 miles among the six billion people living on Earth, each person would get about three inches of space along the ocean's shoreline. (You've probably had fishing days during which the shoreline seemed this crowded!) But if we do a similar calculation involving the entire ocean, including its depth and thus its

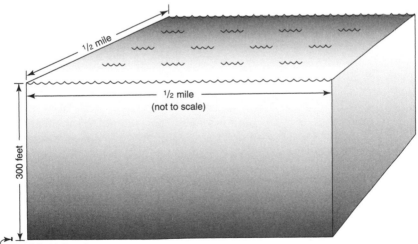

Fig. 1-1 This illustration shows how much of the ocean an individual would receive if the ocean was divided among each of the about 6 billion individuals on this planet. Only the angler (lower left) and the 300-foot line are drawn to scale; if the half-mile lines were drawn to scale they would be about nine times the length of the 300-foot line. Not everyone gets a surface section.

volume, the results are startling. Looking offshore and dividing the volume of the ocean among our six billion friends and neighbors, we see that everyone would have a section that is a half-mile long, a half-mile wide, and about 300 feet high. As I said, the ocean is immense.

The total volume of the ocean is 318 million cubic miles. These 318 million cubic miles of water equal 97.2 percent of all the water on Earth's surface. Another 7 million cubic miles of water are contained in polar ice caps and glaciers. If this ice were to melt and flow back into the ocean, the ocean would then have 99.35 percent of the world's water. Freshwater lakes contain a total of 30,000 cubic miles of water (0.009 percent of the world's water), and all of the rivers and streams of the world contain only 300 cubic miles of water (a mere 0.0001 percent of the world's water).

The average depth of the ocean is about 2,077 fathoms, or 12,464 feet, or 2.4 miles. Think about this average—it means that 50 percent of the ocean is deeper than 2.4 miles. If Earth's surface was completely smooth, without any mountains or valleys on land or under the ocean, the entire planet would be covered by about 8,000 feet of water. If all the water in the ocean were spread over the United States, it would make a layer about 90 miles thick.

These numbers clearly show that the ocean is the dominant surface feature of our planet. Because most of our planet is covered by water, one might wonder whether the name Earth is a misnomer; perhaps our planet should have been named Water. The ocean certainly is one of the last unexplored frontiers of our planet and is actively being studied by marine scientists.

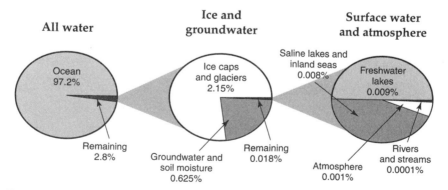

Fig. 1-2 The Earth's water supply. Note the tiny percentage of the total amount of water that is fresh water and drinkable.

CIRCULATION AND CURRENTS

The ocean, as well as the atmosphere above, is constantly moving, being driven by the wind, by density differences, and by gravity. The main force that causes the wind, and produces the density differences in ocean water, is radiant or solar energy from the sun. Solar energy is absolutely crucial to life on Earth, and drives many of the physical and biological processes that occur in the ocean; therefore, solar energy also influences, although perhaps not obviously, many aspects of saltwater fishing.

The atmosphere and the ocean are so closely intertwined that it is hard to ignore one when talking about the other. As atmospheric winds exert stress on the surface of the ocean, the water responds by moving. The product is the wind-driven circulation of the ocean. (The actual direction of the current, however, is often influenced by other factors, such as the position of land and the Coriolis effect.)

Atmospheric winds and ocean currents transport heat from low-latitude (equatorial) regions, where there is more incoming solar radiation, to high-latitude (polar) regions, where there is less solar radiation. Such movement of heat is necessary to preserve Earth's heat balance. Thus the initial unequal distribution of heat is responsible for major ocean currents and the wind system around our planet.

The movement or circulation of ocean water is essential to many ocean processes. One of the most important is that ocean circulation moves nutrients from the deeper parts of the ocean back up to the surface waters, where these nutrients can be used by plants in the process of photosynthesis. If this did not occur, the variety and abundance of ocean life, including the variety and abundance of fish in the ocean, would be considerably reduced. Also, surface currents move heat from the warmer equatorial parts of the ocean toward the North and South Poles, where the water is cooled and eventually transported by vertical currents to the deeper parts of the ocean. This process provides the main source of life-giving oxygen to the deeper waters of the ocean. The movement of heat and water also has a considerable influence on the climate and weather of our planet.

WHAT IS SEA WATER?

Scientists have found about 84 elements in sea water, some of which have important biological effects on fish and other sea creatures. (The ocean probably contains all known naturally-occurring elements, though scientists haven't yet detected all of these elements in ocean water.) Chlorine, sodium, magnesium, sulfur, calcium, and potassium make up more than

How Wind-Driven Ocean Circulation Works

In simple terms, the wind literally drags on the water surface, causing the water to move and build up in the direction the wind is blowing. This buildup of water causes a pressure difference between the lower and higher areas; the higher pressure is at the downwind end, where the water has piled up. Said differently, the wind has forced the water to flow uphill, but gravity is pulling it back down the slope, as shown in Figure 1-3a. In the open ocean, away from the restricting influence of land, the moving surface water will be deflected by something called the Coriolis effect, and will move at an angle of about 45 degrees to the wind direction. This deflection occurs to the right in the Northern Hemisphere, and to the left in the Southern Hemisphere. Over the ocean there is a general balance between the effect of the pressure gradient (or gravity) on the moving water, and the deflection by the Coriolis effect. When this balance is in place, there will be no further deflection of the moving water and the current flows around the high-pressure area, forming a gyre. Remember that because of gravity water cannot flow uphill, and in our Northern Hemisphere example it can only be deflected to the right, due to the Coriolis effect. The outer boundaries of these ocean-circling currents, or ocean-wide gyres, are the continents. The reason the gyres occur only north or south of the equator is that the Coriolis effect is zero at the equator, thus no deflection of the water occurs there.

90 percent of the total elements in sea water. Chlorine and sodium are the principal elements in solution, while nitrogen, oxygen, and carbon dioxide are the main dissolved gases. Oxygen and, to a lesser degree, carbon dioxide play a critical role in many of the biological processes in the ocean; the oxygen content of sea water is crucial for the survival of fish, and it also influences their behavior. These two gases, oxygen and carbon dioxide, are produced and used in the ocean through the processes of photosynthesis and respiration, which I'll discuss a little later in this chapter. Nitrogen as gas is rarely involved in chemical reactions, except as used by some bacteria, but in various compounds it is very important as a nutrient in sea water.

Fig. 1-3 A. Side view of sloping sea surface produced by the wind blowing on the sea, literally "piling up" the water downwind (slope is greatly exaggerated). "L" has lower pressure than "H."

B. Top view of pressure gradient and resulting current produced from the situation shown in A. The direction shown is for the Northern Hemisphere.

C. Top view of high pressure area "H" and the actual motion of the surface water being driven by the wind (in the Northern Hemisphere). The net result is for the water to flow around the high-pressure area, forming a gyre.

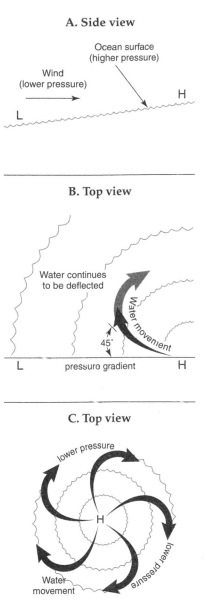

A. Side view

B. Top view

C. Top view

Many organic compounds of biological origin are also found in sea water. They include carbohydrates, proteins, amino acids, organic acids, and vitamins, plus nitrogen and phosphorus, which are chemically combined into organic compounds. Aside from the nutrients nitrogen and phosphorus, little is known about the dissolved organic material in ocean water, except that much of its source is excreta and the decay of dead organisms. Nutrients are critical for the growth and health of plants and animals, including fish, in the ocean.

Sea water itself is a valuable resource. Many chemicals and elements can be extracted from it, including iodine, bromine, potassium, magnesium, manganese, and common table salt. Sea water also can be desalinated (by removing all its salts) and then used as drinkable fresh water—a resource that is in short supply in many parts of the world, especially the Middle East. In some areas, a gallon of fresh water costs more than a gallon of gasoline.

EXAMINING SEA LEVEL

Sea level (or the height of the sea at any given time) and the subsequent position of the shoreline has changed many times through Earth's geologic history. More recently, in the last couple hundred thousand years, the location of the shoreline has gone through several major changes due to the widespread growth and melting of glaciers; the growth of glaciers would lower the sea level, and the melting of glaciers would raise it. These glacial and nonglacial periods were caused by rather dramatic changes in Earth's climate.

The subject of global climatic change is one of the most heavily studied and controversial fields of present-day oceanographic research. The common view seems to be that Earth is in a period of warming, in large part due to the increasing content of heat-absorbing greenhouse gases in the atmosphere. If this view is correct, more melting of glaciers around the world is highly probable and so is a corresponding increase in the height of the sea. This rise, if it occurs, will cause considerable flooding of low-lying coastal areas, as well as damage to coastal environments. The future level of the sea is still hard to predict; however, the past history of sea level is known.

About 18,000 years ago, the sea was as much as 420 feet below its present level, due to numerous large glaciers that existed at that time. Back then, the shoreline was positioned near the edge of our present continental shelf. Since that time, many glaciers have melted or retreated, sea level has risen to its current level, and the position of the shoreline has moved from near the edge of the continental shelf to its present position. Initially the rise in sea level was fairly fast, but it has slowed in the last 7,000 years. Many of the natural fishing structures on the sea floor, especially around the northern United States and Canada, are the result of recent glaciation and subsequent rise in sea level. Examples include major bottom structure such as shoals, banks, and channels.

ASPECTS OF SEA WATER

The ocean provides a saltwater fish's food, oxygen, and entertainment—indeed, everything it needs. An unhealthy ocean makes for unhealthy fish. Fortunately, the ocean can be a very accommodating environment, and if conditions are poor in one area, most fish can simply go elsewhere to find a better habitat.

Although it seems logical that the physical aspects of water should influence the behavior of fish, the data on this subject concerning saltwater fish is sparse; most available information is based on studies of freshwater fish species. Experiments have shown that temperature, light,

Why Study the Ocean's Ecology?

The study of the relationships between organisms and their environment is called ecology. A knowledge of marine ecology is helpful for fishermen because organisms, including fish, rarely live independent of their surroundings or other creatures. (See Appendix 1 for a general classification of the organisms that live in the ocean.) Marine organisms are strongly influenced by the physical and chemical aspects of the ocean, as well as by the plants and animals with which they interact. These interactions, in turn, also affect the ocean environment. So the animals and plants of the ocean are part of a very complex system, called an ecosystem, that involves various physical, chemical, and biological aspects each interacting with the other.

The animals and plants that live in the ocean clearly have adapted to their environment, even though the environmental conditions can vary throughout the ocean. For example, marine creatures living in shallow water and estuaries must withstand the considerable temperature and salinity changes that can occur in these environments. Organisms inhabiting very shallow water may become exposed at low tide, and must be able to avoid or protect themselves from drying out. Benthic (bottom-dwelling) animals that live in nearshore waters typically have streamlined and strengthened shells in order to withstand the crash of waves; other such organisms may burrow into the sediment for shelter. Fish are similarly influenced. For example, most large predators have streamlined bodies, a shape that helps them swim relatively fast.

oxygen, and other aspects of water can affect fish behavior; however, it is difficult to extrapolate what might happen in the well-mixed open ocean, since these experiments are usually performed on freshwater fish in a confined environment. Of course, from spending time on the water, we saltwater anglers can make our own observations on fish behavior. One is that an increase in oxygen (due to mixing of the water by waves or wind) can make fish more aggressive and therefore fight better. Another is that reduced visibility, due to the wind or waves mixing the water, may make fish less wary.

Let's look at some important physical aspects of sea water and how they impact marine life, particularly fish. I'll emphasize the factors that are most important for fishing. (Appendix 2 offers some information on water and how its various aspects can affect the creatures that live in the ocean.)

Temperature

Marine biologists generally agree that water temperature is the most important factor determining where fish will be in the ocean; it also influences many aspects of their behavior.

Some ocean fish can easily move across temperature zones. For example, the migration patterns of bluefin tuna show that they can range over most of the upper ocean. Many other animals, including most fish, are more restricted and spend their entire lives living within a fairly narrow temperature range. (Keep in mind that water-temperature changes can exist both horizontally and vertically, with depth, in the ocean.)

Water has a high heat capacity, which in simple terms means that its temperature will not rapidly fluctuate, but rather water will slowly warm or slowly cool. Because of this, marine organisms are rarely trapped by temperature changes, since the changes in water temperature are slow enough that fish can escape potentially hazardous situations. This is important, as many marine animals are sensitive to rapid water-temperature changes. It also means that most marine organisms, including fish, do not require extensive thermal regulation mechanisms of the kind that many terrestrial animals have, including humans. On the other hand, the lack of such a system can make some marine organisms vulnerable to temperature changes.

Most fish are cold-blooded, which means their internal body temperature is strongly influenced by the temperature of the surrounding water. There have been many instances during which a rapid change in atmospheric temperature rapidly cooled shallow nearshore waters and caused a fish-kill. Warm-blooded fish such as tuna can control their internal temperature in vital parts of their bodies (such as the brain) and are less affected by the temperature of the surrounding water. This is what enables bluefin tuna to range widely, as they are not strongly affected by ambient water temperature; most fish are at the mercy of the temperature of the water surrounding them.

Where do water-temperature changes occur in the ocean? One place is in the vertical dimension, where a zone of rapid temperature change, called the thermocline, occurs between the warm surface water and the

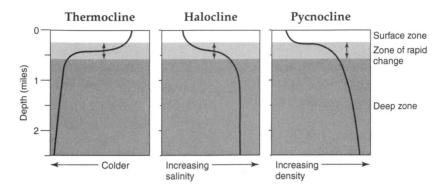

Fig. 1-4 The ocean's temperature, salinity, and density are far from uniform, and they vary with depth. These variations are shown in the three graphs. The thermocline is caused by a rapid change in temperature with depth. The halocline is caused by a rapid change in salinity with depth. The pycnocline can be caused either by unrelated variations in temperature or salinity, or by variations that occur in both together.

cold deeper water. The thermocline will limit vertical movement of temperature-sensitive fish. Strong and distinct thermoclines are not common in shallow, well-mixed waters, though temperature changes do occur in shallow areas. In fact, water temperature can change rapidly in shallow water, which is influenced by mixing, turbulence, and air temperature. Fish that have difficulty adjusting to rapid temperature changes will often leave shallow water during the passage of a temperature front and go to deeper water.

Ocean fronts, or temperature boundaries, can exist between bodies of water that have different temperatures and densities. An example is the Gulf Stream and its boundary with adjacent coastal waters.

Often, fish will congregate or hunt along the edge of a water-temperature change. Research has indicated that larger members of a species have more of a preference for lower water temperatures than smaller fish of the same species. The idea has not been well-studied, but there is considerable anecdotal information on the subject. For example, larger striped bass are frequently found deeper than, and below, smaller stripers. Being deeper usually means being in cooler water; however, there are just too many other environmental and biological factors that could explain this behavior. The bigger and deeper fish may just be maximizing their feeding efficiency by casually sucking in dead and dying prey disabled by the youngsters feeding above. So maybe bigger fish like colder water, maybe they don't.

Water temperature can also affect the development and growth of some species. Fish that live in warmer areas of the ocean tend to develop more rapidly and reach sexual maturity sooner than those that live in colder regions, while fish indigenous to colder areas usually grow larger than warm-water species.

Although most fish can live over a moderate range of water temperature, they usually have an optimal or preferred range, as well as high and low tolerance limits. Fish can, however, live outside of their temperature range for various reasons, such as to find food or to avoid predators. Nevertheless, there are water temperatures above or below which an individual fish or an entire species might not survive. These temperature ranges and limits can change over time for a particular stock or group of fish, and might be different for unrelated groups of fish of the same species. Said another way, the bonefish of Belize and the bonefish of the Bahamas may have different optimal temperature preferences and tolerance limits.

Atmospheric or Barometric Pressure

An interesting question is, Are ocean fish aware of, or sensitive to, changes in atmospheric or (as it is commonly called) barometric pressure?

Some small fish, such as minnows, appear to be sensitive to slight changes in barometric pressure. In general, however, scientific evidence does not prove that a change in barometric pressure is detected by, or influences, most ocean fish. Of course, fish certainly react to factors associated with changes in barometric pressure such as rainfall, strong winds, tidal differences, and temperature fluctuations, which in turn may regulate the amount of oxygen in the water, stir up food, or increase the turbidity of the water.

In many areas, especially on tropical tidal flats, the fishing often changes dramatically before, during, and after the passage of an atmospheric high- or low-pressure area. I suspect that it is the temperature change, as well as the wind and maybe some other factors, that influence the fish, rather than the actual change in pressure. Similarly, a change in barometric pressure will affect the height of the tide, which on tidal flats may restrict or increase access to certain areas for some fish. Less or more water on the flats can also change the water temperature, water turbidity, salinity, and many other factors that in turn will influence where the fish will be.

The actual pressure change associated with the passage of a front is equivalent to the pressure change that a fish would experience by changing its depth in the water by just a few inches. Perhaps this pressure change has an affect on fish in very shallow water, such as bonefish, but it seems as if it should be inconsequential to fish living in deeper water.

Currents

There are a variety of currents in the ocean, and because they move and mix the water they will influence various aspects of the environment, and can affect the fishing in a given area. One especially important environmental impact of currents is that they can move nutrients from deep water to the surface, where these nutrients can be used by plants, in the photosynthetic process, to produce organic matter. Currents can also disperse waste products, eggs, larvae, and adult life-forms. Some fish spawn in or near a current, which may then carry the eggs and young into an environment favorable for growth. By mixing ocean water, currents keep water-temperature changes to a minimum. Turbulence caused by currents adds oxygen to the water—oxygen that fish need.

Currents can be an environmental boundary to fish and thus play a major role in determining where fish concentrate or move to. Some fish, including large sport fish such as tuna and sailfish, often hold and feed near the edge of a current, such as the Gulf Stream along the East Coast of the United States. The edge of a current is usually distinguished by a change in temperature and other physical characteristics of the water, such as a change in water color or by an accumulation of floating debris along the current edge.

Very little is known about why fish respond to or how they behave in currents, largely because it's difficult for scientists to observe fish in natural fast-moving currents. We do know that fish will almost always face into the current flow. There are two main reasons for this. First, when they are facing into a current water easily passes through the mouths and into and over the gills of fish. (Fish obtain oxygen from, and eliminate waste products through, water running over their gills.) Second, it's an easy way for fish to detect and catch any food moving or being carried their way by the current.

Current-produced water motion can also have some nonbeneficial effects on fish, such as carrying them from their natural environment into an unfavorable one. Further, in shallow water currents may reach the bottom, cause erosion of sediments, and change the local habitat. Any sediment lifted from the bottom by currents will increase the turbidity in the water and reduce the penetration of sunlight, which in turn reduces plant growth and the production of food through photosynthesis. In extreme situations, fish may have difficulty breathing in sediment-filled turbid water. Turbid waters can also reduce the survival rates of larval and juvenile fish.

A Look at El Niño

Although much remains to be learned about what initiates El Niños, and how to predict them, it is clear that they start following a change in the wind pattern and direction in the tropical Pacific. This change allows the typically warmer water on the western side of the Pacific to move or literally slosh to the east toward the coasts of Central and South America. When this happens, the warm water usually arrives around Christmas, sometimes a little earlier.

El Niño is Spanish for "The Child," or in liturgical terms "The Christ Child," an appropriate name for a major event that generally occurs around Christmas. El Niños, which have been documented back to 1726 and doubtless occurred before then, generally last about twelve to eighteen months, and develop once or twice a decade. In recent years, however, the incidence, duration, and perhaps the intensity of El Niños have increased. Some scientists believe this is due to worldwide global warming resulting from the increasing amounts of greenhouse gases accumulating in our atmosphere.

In simple terms then, an El Niño is an unusual warm current, initially off the coast of Peru and Chile, that has the ability to cause major weather and climate changes over many parts of the world. How can an El Niño have such far-reaching climatic effects? The answer seems to be that the warmer surface waters in the equatorial Pacific change the overall pattern of the atmospheric jet stream in the Northern Hemisphere. This change causes storms in some regions and mild weather or droughts in other regions.

The 1997 to 1998 El Niño was the strongest of the twentieth century. During its tenure, several states had their warmest and/or wettest conditions ever recorded. Many severe coastal storms and considerable flooding occurred along much of the West Coast of the United States. El Niño conditions in the Pacific usually cause a smaller number of hurricanes in the Atlantic, which is what seemed to happen in 1997.

There are several ways that an El Niño can affect fish. One is that the rising surface-water temperature will cause fish to migrate away from their natural range to seek out cooler water or food. They may eventually reach dangerously cool waters that were unchanged by the El Niño, at which temperatures they may die. Fish that do not migrate and remain in an El Niño area may suffer or die from the increasing water temperature or the lack of food.

Another El Niño outcome may result from an increase in rainfall, which will affect coastal habitats and the fish that live in these waters. The rains will increase river discharge and therefore turbidity in the water, and will reduce salinity. The runoff from land may also carry increased amounts of pollutants into the streams and estuaries where fish live. Any of these changes will badly alter resident fish populations by inhibiting spawning success, or by simply killing fish.

Another impact can result from the changing wind patterns that in turn can restrict or reduce coastal upwelling (a current that brings subsurface waters rich in nutrients to the surface). Less upwelling will mean that there are fewer nutrients in the water, and plants need nutrients to produce organic matter, the basic food of the ocean. A reduction in this food supply will cause problems throughout the food chain, and will make life difficult for marine fish.

Fishery scientists in the National Marine Fisheries Service (NMFS), a division of the National Oceanic and Atmospheric Administration (NOAA), correctly anticipated that the warming of the water off California due to the 1997 to 1998 El Niño would expand the range of tropical marine fish species to the north and bring excellent fishing to California. For example, migrating yellowtail, albacore, and bluefin tuna made an appearance in southern California waters earlier in the season than usual. The warm waters also created favorable conditions for small schooling fish such as mackerel and sardines, and for larger species such as mahi-mahi (dolphin) and billfish. Some species of fish, especially bottom-living fish such as rockfish, were adversely affected by the warmer water, since they do not migrate and cannot avoid the changing water temperatures. Large numbers of migrating sockeye salmon died because of warmer-than-usual waters along their migration path.

It is clear that a strong El Niño, such as the one from 1997 to 1998, will dramatically affect global weather patterns and inflict consid-

(continued)

A LOOK AT EL NIÑO *(Continued)*

erable damage, as well as have a major impact on the distribution, movement, and survival of many species of marine life. Unfortunately, the biological impacts of an El Niño are not always obvious or can take years to be discovered. Scientists have started to examine old fishing records and have noted that some anomalies, such as low or outstanding harvests of a particular species, seem to correlate with times of past El Niños.

It seems probable to me that El Niños and fish-population numbers and fish harvest ultimately will be found to be more closely related than previously anticipated.

As if El Niños didn't cause enough problems, there is a similar but opposite phenomenon called La Niña. La Niña is the Spanish name for a female child, and refers to an event that can cause more trouble for the United States than its better known "brother." La Niña will occur after an El Niño, when the more typical wind pattern returns to the eastern Pacific, causing colder and deeper water to replace the warmer waters that resulted from the El Niño. The most recent La Niña, starting in 1998, caused lower surface-water temperatures than usual. One of the effects of La Niña is that the jet stream over the United States is pushed northward toward Canada and Alaska, and then returns carrying cold air south into the United States. This could mean colder and wetter winters for the central and western states, and mild and dry conditions for the southern states. Of most concern is the possible increased incidence of hurricanes along the Atlantic seaboard during summer and autumn, and more tornadoes and very dry conditions in the southeastern parts of the United States in spring.

Salinity

This is a measure of the amount of the various salts that are dissolved in sea water, and is expressed in parts per thousand (‰). The average salinity of offshore ocean water is about 34.7 ‰. This value remains generally constant in offshore waters, whereas it can vary considerably in coastal waters. Usually, the greatest range in salinity (both horizontally and vertically) occurs in estuaries, where the level can go from 0 ‰ to 30 ‰ or more. Sometimes, the salinity range in a given area is profound, such as when low-density and low-salinity river water overlays denser high-salinity sea water.

Salinity is an important ecological factor and clearly affects the distribution of fish in the ocean. Salinity variations can be a barrier to the movement of many species of saltwater fish. (Only about 1 percent of the known fish species can exist in both fresh- and saltwater environments.) The reason is that the salt content of the internal fluids of fish and other marine creatures must maintain a balance with the salt content of the waters in which the animals live. If the salinity of the waters of an environment were to change and a fish could not adjust to the change, it would be under considerable stress—stress that could eventually be fatal.

Some fish, however, can tolerate salinity changes by regulating the salt content of their internal fluids. The species that can tolerate a broad range of salinity are typically found in coastal and estuarine waters, where salinity fluctuations are common. Striped bass and tarpon are excellent examples, often going into an estuary to feed, and later going offshore to rest. Other fish that can move between fresh water and sea water include, snook, salmon, permit and some other jacks, and herring.

Oxygen

In sea water, oxygen is present in relatively small amounts compared to its concentration in the atmosphere. Still, to breathe, fish need oxygen in the water. (The oxygen in water is not the oxygen that has combined with hydrogen to make H_2O, but rather is oxygen gas, called free oxygen, and is dissolved in the water.)

Sea water usually contains between 0 to 8 milliliters of free oxygen dissolved in a liter of water. The oxygen content in the atmosphere is considerably higher, about 210 milliliters per liter. In the atmosphere the oxygen content is essentially constant, so land animals rarely have to worry about getting their needed supply. In the ocean, however, not only is the oxygen content low, it can vary from one area to another, as well as change over time in any given area.

There are two main processes that supply oxygen to sea water. The first involves the atmosphere. Because the surface water of the ocean is in direct contact with the atmosphere, winds and waves will mix these waters with the relatively oxygen-rich air of the atmosphere, and in this manner put oxygen into the water and increase its oxygen content. The second involves photosynthesis and respiration. (See Appendix 3 to refresh your memory about how these processes work.) During photo-synthesis, plants produce organic matter and release oxygen. The result-ing oxygen and organic matter are used by other marine organisms in a process called respiration or oxidation, which removes oxygen as a gas from sea water. In some instances, the oxidation process can remove so much oxygen from the water that it leaves oxygen levels dangerously low.

Warm water is able to hold less free oxygen than cold water can, which unfortunately is just the opposite of what fish need. At higher tem-peratures the metabolic rate and oxygen needs of fish increase; the oppo-site is true at lower temperatures. If the oxygen content of the water gets too low, fish may die, though they usually first reduce their activities to decrease their need for oxygen. Apparently, fish stop growing and repro-ducing below a certain oxygen-content level.

The oxygen content can be low (or even nonexistent) in waters con-taminated by pollutants, especially sewage, or where water circulation is restricted and the bottom has a high content of organic matter. In either instance, the decaying organic matter can, by being oxidized, use up the available free oxygen in the water. Algal blooms or red tides can also rapidly consume the oxygen in the water, causing extensive fish-kills.

Because there is such a relatively small amount of free oxygen in sea water, fish need an efficient system by which to obtain the oxygen they need for their survival. Most fish have such a system: they get their oxy-gen directly from the oxygen dissolved in sea water. Water is taken in at the mouth and passed over fine membranes arranged in a tightly packed series of filaments in the gills. (These membranes are very delicate; a fish can bleed to death if its gills are cut or penetrated by a hook.) Carbon dioxide (CO_2) is a waste product of this process, and is diffused into sea water.

The more active the fish, the more oxygen it needs, and the more CO_2 it must eliminate. Some active fish accomplish this by having an increased surface area of their gills which, in turn, increases the efficiency of the oxygen-diffusion process. A few active fish are able to remove more than 80 percent of the dissolved oxygen in the sea water that flows over their gills. A typical air-breathing vertebrate, living on land, generally will remove less than 30 percent of the oxygen in the air it inhales.

When the oxygen content of the water is low, fish can obtain more oxygen by increasing the volume of water flowing over their gills. They accomplish this by increasing the number of strokes with which they take in water, or by increasing the volume of water taken in per stroke. Though the gills of most fish are extremely efficient at removing dissolved oxygen from sea water, there are situations in which the oxygen in the water is low enough to restrict metabolic processes. A few fish, tarpon for example, have the ability under such low-oxygen conditions to breathe air from the atmosphere.

The efficient manner of exchange of chemicals via the gills and blood of fish from the surrounding water also has the potential for harm. In the exchange process, fish can take up harmful substances, such as pollutants dissolved in the water. Pesticides and mercury compounds that entered sea water and were taken in by fish have led to large fish-kills.

LIGHT IN THE OCEAN

Light is critical for healthy marine life. Sunlight is a major part of the photosynthetic process, and without it plants could not produce the organic matter that is the primary source of food in the ocean. Because light can penetrate sea water, to some degree, photosynthesis is not restricted to the upper few feet of the ocean but can take place in the upper hundred feet or so, depending on water clarity. (Though no sunlight reaches the deeper parts of the ocean, some light is present in the depths due to the process of bioluminescence.) In the upper parts of the ocean, light is important to fish in several ways. Certainly fish need light to see, and for many fish the amount of light present determines when they feed.

The duration and amount of light that reaches the ocean is influenced by the season—there will be more light, and longer duration of light, during the longer days of summer, and less of each on the shorter days of winter. The duration and intensity of light can initiate fish migration, reproductive cycles, and growth. At night the lack of light will cause most schooling fish to disperse, to some degree.

Some fish are attracted to light, some are repelled by or avoid it, and others are ambivalent to it. (The scientific word for the attraction to or avoidance of light is phototaxis.) Fish that find their food by using their vision require some light. Many of these fish hunt during low-light periods such as dawn or dusk. In the laboratory, fish often respond to light stimuli, even when the light is of low intensity. A few experiments have shown that a fish's ability to recognize color can be affected by the brightness of light—in other words, below a certain level of illumination the fish will not recognize color. Some fish appear to favor certain colors of light, although much remains to be learned on this subject. (Chapter 7 contains more on this subject.) Laboratory experiments have also shown that many fish will be most active at a specific level of light intensity, and that artificial light is generally less attractive to fish than natural light.

Absorption of Light

The visible light that reaches the ocean's surface is part of a broad range of radiation emitted by the sun. This visible light, including that which is reflected off the moon, undergoes changes when it reaches and passes into the ocean. Several of these changes come to bear on how fish see.

As light enters and moves through the ocean the various colors that comprise visible light are quickly and differentially filtered out or absorbed with depth or distance through the water. Visible light, also called white light, actually is formed by a combination or spectrum of several colors: red, orange, yellow, green, blue, and violet. You can see this spectrum when light is refracted by a prism or a diamond. These individual colors differ by their wavelengths—reds have the longest wavelength,

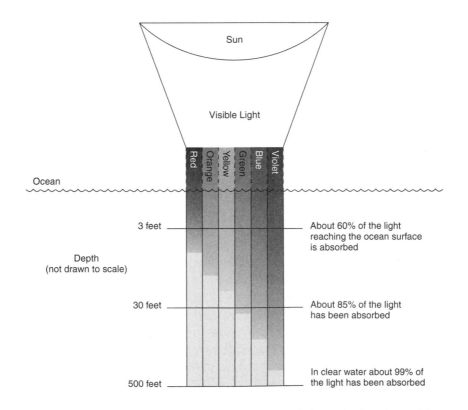

Fig. 1-5 Visible light occupies only a small portion of the total radiation coming from the sun; it is a combination of the colors red, orange, yellow, green, blue, and violet. This figure shows that little visible light penetrates below the surface of the ocean and that the reds, oranges, and yellows are absorbed before the greens, blues, and violets.

blues and violets the shortest—and water absorbs each wavelength differently. As light enters the ocean the longer wavelengths of visible light, the reds and oranges, are the first ones absorbed, thus these colors penetrate shallower than the shorter green, blue, and violet wavelengths.

In most cases, the color red is almost totally absorbed in water, and orange nearly so, usually by 10 to 20 feet below the surface. A red or orange object at this depth will appear gray and eventually black in deeper water; the intensity of the color also decreases. This explains the initially surprising fact that some deep-water fish are red. Their conspicuous color, when viewed at the ocean surface, would be an inconspicuous dark gray or black at the depth they inhabit.

At 30 or more feet (depending on the turbidity of the water) usually just the blues and greens remain. In very deep water, most objects appear to be blue, violet, or black. Black results when all other colors have been absorbed. The filtering out or absorption of color also works horizontally, so again red will not be seen as red beyond a distance of 10 to 20 feet.

Underwater studies on the visibility of various colors showed that the fluorescent version of a color was seen better, and was more visible from a distance, than the nonfluorescent version of the color. Fluorescent chartreuse was the most visible of the colors tested, which may explain why this is such a popular and successful color when used in flies.

Reflected Light
The color of an object, as we see it, comes from the wavelengths of light that are reflected back to us, not from the ones that are absorbed. Indeed, the color we perceive the ocean to be depends on which wavelengths are reflected back to our eyes. Generally, we see the clear offshore ocean as being blue-green. Here's why: light penetrates clear offshore waters deeply because of the relative absence of suspended material, so the reflected light comes from the deeper-penetrating blue and green wavelengths, and we thus see the water as blue-green. The other spectral colors are absorbed in the water near the surface and therefore have less chance of being reflected back to us.

In relatively shallow coastal areas, sea water often appears to have more of a green, yellow, or even red hue. This is due to the relatively high quantities of suspended and floating material in these waters. Such materials restrict the penetration of light, and therefore more of the light is reflected from the upper layers of the water, where the longer red, yellow, and green wavelengths predominate. There typically are more suspended particles in coastal waters than in offshore waters. This is because coastal waters contain material carried in by rivers, sediment stirred up from the bottom by waves and currents, and a relatively high amount of plant and animal growth. Some coastal waters and rivers can have such a high concentration of suspended sediment and floating plant material that light only penetrates the surface a foot or so. In this case, the water may appear brown, red, or even black.

Attenuation of Light

Another important change that occurs as light moves through the ocean is that its intensity decreases as it moves away from its source. This decrease in intensity is not linear, as in increments of 1, 2, 3, 4, 5, and the like. Rather, it is exponential as in increments of 2, 4, 8, 16, 32, and so on. This loss in intensity is called attenuation.

Attenuation is due to two processes: light is scattered off particles suspended in the water (the more particles in the water, the greater the scattering); or light (really radiant energy from the sun) is converted into heat through absorption or into chemical energy during photosynthesis by floating plants, mainly phytoplankton. That water absorbs radiant energy is evident by the fact that the surface layers of the ocean are warmer than deeper layers.

Suspended material in the water not only reflects light, it also scatters it, which reduces visibility underwater. In a manner of speaking, suspended material scatters and blocks light similar to how smoke or fog does in the atmosphere. Visibility in very turbid water can be just a foot or two, or even less.

About 60 percent of the light that actually penetrates the ocean's surface, either from the sun in the daytime or reflected off the moon at night, will be absorbed by the time it passes through the upper 3 feet of sea water; by 30 feet about 80 percent is gone. In very clear water, such as that generally found only hundreds of miles offshore, less than 1 percent of the light will reach a depth of 500 feet. It is somewhat ironic that the clear offshore waters, which have the best clarity and light penetration (the best conditions for vision) hold relatively small numbers of fish species. This is due, in large part, to the lack of an adequate food supply.

Light at the Ocean Surface

The ocean surface is an important place for many fish, since this is where they often feed. The surface can also be a dangerous place because of the threat of fish-eating birds and fish-searching anglers.

The convex and concave parts of the moving water surface will respectively focus or diffuse light, causing bright or dark spots to appear in the water, and also on the bottom if the water is shallow. Also, surface waves blur images and distort the brightness of objects in the water, in effect shielding fish from predators. The more the water's surface is disturbed (usually due to wind and waves, or both), the harder it will be for predators to detect bait, and vice versa.

If the surface is relatively smooth, as much as 80 percent of the incoming sunlight may be reflected off the water. The exact amount reflected also depends on the angle at which the incoming light hits the surface. When the surface is disturbed or rough there will be a considerable variation in the amount of light that penetrates the ocean at any particular place, regardless of the angle of the incoming light.

Once the rays of light enter the water, they are bent or refracted following what is called the Law of Refraction, or Snell's Law. Refraction is caused when there is a change in the speed of light as it goes from one

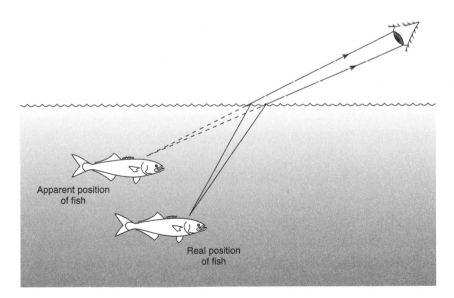

Fig. 1-6 A simple illustration showing the process of refraction of light; here the light is bent going from the atmosphere into the water. Refraction makes an object in the water, the fish in this example, appear both larger and closer to the surface. This, of course, gives a scientific explanation of why the fish you see but do not catch appears bigger than it really is. The apparent distance to an object is about ¾ of the actual distance. In other words, if the bottom is actually 4 feet below the surface, it will appear to be only 3-feet deep. The path of the light actually goes from the "real" position of the fish to the water surface to your eye, but your eye deceives you by telling your brain that the light is traveling a straight path to your eye that starts at the "apparent" position of the fish.

medium to another medium, for example, going from the atmosphere into sea water, or vice versa. Light travels slower in water than in air. The process of refraction will not happen if the light hits the water straight on, but it does happen when the light intersects the water at an angle. The process of the refraction of light is similar to what happens to waves when they enter shallow water. (See Figure 4-4 on page 84.)

A light wave will be bent both when entering and when leaving the water. In other words, refraction works both ways; when the light leaves the sea water it will be refracted down toward the horizon. This bending or refraction of light can create some interesting illusions. One is the well-known "bending" of a stick when it is partially submerged in water; the stick will appear to be bent or almost broken at the water's surface.

Another illusion occurs when we see a fish in the water. Refraction makes the fish appear both closer to the surface and also bigger than it really is. This may explain why the fish that got away always appears to be larger than it really is. This illusion also makes the bottom appear closer, or in other words, the water to be shallower than it actually is. If the water were 4 feet deep, it would, because of refraction, appear to be only 3 feet deep. This is probably where the saying "water depths can be deceiving" comes from. So keep this in mind next time you jump off your boat—check the depth first, otherwise you might be very surprised, and wet.

PLANTS AND ORGANIC MATTER IN THE OCEAN

Plants are critical for life in the ocean. If plants were removed from the ocean, food chains would collapse, animals would starve, and the ocean would be a lifeless body of water, except for bacteria and those organisms that feed on bacteria. Plants are the primary producers of organic matter, and essentially all other forms of marine life are dependent on this organic matter for their food. Photosynthesis is the process that produces organic matter, and this process is used by all plants, whether they are microscopic and float in the ocean, are anchored to rocks in the shallow sea, or are rooted in soil on land.

The photosynthetic process by marine plants is the most important biological process in the ocean. Without it, marine life as we know it would be impossible. The photosynthesis process combines carbon dioxide, water, and solar energy (sunlight), in the presence of chlorophyll, to produce organic matter and oxygen. Growth rates of plants generally are controlled by the availability of nutrients and the amount of sunlight. In areas where the water is well-mixed, either seasonally or continuously, the production of organic matter can be high due to continued replenishment of nutrients to the near-surface layers from deep waters.

Organic-matter production can vary considerably with time of day or year, and also with location. In polar regions, for example, production is very high in the summer months because the sun shines almost twenty-four hours a day. During the polar winter, however, the days are essentially dark and organic-matter production in the ocean is very low. In the tropics, where the sunlight reaching the ocean is fairly constant, production proceeds at a relatively constant rate throughout the year. Areas of high production, such as Georges Bank off the Northeast coast of the United States, can produce 300 grams of carbon per square meter per year. In other areas, organic production can be one-hundredth of this amount.

In the ocean, organic matter can be produced essentially everywhere within the photic zone (the zone in which there is sufficient light for photosynthesis). On the other hand, the nutrient concentration in the ocean is considerably less than it is on land.

BIOCHEMICAL REACTIONS AND NUTRIENT CYCLES

Many of the most important chemical reactions in the ocean are the result of the various life processes of the creatures that live there. Collectively, the organisms and these reactions form what's called the ocean's biochemical cycle. The biochemical cycle results in a flow of nutrients, going from the organic matter formed by plants during photosynthesis, through the life cycle of the various organisms in the ocean, and ultimately back into the photosynthetic process.

You might expect that all of the organic matter floating around in sea water would eventually collect and pile up on the seafloor, but actually very little accumulates there. The reasons are simple: organic matter will either decay or be eaten while falling through the water; or, when it reaches bottom, it will be digested by bottom-dwelling organisms. When organic matter eventually decays through the respiration process (the reverse of photosynthesis), the nutrients it contains are released into the water. Respiration, unlike photosynthesis, does not require light energy and can therefore occur at any depth, at any time. If the organic matter does accumulate on the seafloor and is buried under sediments, it may eventually be converted to petroleum. Of course, the petroleum-conversion process is very complex, and several million years may pass before the process is complete.

Upwelling, which brings subsurface water containing nutrients to the surface, or other forms of vertical mixing of the ocean often result in an increased supply of nutrients in the surface waters. This in turn may cause a large growth of phytoplankton (floating plants). The phytoplankton growth often attracts other organisms, including fish, which feed on

Energy Input to Drive the Biochemical Cycle

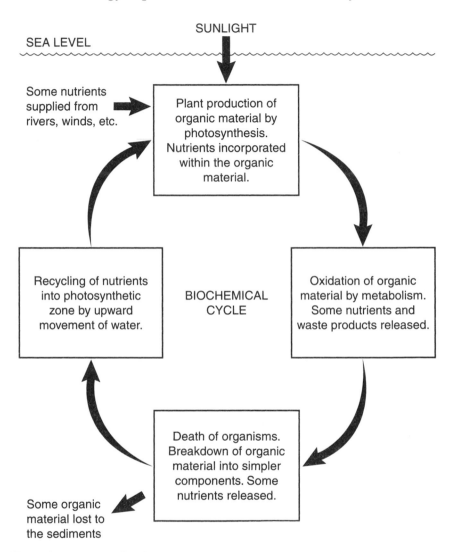

Fig. 1-7 The basic parts of the biochemical cycle.

the plankton. In simple terms, this is why coastal regions, whose waters are usually well mixed, have large numbers of fish. On the other hand, if an area has an insufficient supply of nutrients, there will be a limited growth of phytoplankton and a corresponding absence of fish. Seasonal changes in nutrient content in sea water are most obvious in temperate

Human Input

The effect of human activity on the chemical composition of the ocean is slight, but it is observable and sometimes very damaging. From one viewpoint, the ocean is highly polluted and, in a manner of speaking, it has been so for hundreds of millions of years. This "pollution" results from the large quantity of various elements, or salts, present in sea water. Salinity is important to the organisms that live in the ocean, but represents no risk to them. Of course, salinity prevents us from drinking sea water, or using it for agriculture or many industrial purposes, until the salts are removed. Humans also have introduced many true pollutants into the ocean. In some areas, our pollution input has had devastating effects on marine organisms. Fortunately the ocean does have a considerable healing ability, and the effects of some but not all types of human-introduced pollution can be reversed.

areas, where phytoplankton generally have two major growth periods each year—spring and early autumn.

THE FOOD CYCLE

In the ocean, production by plants of organic matter is just the first part of a complex nutritional system involving all marine organisms. The system can be simplified as follows: at the bottom are plants, which are the primary producers of organic matter, which is consumed by herbivores (mainly zooplankton or floating animals), which in turn are consumed by carnivores, such as fish, or mammals, such as whales. Zooplankton convert the organic matter in plant tissue to animal tissue, which in turn becomes food for higher-order organisms. Humans become part of this system when they eat ocean carnivores.

The pattern or sequence of each organism being eaten by the one above it is called a food chain. The food chain ends with the animal that does not have a predator. A highly simplified food chain, including the trophic (or feeding) levels and the energy gradient, is shown in figure 1-8. This simple trophic scheme assumes a 10 percent efficiency in energy conversion, going from one feeding level to the next higher feeding level. For example, for a large fish such as a tuna to add 1 pound of weight it must consume 10 pounds of a moderate-size fish such as a bluefish. With

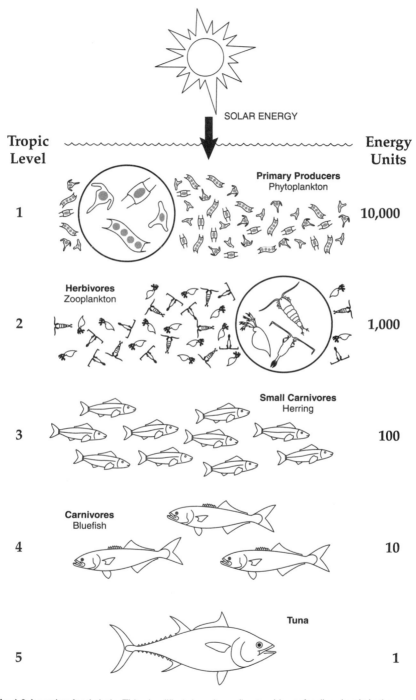

SOLAR ENERGY

Tropic Level

Energy Units

Primary Producers
Phytoplankton

1   10,000

Herbivores
Zooplankton

2   1,000

Small Carnivores
Herring

3   100

Carnivores
Bluefish

4   10

Tuna

5   1

Fig. 1-8 A marine food chain. This simplified view shows five trophic, or feeding, levels in the ocean. The process is driven by solar energy, which phytoplankton use in the photosynthesis process. A 10 percent efficiency is assumed in going from one trophic level to the next trophic level.

this model, 10,000 pounds of phytoplankton are needed to produce 1 pound of tuna for human consumption. The 90 percent "loss" of energy at each level results from the organism using some energy to feed, breathe, move, reproduce, and do other fishy things.

A trophic diagram shows the biological efficiency of the ocean. In reality, however, the system is a more complex relationship between organisms that produce organic matter, those that consume it, and those that decompose it. This complex system is called a food web. In a food web, organisms, especially those higher up in the chain, feed on a variety of organisms, not just one. A food web is advantageous for higher organisms, such as most marine game fish, since they are not as vulnerable to changes in their food supply as are organisms that feed on only one species.

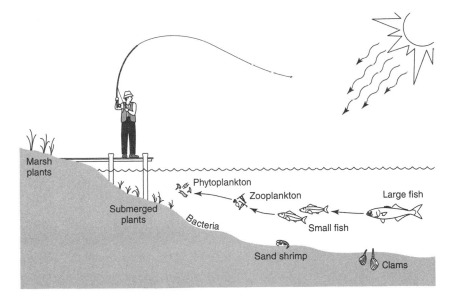

Fig. 1-9 A simple food web for a coastal estuary. The arrows indicate some of the motion of the food and energy through the system. This figure is a simplification of a fairly complex process. (The organisms and the dimensions are not drawn to scale.)

Chapter 2

Tides, Tidal Currents, and Waves

Why should saltwater anglers be concerned with moving water? The answer is simple: marine fish tend to feed when the water is moving, and you will catch more fish when the fish are feeding. Tides and their associated tidal currents and breaking waves are among the main forces that move water and influence fishing in the ocean.

Ocean fish are part of a complex food chain. Baitfish feed on plankton, which cannot swim and are moved about by the currents, so when plankton are concentrated in a certain area baitfish will follow, and they in turn will attract the game fish we want to catch. Furthermore, strong currents caused by the tides overpower baitfish and concentrate them in dense schools. If you know where the baitfish are, or can predict where they will be, you have a tremendous advantage in finding game fish.

Most saltwater fish are wanderers, following the currents or the food that is carried with the currents. Therefore, an area with moving water is generally a good place to fish. The reverse is also true in the ocean—fishing tends to be poor in areas where the current isn't moving; during slack water, there is no current to concentrate either the plankton or baitfish, and they disperse.

Simply put, tides give us a timetable with which to deduce when the water is moving, which is when the fish are most likely to be feeding.

WHAT ARE TIDES?
We can define tides as the rhythmic rise and fall of sea level. This pattern should be familiar to anyone who has fished from the beach, or has lived or vacationed near the seashore. It's easy to see tides near the shore, but they also occur to a lesser degree offshore, where the lack of a fixed reference point makes their up-and-down motion difficult to observe. Even out at sea, however, tides and tidal currents become visible when they flow over shallow areas of the seafloor, forming turbulent areas called tidal rips.

TIDES FOR POINTS ON VINEYARD SOUND, BUZZARDS BAY

		Popponesset Bay		Succonnesset Point		Falmouth Heights		Woods Hole (WHOI)		West Falmouth		Canal (RR Bridge)		Canal Current (RR Bridge)		Robinson's Hole Current (Middle)		Woods Hole Current (S. End)	
		High Tide	Low Tide	High Tide	Low Tide	High Tide	Low Tide	High Tide	Low Tide	High Tide	Low Tide	High Tide	Low Tide	Turns West	Turns East	Turns West	Turns East	Turns West	Turns East
TUESDAY JULY 28	AM	5:06	11:10	3:57	9:57	2:47	9:09		7:01		5:20	12:44	7:49	1:18	7:24	2:20	8:54	2:35	7:53
	PM	5:37	11:30	4:28	10:17	3:18	9:29		7:19		5:38	1:13	8:07	1:57	7:44	2:59	9:14	3:14	8:13
WEDNESDAY JULY 29	AM	5:52	11:54	4:43	10:41	3:33	9:53	12:20	7:34	12:19	5:53	1:29	8:22	2:03	8:06	3:05	9:36	3:20	8:35
	PM	6:22		5:13	11:05	4:03	10:17	1:08	7:59	1:07	6:18	2:01	8:47	2:40	8:29	3:42	9:59	3:57	8:58
THURSDAY JULY 30	AM	6:40	12:18	5:31	11:26	4:21	10:38	1:24	8:12	1:23	6:31	2:17	9:00	2:51	8:51	3:53	10:21	4:08	9:20
	PM	7:08	12:39	5:59	11:55	4:49	11:07	1:58	8:45	1:57	7:04	2:51	9:33	3:25	9:18	4:28	10:48	4:43	9:47
FRIDAY JULY 31	AM	7:31	1:08	6:22		5:12	11:26	2:15	8:55	2:14	7:14	3:08	9:43	3:44	9:40	4:46	11:10	5:01	10:09
	PM	7:57	1:27	6:48	12:14	5:38		2:50	9:38	2:49	7:57	3:43	10:26	4:16	10:11	5:18	11:41	5:33	10:40
SATURDAY AUG. 1	AM	8:24	2:01	7:15	12:48	6:05	12:00	3:09	9:45	3:08	3:04	4:02	10:33	4:41	10:33	5:43		5:58	11:02
	PM	8:47	2:17	7:38	1:04	6:28	12:16	3:44	10:40	3:43	3:59	4:37	11:28	5:09	11:08	6:11	12:03	6:26	11:37
SUNDAY AUG. 2	AM	9:19	2:56	8:10	1:43	7:00	12:55	4:06	10:41	4:05	9:00	4:59	11:29	5:42	11:30	6:44	12:38	6:59	11:59
	PM	9:39	3:09	8:30	1:56	7:20	1:08	4:37	11:47	4:36	10:06	5:30		6:04		7:06	1:00	7:21	
MONDAY AUG. 3	AM	10:13	3:50	9:04	2:37	7:54	1:49	5:01	11:42	5:00	10:01	5:54	12:35	6:41	12:05	7:43	1:35	7:58	12:34
	PM	10:30	4:02	9:21	2:49	8:11	2:01	5:29		5:28	11:10	6:22	12:30	6:57	12:28	7:59	1:58	8:14	12:57

July 31, 1998 – Sunrise is at 5:36AM; sunset is at 8:01PM. Moonrise is at 1:23PM.
August 3, 1998 – Sunrise is at 5:39AM; sunset is at 7:58PM. Moonrise is at 4:14PM; moonset is at 1:34AM.
Source: National Ocean Survey Tide and Tidal Current Tables. Compiled by: W. T. Elbow

Fig. 2-1 An example of a tide table that appears in local newspapers. Typically included are the times of high and low tides and, for some areas, when the tide turns or changes direction. You cannot tell from this information the time of maximum tidal current or slack water. You might be surprised to see that two areas about 7 miles apart (Falmouth Heights and Popponesset Bay) have more than two hours between their high tides. Falmouth Heights and Woods Hole are about 5 miles apart and they have a three-hour difference between their high tides. The reasons, described in the text, are the differing effects on the tide from the shape, depth, and configuration of the coastal areas.

Tides are important to the health of the ocean for many reasons. For example, they cause currents that flush and clean harbors and estuaries, as well as mix nearshore waters, thereby diluting water-borne pollutants. Tides help recirculate the nutrients needed by floating plants (phyto-plankton) to produce the primary source of food for all the organisms in the ocean. Tidal currents move small animals and plants to and from their shallow-water breeding or growth zones to offshore areas and deeper parts of the ocean. Many biological activities of marine animals, includ-ing reproduction cycles, are linked to various periods or times of the tide. Indeed, the health of the sea and all its creatures depends on the cease-less movement of water.

A knowledge of tides is vital for anyone fishing in the ocean—for success, and for safety. Boating anglers and shore fishermen alike can use the tides to their advantage. Many nearshore-fishing techniques depend on what the tide is doing, especially when fishing on tidal flats, in estuar-ies, and around inlets. As I mentioned earlier, the tide-produced move-ment of water often dictates where game fish will be.

Predicting tides is both an art and a science. People who do so make long-term measurements at a few specific areas, and then extrapolate (nowadays using computers) these measurements to other coastal areas and into the future. These predictions become less accurate the farther one goes from the areas of the original measurements; in coastal and inshore areas, tidal conditions can vary considerably in areas just a few miles apart. At its basic level, tidal prediction includes determining the times and heights of high and low tide for a specific location, and sometimes the direction and speed of the tidal current.

For the fisherman or oceanographer, many aspects of the tides are relatively easy to understand, but some, such as tidal currents, can be complex. Fortunately, anglers don't have to understand all the tricky fac-tors; knowing the ramifications and effects of tides is good enough when we fish.

CAUSES OF THE TIDES

Tides are caused by two types of forces acting on our rotating Earth: *gravity* and *inertia*. Gravity can be defined as the attraction between two objects—Earth and the moon, for example. As you might remember from science class, this attraction is directly proportional to the product of the masses of the two objects and inversely proportional to the square of the distance between the objects. Inertia is the tendency of a moving object to continue moving in a straight line; it is this force, sometimes called centrifugal force, that holds water in a bucket when you swing the bucket in an arc overhead. The relative orbits of Earth, moon, and sun are dependent on these two forces. Without inertia, Earth, the moon, and the sun would crash together because of gravity. Without gravity, inertia would make them fly apart from one another into outer space.

In considering tides and gravity, the principal objects involved are Earth, the sun, and the moon. Earth and the moon are about a quarter of

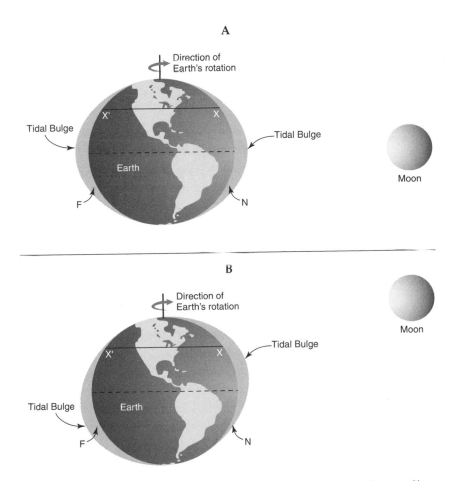

Fig. 2-2 This illustration shows the gravitational attraction between the Earth and the moon (the dimensions and size of the tidal bulge are greatly exaggerated). In the upper figure (A) the moon is parallel to Earth's equator. Points X and X' indicate the change in position of a point on Earth's surface after half a lunar day (12 hours, 25 minutes). With the moon parallel to the Earth's equator there will be two equal or almost equal high and low tides per 24 hours and 50 minutes at positions X and X'. In the lower figure (B) the moon is inclined to Earth's equator. In this situation there will be two unequal high and low tides at positions X and X' per 24 hours and 50 minutes. This is not as complicated as it looks or sounds. If you are having trouble with it, give it another reading and check the text again.

a million miles apart, whereas Earth and the sun are about 93 million miles from each other. The mass of the sun is about 27 million times that of the moon. The moon, however, is about 400 times closer to Earth than the sun is, and this proximity gives it a greater gravitational effect. (Remember, the power of gravity is inversely proportional to distance *squared*.) As far as tides are concerned, the gravitational attraction between the moon and Earth is about twice that between the sun and Earth.

Let's first consider the simpler case of the gravitational attraction between just Earth and the moon. The gravitational attraction between the two occurs everywhere, but is strongest on the side of Earth that faces the moon, simply because that is where the two spheres are closest. Inertia is also active here, but the gravitational force slightly exceeds it and pulls the water on Earth toward the moon. This causes a "bulge" of water on the side of our planet closest to the moon (labeled N in Figure 2-2).

On the opposite or far side of Earth (labeled F), the gravitational attraction of the moon is at its weakest. Here, the inertial force slightly exceeds the moon's gravitational force. The water tries to keep going in a straight line—it wants to fly off the planet and into space, but Earth's gravity won't let it—and forms a second bulge. The two bulges of water formed by gravity and inertia are situated on opposite sides of Earth: one forms where Earth and the moon are closest, and the other forms where they are farthest apart.

Because water is a fluid, the two bulges remain oriented to the moon as Earth rotates and as the moon revolves around our planet. During one rotation of Earth (relative to the moon), a marine area will generally experience a pattern of two tidal highs as it passes through the two bulges on opposite sides of the planet, and two relative lows when outside the bulge areas. Since the moon is generally not perpendicular to Earth's axis of rotation—that is, it's not aligned with our equator—the two high tides at a particular spot are usually unequal; one high tide is higher than the other. (Compare X and X' on the lower and upper parts of Figure 2-2.)

Earth completes one rotation every 24 hours, relative to the sun. But because the moon revolves around Earth as the planet rotates, it takes Earth a little longer (an additional 50 minutes) to complete one rotation relative to the moon. In other words, a point on Earth's surface passes closest to the moon every 24 hours and 50 minutes; thus, in general the passing of the two tidal bulges on Earth's surface will produce two high tides about 12 hours and 25 minutes apart.

Because the time interval between each high tide is about 12 hours and 25 minutes, on a *daily* basis the high or low tides will occur about 50 minutes later every day (two times 25 minutes). Or, to put it differently, the entire tidal pattern will repeat itself every 24 hours and 50 minutes. This simple fact clearly shows that tides are primarily influenced by the moon; if they were primarily controlled by the sun, the pattern would occur at the same time every day, based on our normal 24-hour solar day.

The effect of the sun on tides becomes important when it and the moon line up together to pull on Earth. Their combined gravitational attraction on Earth causes a relatively strong tide, which is said to "spring forth" onto the coast, and is therefore called a spring tide. (Spring tides have nothing to do with the season.) Spring tides (also called moon tides) occur roughly every two weeks, at about the times of new moon and full moon. There usually is little or no difference in the total range or strength of the spring tides during full moon or new moon. The dominant image of the moon in the sky during a full moon might make you think that the tides are stronger at this time than they are during a new moon, when the moon is barely visible. This is not the case; the tides are about the same strength during both moon phases.

Relatively weak tides, called neap tides, occur when the gravitational forces of the sun and moon form a right angle relative to Earth. In this position, they work against each other. (The term "neap" comes from an old word that means "inactive.") Neap tides also occur about every two weeks, at first-quarter moon and last- or third-quarter moon. An observant fisherman can easily become familiar with these different phases of the sun and moon and their resulting influences on tides.

The typical tidal sequence is a spring tide followed by lower tides, leading about a week later to a neap tide, which in turn is followed by rising tides leading a week later to spring tides—and so on. The general tidal sequence will repeat itself about every fourteen days. The spring-tide range tends to be about 20 percent above the average tidal range, while the neap tide range is about 20 percent below the average range. In other words, the tidal range (the maximum water height at high tide minus the minimum water height at low tide) is more than average during spring tides and less than average during neap tides. The time between an entire tidal cycle, or between one new moon and the next one, is 29½ days.

TIDAL CHARACTERISTICS

Continents can interfere with, change, and block the tidal bulge (which oceanographers prefer to call the tidal waveform) as it moves around Earth. This causes many complications in the tides, their patterns, and related currents, especially in coastal areas. (If there were no continents—in other words, if our planet was all ocean—the tides would be a lot easier to understand and predict.)

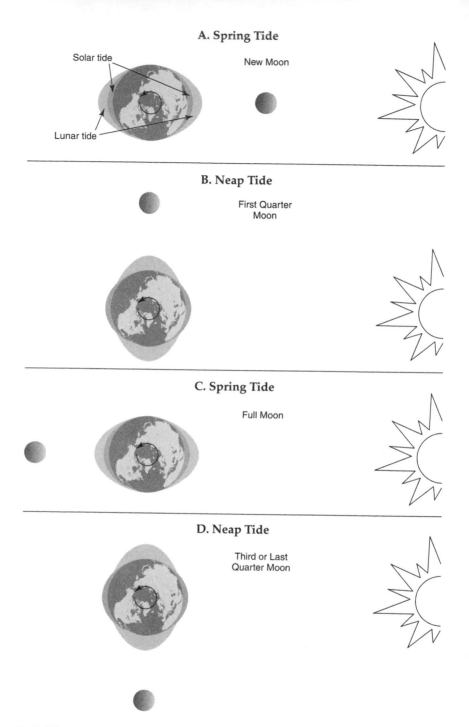

Fig. 2-3 The four phases of the moon and how they and the sun produce the spring and neap tides (the dimensions and size of the tidal bulges are greatly exaggerated). Neap tides occur when the trough of the solar tide is aligned with the crest of the lunar tide or when the trough of the lunar tide is aligned with the crest of the solar tide. Spring tides occur when the crests of both lunar and solar tides are aligned. The view is looking down from the North Pole and the tides are greatly exaggerated. The arrow indicates the direction of Earth's rotation.

Defining Tidal Stages

The term high water means the maximum tidal level during a tidal cycle; low water means the lowest level. The term slack water indicates when the tidal current is not flowing. The term "stand" or "stand of the tide" indicates when the tide level is stationary. When the tide is rising, when water is coming in toward the shore, we say it's flood tide. Eventually the incoming water attains its high tide level and starts to withdraw or fall. The falling tide is called the ebb tide. The short period of time when the tide stops, before changing direction, or when there is no horizontal motion, is usually called slack water.

Most coastal areas have two high tides and two low tides a day. If the two highs and the two lows are each about the same height, the pattern is called a semidaily or semidiurnal tide. When the highs and the lows each differ in height, the pattern is called a mixed tide. Some areas, such as the Gulf of Mexico, have only one high and one low tide each day; this is called a diurnal tide. The West Coast of the United States tends to have mixed tides, whereas a semidiurnal pattern is more typical of the East Coast.

An area with either a mixed or semidiurnal tidal pattern will have ebb tides twice, flood tides twice, and slack water four times over a 24 hour and 50 minute period. Sometimes, one of the two high tides during a day is higher than the other. This is due to the moon's inclination to Earth's equatorial plane (compare the position of X and X' on the bottom of Figure 2-2).

In many areas, especially those with a semidiurnal tide, the highest tides occur a day or two after a full or new moon rather than during those exact lunar stages. The same delay will occur with neap tides—they'll arrive a day or two after the quarter moons. This effect, called "the age of the tide," is due to such factors as the shape of the ocean basin and friction of the tidal waveform with the seafloor.

Many coastal fishing areas, including inlets, small estuaries, and bays, contain a small volume of water compared to the open ocean; thus, the gravitational attraction between this small amount of water and the sun and the moon (the causes of the tide) is relatively weak compared to what occurs in the open ocean. Still, coastal bays and estuaries have tidal rhythms. The tides here, called "forced tides," are caused by water being

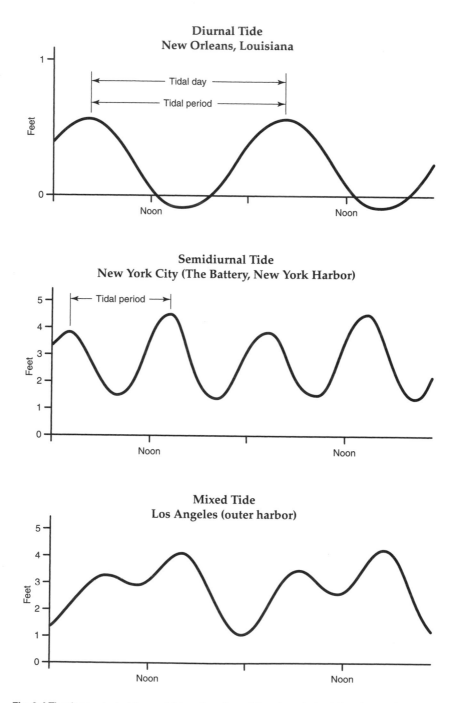

Fig. 2-4 The three principal types of tides: diurnal, semidiurnal, and mixed. See the text for more details.

Fig. 2-5 The types of tides and the spring tidal range around North America and parts of South America. The largest tidal range, up to 50 feet or more, is located in Canada in the Bay of Fundy, between Nova Scotia and New Brunswick. Its high tidal range is due to its funnel shape and its position to the direction of tidal flow.

forced into or out of inlets by the tidal changes in the open ocean. Forced tides, like any variety of tidal change, cause tidal currents that influence where the fish will be.

OTHER FACTORS

We've looked at the basic forces influencing the tides, but there are complicating factors. For example, neither the moon nor Earth have perfectly circular orbits. The orbits are ellipses (elongated circles), and they cause the distance between Earth and the moon to vary during the year. In turn, the relative heights of spring, neap, and other parts of the tide will vary.

When the moon is farthest from Earth (called the lunar apogee), the tidal range will be less than average; when the moon is closest (at the lunar perigee), the range will be higher than average. This is because the gravitational effect of the moon on Earth is greater when they are closer to each other, and vice versa. (The period of time between apogee and perigee is 27½ days.) When the lunar perigee and the spring tide coincide, very high and very low tides will occur. Under certain conditions, when the sun and the moon are closest to Earth and aligned, extreme tides can occur.

The character and timing of the tide in coastal waters is strongly influenced by the width, shape, and depth of the continental shelf. For instance, the continental shelf width off Newport, Rhode Island, is less than it is off Boston, which is only about 50 miles to the north on the Atlantic coast. Because of this, high tide occurs about 3½ hours earlier in Newport.

The weather, especially winds and barometric pressure, can effect the timing of the tides, as well as the tidal range. A strong wind blowing in the direction of the tide-caused current may obscure the tidal effect. Conversely, winds blowing in the same direction as the tidal current will increase the speed of the current. A change of 1 inch in the barometric pressure in a stationary low-pressure system can result in a 1-foot rise in the level of the tide; if the tidal range is small, this meteorological effect can be even larger than the normal tide, and obscure its effect. Storms blowing onshore can considerably increase the height of a tide, sometimes causing damage in coastal and inland areas. For example, in 1900 more than 6,000 people were drowned by a storm surge in Galveston, Texas. Bangladesh, because of its location and shallow topography, has been especially vulnerable to such storms; more than 100,000 died in 1970 due to such a storm effect, and similar events have occurred since.

TIDAL CURRENTS

The tides produce a vertical rise and fall of sea level. This up-and-down movement will cause a difference in the height of sea level between one area and another. This difference in water levels, in turn, initiates a flow from one area to the other to bring the water level back to horizontal. The bigger the difference in the height of the water between two areas, the stronger the flow. Think of what happens when you disturb the water level in a bathtub. When the tides cause such a difference in water-level height (winds can have a similar effect), the resulting flow is called a tidal current.

Unlike most other ocean currents, tidal currents are not restricted to the surface or near the surface, but generally maintain a similar speed

Expressing Current Speed

Among sea captains and oceanographers, the speed of a current is often expressed in knots. A knot is equal to the speed of 1 nautical mile per hour, so we never use the expression "knots per hour." A nautical mile (6,080 feet) is longer than a normal or statute mile (5,280 feet) by about 1.15 times. Thus, a current of 3 knots is equal to 3 nautical miles per hour or 3.45 statute miles per hour.

almost down to the seafloor. This is an important consideration for fishing. Tidal currents are a horizontal movement of the water, whereas tides themselves are a vertical movement. Like the tides, tidal currents can be semidiurnal, diurnal, or mixed, and will usually be similar to the pattern of the tide in the region.

Out in the open ocean, away from the influence of land and shallow water, tidal currents move fairly slowly. Near the coast, however, tidal currents are restricted by land, channels and inlets, and bottom structure or the bottom proper. These restrictions increase the water's rate of flow, which causes the current to intensify. Consider water flowing from an area 20-feet deep onto a 10-foot shoal. For the flow to continue—for it to "climb" the shoal area—the current speed must increase. The increased flow over this shoal will frequently become turbulent, forming what we call a tidal rip. Even offshore, you can identify bottom structures by noting the tidal rips that occur over them.

As an angler, you'll benefit from knowing when maximum tidal current and slack water occur. Often, when the tides reach either their high or low mark, the water will go slack and the current will reverse or change direction. This general rule, however, rarely applies to nearshore or inshore areas, where the land or the continental shelf interferes with the tidal waveform. In these regions, the relationship between tide height and strength and the direction of the current is more complex.

To make sense of the varying tidal-current conditions along the coast, oceanographers characterize the tidal waveform as being either a progressive wave or a standing wave, or some mixture of the two. In a progressive waveform, the maximum currents occur at high and low tides. The tidal current weakens, stops, and reverses at the midtide position. A progressive wave is the waveform typically found in the open ocean and sometimes

Progressive Waveform

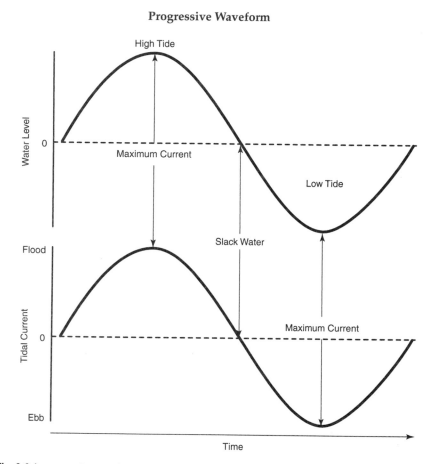

Fig. 2-6 A progressive waveform. The upper part of the figure shows the tidal curve. The lower part of the figure shows the direction of the tidal current. Note that the tidal current essentially stops about midway between high and low tide and then reverses direction. Maximum currents are at high and low tide. This is the common tidal pattern offshore, beyond the influence of land and shallow water.

close to shore, especially when the tide comes in parallel to the coast. The maximum current of a progressive wave will be near the high and low tides.

Commonly, the path and character of the progressive waveform is affected by the shape of the coast, especially when the tides enter an inlet, an estuary, or a large partially enclosed coastal area, such as the Gulf of Maine. Here, the progressive wave behaves more like what is called a standing wave. To put the concept in more familiar terms, when you disturb the water in a half-filled bathtub, a standing wave results. The water will be high at one end, low at the other end, and will slosh back and forth with corresponding changes in the water level. A standing wave, and the water flow (or current), will be from the end that is falling toward the end that is rising. The maximum current will be at the midpoint (or midtide), when both ends of the wave are at the same level; slack water will occur at the high and low ends (or high and low tides).

As you can see, the current patterns—when the current slackens and when the maximum current occurs—of progressive and standing wave-

Standing Waveform

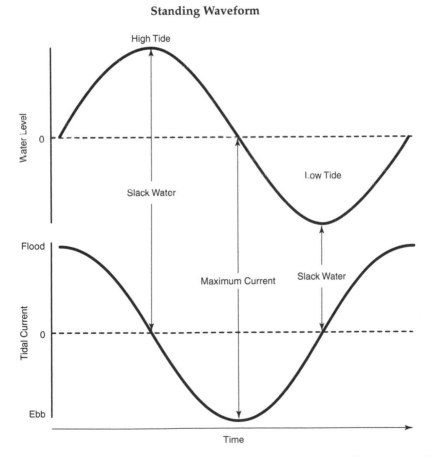

Fig. 2-7 A standing waveform. The upper part of the figure shows the tidal curve. The lower part of the figure shows the direction of the tidal current. Note here that the maximum tidal flow occurs at midtide and that the tidal flow is at a minimum at the high- and low-tide positions. This type of tidal pattern is common in restricted areas, such as bays, inlets, and estuaries.

forms are roughly the opposite. To know which waveform is active, you must study the tidal pattern. When you're fishing an estuary or similar coastal body of water, you can observe if slack water occurs at midtide (progressive) or at high and low tide (standing). Alternatively, if high and low tide occur at the same time everywhere in an estuary, a standing waveform will be present; if the highs and lows happen at different times throughout the estuary, you'll be observing a progressive waveform.

Unfortunately, these examples only apply if the progressive or the standing wave dominates the tidal flow. Often, neither a pure progressive nor a pure standing waveform dominates; instead, you'll see a mixture of the two. Also remember that the wind can interfere with or compound the effects of tidal currents. Every coastal location is different. You should observe what's going on in the areas you fish; getting to know the tidal patterns, and the resultant current patterns, will lead to more fruitful angling.

HYDRAULIC CURRENTS

Often, the tidal pattern at either end of a strait or inlet of water, such as between an estuary and the open ocean, is not in phase. This results from what is called a hydraulic current, which is caused by the differences in water height at either end of the strait or inlet.

A hydraulic current can create situations in which the offshore ocean tide is rising but the water in the estuary is falling, resulting in an out-flowing, or ocean-flowing current, in the strait. The outgoing or incoming flow through the narrow inlet or strait cannot keep pace with the rising or falling tide outside in the ocean. As a result, the water level inside the inlet, in the estuary, lags behind the water level of the ocean. For just how long the water is out of phase depends on the dimensions of the inlet, the size and shape of the bay or estuary, the strength of the tide, and the weather conditions. (The subject of hydraulic currents, and how they relate to fishing, is discussed further in Chapter 9.)

Hydraulic currents cause the current flow inside the estuary to differ considerably from the flow outside the estuary in the ocean. In some small estuaries, the difference in the times of the tides within the estuary and outside the estuary's strait can be as much as an hour or two. The fishing may be considerably different in the two areas, too.

OFFSHORE TIDES

In offshore waters, where land or shallow water do not restrict the direction of flow of the tide, tidal currents often follow a rotary pattern and the tidal flow will be in all directions. The rotation of the offshore tidal current is caused by the Earth's rotation; unless influenced by other factors such as weather, the current moves clockwise in the Northern Hemisphere and counterclockwise in the Southern Hemisphere. Interestingly, in deep water, some fish can use the tide to migrate. At the appropriate tide stage, they rise from the bottom and then swim along with the tidal current.

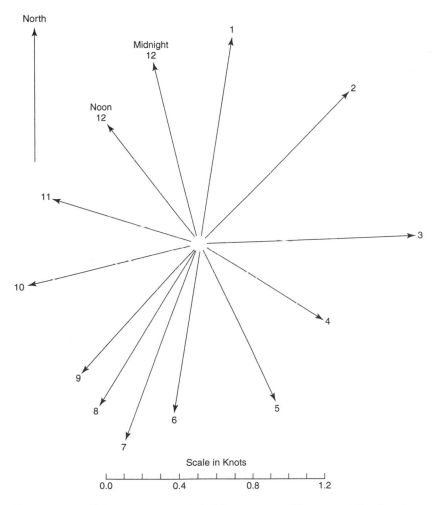

Fig. 2-8 A rotary tidal current pattern typical of the open ocean. This representation of a rotary current, also called a current rose or a current ellipse if the flow pattern is irregular, is by a series of arrows that depict the current direction and speed at each hour. The illustration shows the speed and direction of the current at the beginning of each hour starting at noon for a typical day at the Nantucket Shoals Lightship, stationed off the coast of Massachusetts. A rotary current flows continuously, with its direction changing through the entire 360 degrees of a compass over the 12 hour and 25 minute tidal period. An important characteristic of a rotary current is that it does not have a period of slack water. The length of the arrows are proportional to the current velocity.

The speed of the rotary current flow will vary throughout the tidal cycle, with two maximums and two minimums in each cycle; the maximums and minimums are usually in approximately opposite directions and are separated from each other by about three hours. This rotary pattern circulates around a position called an amphidromic point, which has no tidal height. The general pattern is similar to water sloshing around a bucket.

Rotary currents can have the same periodic variations as those of normal tides, but their tidal range is usually fairly small, usually less than 2 feet. During full and new moons, the rotary currents will be stronger than average, and will be less than average during the quarter moons. Likewise, the rotary currents will be stronger when the moon is closer to the Earth than when it's farther away.

If the coastal waters are relatively deep, the offshore rotary pattern can come close to shore, but the shoaling bottom and the presence of the coast will change the rotary tidal waveform as it approaches land. As the shoaling bottom and the presence of the coast restrict the offshore rotary pattern, the tidal currents will flow in a back-and-forth manner, rather than in the rotary pattern. The restricting influence of the coastal region will increase the rate of the tidal flow and the resulting currents.

FACTORS INFLUENCING TIDAL CURRENTS

The moon phase influences the strength of tidal currents, though often that effect lags just a bit. (The same is true for the tide.) In general, spring (maximum) tidal currents may occur a day or two after the full and new moon, and the ebb, or minimum, tidal currents may occur a day or two after the quarter moons. The same as the tide, tidal currents are also affected by the relative closeness of the moon—currents are stronger when the moon is closest, at its perigee, and weaker when the moon is farthest away, at its apogee.

The water movement associated with a tidal current also has non-tidal influences, namely the wind or local river flow. Winds can delay the turning of the tide, and increase or decrease the speed of the tidal current. During periods of strong winds and weak tidal currents, the current may be very different from what the tide alone would cause it to do.

The speed of the tidal current, and the time at which the current begins, can vary considerably over short distances due to changes in bottom topography and the shape of the coast, in about the same way as the tidal range varies. In other words, when the tidal range is high the currents will be relatively strong, and when the tidal range is low the currents will be weak. Still, the relative strength of the tidal current can differ, meaning that the overall currents can be relatively weak in an area even though the tidal range is high, and vice versa. An example of this phenomenon occurs along the New England coast. The Gulf of Maine has a large tidal range, but weak tidal currents. In nearby Nantucket Sound, however, the tidal range is small, but the tidal currents are strong. The strength of the current in each of these places is a result of the volume of water that enters the area, and the size of the opening to the area. A lot of water flowing through a small opening will produce a relatively strong current. Because the large volume of water entering the Gulf of Maine passes through a large opening, the tidal currents are relatively weak, whereas in Nantucket Sound the opening is relatively small, causing faster tidal currents. Nevertheless, the relationship between the speed of the tidal current and the tidal range holds true in most areas.

PREDICTING TIDES
Published tidal information typically indicates when the current turns, changing from flood tide to ebb tide, or vice versa. You can find this information in tackle shops, in the newspaper, in books such as the *Eldridge Tide and Pilot Book*, or from the National Oceanic and Atmospheric Administration (NOAA). Several computer programs give tidal curves for locations around the United States. (I have described some of these in Appendix 4.)

These sources can be useful, but they are based on information from a few localities that has been extrapolated to apply to other areas, so you might not be getting accurate data; in coastal areas, tides can vary greatly in spots just a few miles apart. Unfortunately, there often is little or no high- or low-tide information published for offshore areas. In open-water areas, away from land, you'll be fairly safe to assume that the tidal current follows a progressive waveform, with maximum currents near high and low tides.

Even with the best tide tables, tide watches, or computer programs, it's likely that the times of high and low tide, and the times of maximum currents, in the area you plan to fish will be somewhat different than predicted. It's also true that the most difficult areas in which to predict tides are harbors, estuaries, inlets, and bays—just where we frequently fish. If no data exist, or if the available information isn't accurate, you'll have to depend on your own observations. One thing you can do is to keep a log, noting the times of high tide, low tide, and maximum current. You can compare this information with the published tide tables for a nearby area, and adjust the times from the tide table to apply to your area.

If you really want to get serious, you can make your own tidal curve by plotting on a graph hourly measurements of the tide's position. You

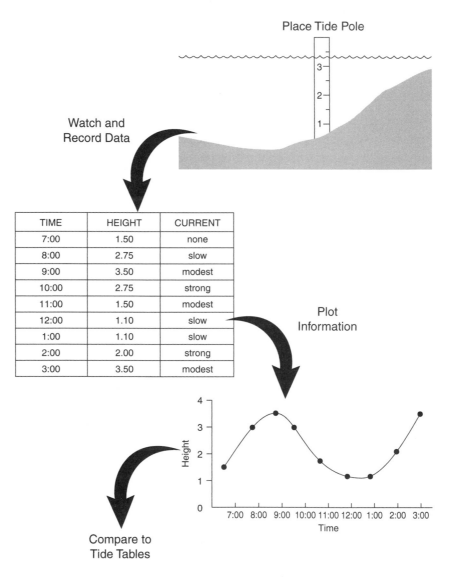

TIME	HEIGHT	CURRENT
7:00	1.50	none
8:00	2.75	slow
9:00	3.50	modest
10:00	2.75	strong
11:00	1.50	modest
12:00	1.10	slow
1:00	1.10	slow
2:00	2.00	strong
3:00	3.50	modest

Fig. 2-9 A simple method to develop a tidal curve for your favorite area—just follow the arrows. See the text for more details.

can do this by measuring the tidal height against a fixed object, such as a stick marked in 1-foot intervals or a bridge piling. Begin by observing the tide over a twelve-hour period (or whatever time is needed for one high-to-low-tide cycle to pass). You can estimate the current speed as slow, fast, or slack, and note this on your graph. Later, you can plot another tide cycle; the tidal heights of the two cycles will be different, but the information will better define the general shape of your tidal curve. This curve will help you to predict when the current is active or slack in your area. Once you know the difference between the tide in your area and what's published in the newspaper, you can add or subtract the appropriate time correction to or from the published tide information to predict future conditions in your area.

WHICH TIDE OR CURRENT IS BEST FOR FISHING?

The answer to this question depends on what species of fish you'll be going after, what type of fishing method you plan to use, where you'll be fishing, the weather conditions, and if you plan to fish during day or night.

Some anglers feel that the roaring currents during a spring tide are the best for fishing; many anglers who fish at night for striped bass fall into this category. Striper fishermen often say that the spring-tide currents will trap, hold, and confuse large amounts of bait, creating a situation in which the striper's appetite kicks into high gear.

Even ardent striper anglers, however, question *when* to fish during a spring tide. Some say that the fishing is best when the current is the strongest, others prefer the point when the tide is just beginning to flow or ebb. (Most agree that it's best to fish after dark.) I favor the latter perspective, because fish avoid extremely strong currents to conserve their energy, or at least stay on the edge of the current as much as possible.

Other anglers believe that we should avoid fishing during spring tides altogether, especially during a bright, full moon; many offshore anglers fall into this group. These anglers believe that daytime feeders such as bluefin tuna and marlin will feed at night under the bright light of the full moon, and thus be less apt to bite during the day.

The strong tidal currents associated with spring tides can cause problems for bottom fishermen: the stronger the current, the harder it is to keep your bait or lure at the appropriate depth. Strong currents can also frustrate boating anglers who wish to hold their position over a certain part of the bottom.

High tides can give flats fishermen fits because the strong tide allows fish to get deep into mangrove swamps, off the flats. This will make the fish more difficult to catch, and more difficult to land. At the same time, high tides open up new areas for predators to explore. And as the high current ebbs, it will drain bait off the flat, carrying food to waiting predators. This situation—large amounts of water full of bait during an ebbing spring tide—also occurs at the inlets or mouths of estuaries or bays. Obviously, the fishing can be very good at these times.

Some fishermen feel that the period leading up to a spring tide is considerably better for fishing than the period after the spring tide. This is called "fishing up the moon" versus "fishing down the moon." There may be some truth to this idea—if spring tides stimulate fish to feed more aggressively, it would seem that "up the moon" has more potential than "down."

I know many anglers who don't like their chances for fishing success during neap tides. Though the fishing might be better during spring tides, it still can be pretty good during neap tides—it just may be a little harder. But let me assure you that fish don't fast as they wait for the higher tides and stronger currents. Nor do they feed only during a fleeting part of a specific tide. Marine fish are almost always looking for food; they will continue to feed throughout the monthly tidal cycle, through the highs and lows and changing tidal currents.

Offshore, fish slow down and even stop their feeding on or around rips when the current stops, and will start again when the current returns. You may have a more difficult time finding fish when the currents aren't strong—but that's part of the challenge of ocean fishing.

Periods of slack current are probably the least favorable times to fish in the ocean, as slack currents generally do not carry the amount of bait that moving water does. Nevertheless, the game fish are somewhere—they're probably just spread out. If they see food (or a lure, fly, or bait), they may well take it. I caught my largest false albacore (little tunny is the more appropriate term among biologists), a 14-pounder, on a fly during slack current. I made a lucky, blind cast, and I'll never forget it.

So what is the best tide or current to fish? Well, it depends. You can probably catch fish during any tide or current; some part of the tide will produce good fishing somewhere along the coast, or offshore. The challenge is to match the location with the right tide for fishing.

If you have good fishing during a specific tide, keep in mind that similar tidal conditions will be present 12 hours and 25 minutes later. If you want to fish a similar tide the following day, fish 50 minutes later. (In other words, visit the area 24 hours and 50 minutes later.) This is sometimes called the "hour-after principle"—if the tide is right for fishing at 8 A.M., it should be okay at 8:50 A.M. the next day. The principle works most of the time, though some fish prefer to eat at dawn or dusk regardless of the tide.

Once you start paying attention to the phases of the moon you should be able to estimate the relative strength of the tide. If you fish in an area where the tides are of the mixed or semidiurnal variety, note which of the two daily high tides is the highest—it will occur 50 minutes later each subsequent day. Fishing the stronger (higher) high tide when it occurs at dawn or dusk often yields especially good fishing.

Always remember that the tides and tidal currents vary along coastal areas, and that the actual tide may not correspond to information in published tide tables. Also remember that generalities about tides, such as that the tidal current is stronger at a certain hour after a certain tide, are not always the rule. It's worth your time to know the tides and tidal currents where you fish. This information will make your fishing more productive—and you'll have more fun when you're aware of the processes at work around you.

A LOOK AT OCEAN WAVES

Waves in the ocean can be less than an inch high to more than 100 feet tall, and can be less than a foot long or stretch thousands of miles. The most common waves are caused by the wind, and not surprisingly are called wind-driven waves. When we see a wind-driven wave, we see a moving shape called a waveform; the water is forced to take on this shape by the energy of the wind. The water itself is moving, but more slowly and in a different manner and pattern than the waveform. (The main exception to this is when waves break near a beach.) One way to visualize this is to hold a sheet of paper, one end in your right hand, the other in your

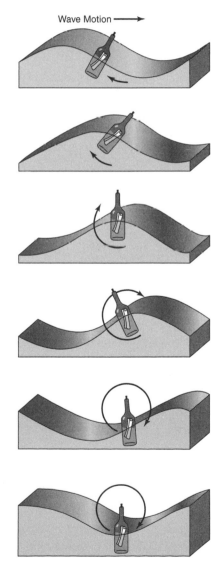

Wave Motion ⟶

Fig. 2-10 An object (a bottle in this example) floating on the surface (in deep water) as a wave passes. The movement of the bottle clearly shows the orbital motion associated with the waveform. Note that the waveform moves forward, but the water particles only move in an orbit or circular pattern. (Deep water, in an oceanographic sense, means a water depth of ½ or more of the wavelength. In other words, for a wave 50 feet long, it is considered to be in deep water if the depth is 25 feet or more.)

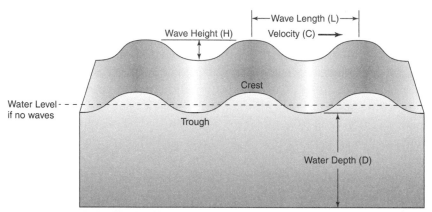

Period (T) = Time for two successive wave crests to pass a reference point

Fig. 2-11 Some of the important characteristics of a wave in deep water. Any ocean wave, including the common wind-driven variety, can be defined by its length, its height, its period, or its speed or velocity. The length of a wave **(L)** is defined as the horizontal distance between successive wave crests. Wave height **(H)** is defined as the vertical distance from the top of a wave (its crest) to its low point (the bottom of the trough). The period **(T)** of a wave is the time it takes for successive crests to pass by a given point. Wave speed or velocity **(C)** is the wavelength **(L)** divided by the period **(T).** In other words, **C= L/T.** This equation is similar to the one used to determine velocity or speed of a moving car: distance divided by the time needed to travel the distance.

left. Move one hand up and down to form a wave that travels along the length of the paper. The paper is not moving forward—only the wave-form is. The process is similar to the wave performed by fans in a football stadium; the people move up and down and the "wave" seems to travel around the stadium.

When waves reach shallow water and eventually break, the water is now moving forward, toward the shore, at the same speed as the wave-form had been traveling. The rapid shoreward movement of water causes various currents in the nearshore area that can produce some excellent fishing. Also, if you've ever been in a small boat between the beach and breaking waves, you know how dangerous this area can be.

The general characteristics of wind-driven waves are determined by three related factors:
1. Duration—the time the wind has been blowing.
2. Velocity—the speed of the wind.
3. Fetch—the unobstructed distance over the water that the wind has blown.

A wave's height and its wavelength generally increase as wind velocity and wind duration increase. Waves generally have shorter wavelengths in lakes, where the fetch is relatively short, whereas in the open ocean the fetch can be hundreds to even thousands of miles. (The fetch is important in determining the length of the wave.) Scientists don't know if ocean waves have a maximum height. Waves as high as 112 feet have been recorded, but scientists suspect that waves can get even larger than that.

Wind-driven waves go through three stages: sea, swell, and surf. Sea refers to the waves found where they are being formed out in the ocean, usually by a storm or strong winds. Within the storm area, the waves have no systematic pattern—waves of different periods and heights are traveling in various directions. Each of these waves is the product of an individual incident of wind dragging over the water. Waves in the sea

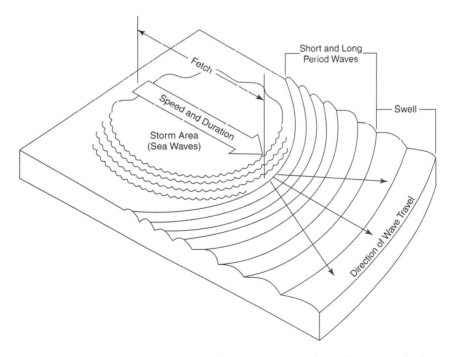

Fig. 2-12 The three main factors that influence the height and period of wind-driven waves: fetch (distance over the water that the wind has blown), wind velocity, and wind duration. Wave size will increase with wind speed, wind duration, and fetch. Waves advance across the ocean as "swell," no longer powered by the wind that spawned them but by the energy they acquired from the wind.

Wave-Trains

Waves travel as groups or wave-trains. You can see this by tossing a rock into quiet water. Several sets of small waves will move away from the impact area. As the group of waves move, the lead one will eventually disappear or die, and will be replaced by the next in the sequence, while a new one will appear at the end of the wave-train. In a manner of speaking, an individual wave will move through the wave-train, disappear, and be replaced by a new one at the end.

stage are sometimes referred to as being "confused." If you are ever caught in such conditions, you will know why the term is appropriate.

As sea waves move away from the storm area, they start to sort themselves out. The longer and faster moving waves move ahead of the waves with slower and shorter periods. (The longer the wave, the faster it travels—remember, $C=L/T$.) Eventually, a relatively uniform wave pattern is established, where groups of waves have similar dimensions and travel at the same speed in the same direction. This uniform pattern is called swell (see Figure 2-13b). One way to visualize this sorting of waves is to imagine cars leaving a full parking lot, with some traveling at 20 mph, some traveling at 40 mph, and some at 60 mph. Eventually, all of the cars traveling 20 mph will be grouped together, as will the ones traveling 40 mph and 60 mph—in other words, they have sorted themselves out according to their speed.

As waves continue to travel away from the area of their origin (the storm area), they will slowly lose energy and get smaller, but their period will remain the same. Actually, swell can travel considerable distances. For example, in one instance the effects of a storm off Antarctica were detected about a week later as swell along the Alaskan coast.

The third stage of wind-driven waves is called surf, which occurs near the shore as the bottom shoals. In the surf stage, shallow water causes the wave's height to increase, after which the wave eventually breaks. Breaking surf waves differ from sea and swell waves in a distinctive way. In the surf stage, the water no longer travels in an orbital motion with a slow forward motion, but moves rapidly directly toward the beach. Energy from the forward-surging water pounds the beach—and any anglers standing in the surf. This energy also causes beach erosion, grinding down and

Fig. 2-13A Sea—Waves in the generation (storm) area.

Fig. 2-13B Swell—Note how the wave pattern has become more uniform.

Fig. 2-13C Surf—The waves are breaking.

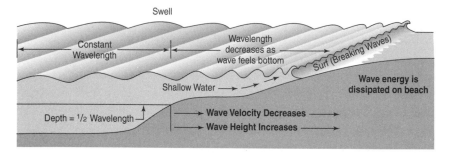

Fig. 2-14 Waves entering the surf zone. Note the decrease in their wavelength and increase in wave height when the waveform reaches shallow water (water depth less than ½ the wave length). The period remains the same. After the wave breaks, its energy will be spent on the beach, sometimes causing erosion.

removing massive areas of beachfront and rocks from the coastal areas of the world. When waves break in the surf zone, a pattern of currents is formed, which, along with the breaking waves, will change the character of the bottom and lead to a unique circulation pattern of the surging water, often creating good opportunities for fishing.

When you're fishing from a boat, it's important to watch both the wave pattern and how it changes, as well as the wind speed and duration. If you start to fish during a 20-knot onshore wind, initially the waves may be only 2- to 3-feet high. After a few hours, with no change in conditions, the waves could easily build to 5 to 6 feet because of the wind duration. My general rule is that once whitecaps appear, which indicate a wind speed of 15 knots or more, I think about returning to port. (I have a heavy and very stable 21-foot boat, by the way.) If conditions continue to build, or stay constant, I definitely return to port.

Once waves are formed, winds, tides, or currents can influence them locally. For example, the sea will increase when the wind is blowing against the direction of wave motion, the current, or the tidal flow. This is common along the edges of major currents, such as the western side of the Gulf Stream off the East Coast of the United States. A nautical situation that boating anglers should be aware of is "wind against the tide." Let's say you start a trip with the tide and wind moving in the same direction. A few hours later, however, the tidal direction may reverse and oppose the wind. As a result, you'll experience rougher sea conditions.

The wind direction, since it determines the fetch, also affects waves. For example, you'll be more comfortable fishing near land with a breeze coming from the land (thus limiting the fetch) than during an offshore blow of the same strength.

Chapter 3

Inshore and Estuarine Environments

From a fisherman's point of view, the marine environment can be divided into three broad regions: the inshore or estuarine waters, the beach and nearshore waters, and offshore waters. In this chapter, and the following two, we'll look at the general characteristics and marine processes that shape and influence each region. Fishing strategies and techniques for each of these regions are covered in Part III.

Nearly 90 percent of the saltwater fish caught by recreational fishermen in the lower forty-eight states of the United States depend on some aspect of the inshore and coastal environment for their survival. Simply said, without healthy estuaries, marshes, bays, tidal flats, and other inshore areas, many species of ocean fish could not endure.

The inshore environment is complex and undergoes frequent change. Because of its proximity to land, the region is exposed to many types of human activity, few of which are beneficial to the ocean or its inhabitants. About 40 percent of the world's human population lives within 60 miles of a coast, and this percentage increases each year. In the United States the number is even higher—about 75 percent of our population lives within 50 miles of a coast (if we include the Great Lakes). Further, about 40 percent of U.S. manufacturing, and about half of all construction, occurs in coastal counties. Rivers passing through inshore regions carrying nutrients (and other elements) needed for plant and animal growth also carry harmful industrial pollutants and municipal discharge.

Despite such hazards, marine fish remain inexorably drawn to the inshore region. One type of coastal area in particular stands out as being vital to the health of marine life: estuaries. Actually, if we had to pick the most vital environment of the entire ocean, the winner would probably be estuaries, and their associated marshes, swamps, tidal flats, and inlets. A large percentage of the fish we anglers are interested in catching rely on some portion of an estuary for their very survival—for their growth, for their food, as an area in which to breed, or just as a place to hang around. Many species of marine fish move through or spend a major part of their lives in estuaries. So do humans—indeed, twenty-two of the thirty-two largest cities of the world, including New York and San Francisco, are situated along estuaries.

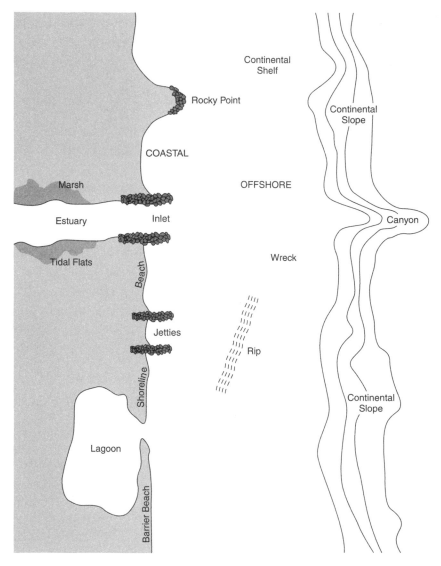

Fig. 3-1 General aspects of the inshore, nearshore, and offshore parts of the marine environment. Coastal waters can include both the inshore and nearshore parts of the ocean. Definitions are somewhat arbitrary and some provinces can occur in more than one region; for example, tidal flats can occur in either inshore or nearshore waters. (The figure is not drawn to scale.)

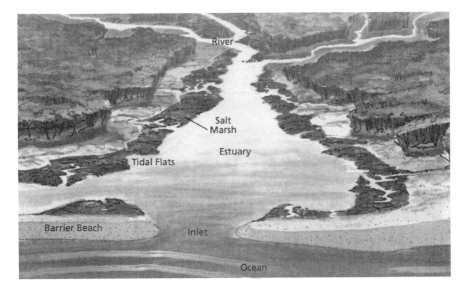

River

Salt Marsh

Estuary

Tidal Flats

Barrier Beach

Inlet

Ocean

Fig. 3-2 Some of the features common to a typical estuary. Note the small creeks and rivers that drain the salt marsh and upland areas. Often the inlet to the estuary is lined by a series of jetties. The features shown here are common to most estuaries regardless of their size; this figure is not drawn to scale.

AN INTRODUCTION TO ESTUARIES

An estuary can be defined as a coastal body of water partially enclosed or surrounded by land, usually connecting a river to the ocean. Many bays and sounds located behind barrier islands are also classified as estuaries. The terms backwaters, tidewaters, back bays, tidal marshes, swamps, wetlands, deltas, and drowned river valleys are frequently used to refer to part or all of an estuary.

Estuaries are the transition areas between the biological, chemical, physical, and geological processes of the ocean and these same processes in adjacent freshwater environments, and on land. Because they are transition areas, estuaries may be the most complex environments in the ocean. They are the breeding and growing grounds for many species of shellfish and baitfish, and therefore are excellent areas in which to find and catch a wide variety of marine game fish. Redfish, snook, white perch, seatrout, bluefish, tarpon, sheepshead, flounder, and striped bass are all found in estuarine environments, though the presence of many of these fish in estuaries often changes seasonally.

Estuaries can vary in size from the Chesapeake Bay system, which stretches 4,000 square miles and is the largest estuary in the United States, to those associated with the smallest coastal rivers. Regardless of their

Fig. 3-3 At low tide, the view across the salt marsh and tidal flats of a small estuary toward its main channel.

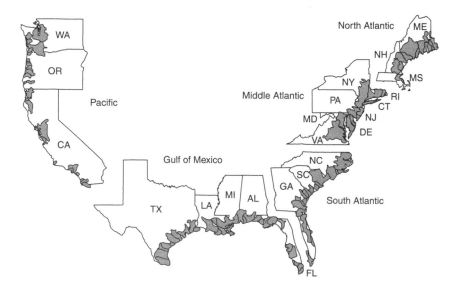

Fig. 3-4 The main U.S. estuary regions and their drainage areas based on a 1990 NOAA report. There are about 900 estuaries in U.S. waters. Apologies to Alaska and Hawaii, whose estuaries were not part of the NOAA study.

size, all estuaries tend to have distinct characteristics, in the same way that no two mountain ranges are the same. Indeed, the makeup of an estuary is influenced by many factors, including the estuary's own size and general shape, the amount of fresh- or saltwater input, the tidal range, the general geology and nature of the surrounding land, and the estuary's location or geological history. The basic marine processes operating within estuaries, however, are similar and common among most.

Most estuaries owe their existence to the recent (in geological terms) rise of sea level that began about 18,000 years ago. The rise in sea level (about 420 feet) literally drowned the previously exposed coastal portions of most rivers. Prior to this, few estuaries, if any, existed along the coast, and most rivers flowed across the then-exposed outer parts of the continental shelf to reach the ocean. Today, these rivers flow into their ancient upland valleys before reaching the ocean proper. The Hudson River estuary of New York and the Umpqua River estuary of Oregon are excellent examples of such drowned river valleys.

If a coastal area was stable during this sea-level rise, an estuary usually formed. If the region had some tectonic activity, however, such as faulting and upward movement of the land, it's less probable that an estuary developed—which explains why few estuaries exist along the tectonically active West Coast of the United States. (Some have formed where subsidence or downward movement of the land occurred, such as San Francisco Bay.)

The sea water within an estuary is usually diluted by the fresh water coming from the adjacent river, reducing the water's salinity below the average 35 ‰ (parts per thousand) of the open sea. The farther one goes up into an estuary, the fresher the water usually becomes, eventually reaching the 0 ‰ salinity of fresh river water. Such a change in salinity is mainly controlled by the amount of river inflow, the tide, and the wind. Fresh water is less dense than salt water, and often flows or lays over salt water until some mixing occurs.

The salinity of estuarine waters, as well as the water temperature, can change sharply, sometimes over short distances, due to the interplay of tides and the mixing of fresh river water with sea water. Significant changes in temperature and salinity in an estuary can develop in just a few hours, whereas comparable changes in the open ocean can take weeks or months.

In some large estuaries, there may be more fresh water on the left side (looking upstream) of the surface, and saltier water on the right side. This pattern is due to the Coriolis effect, which will move the fresh water of the river to the right as it flows toward the ocean, and the sea water

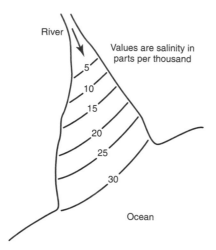

Values are salinity in parts per thousand

River

5
10
15
20
25
30

Ocean

Fig. 3-5 The Coriolis effect can influence the distribution of salinity in a large estuary by deflecting the incoming water to the right side on the incoming tide and the outgoing fresh water to the left side on the outgoing tide. This effect is less obvious in smaller bodies of water, where it can be obscured by the wind or by topographic effects. The Coriolis effect can also influence the current patterns in large estuaries.

from the ocean to the right as it moves into the estuary. One effect of such water movement is that a counter-clockwise circulation develops within the estuary. Let me emphasize that this pattern is only observable in fairly large estuaries, such as Chesapeake or Delaware Bay.

Perhaps the most distinctive feature of estuaries is that they are areas of change, and these changes often are of marked biological consequence for the estuary inhabitants. For example, at night the oxygen content and the pH of the water in an estuary often drop significantly due to respiration by plants and animals. (Respiration occurs in the day, too, but during the day the process of photosynthesis supplies oxygen back to the water.) Changes can occur daily with the tides or wind, which will move saline water in or out of the estuary depending on the direction of the tidal flow or wind. Seasonal changes also occur, as well as long-term changes or impacts due to human activity. In many ways, such changes produce a harsh and rigorous environment for estuary inhabitants, which can limit certain species from living in or moving through an estuary.

On the other hand, the abundance of nutrients in most estuaries, and thus the high food content, generally means that the population of a particular species living within a given estuary can be high. This abundance of food results from the often turbulent mixing of the fresh and salt water, input of nutrients from the adjacent river, organic material carried in from adjacent marshes, the decay of plants, and sometimes even from pollution.

TYPES OF ESTUARIES

Scientists generally classify estuaries by general topography, or by the water flow in the estuary.

Topographic Classification of Estuaries

Using the topographic approach, there are three types of estuaries: drowned river valleys, bar-built estuaries, and fjords. Drowned river valleys have resulted from the rise in sea level over the past 18,000 years due to the melting of glaciers. Within this type of estuary, sedimentation has not kept pace with the rising sea level. In drowned river valley estuaries, the tidal inflow is usually greater than the river flow. The Hudson River estuary and the Chesapeake Bay estuary system are examples of drowned river valleys.

Bar-built estuaries are similar to drowned river valleys, only here sedimentation has kept up with the rising sea. River flow that carries a large amount of sediment is common in bar-built estuaries. The sedimentation typically results in some sort of bar forming across part of the mouth of the estuary, the size and shape of which usually changes with time. Bar-built estuaries are shallower than drowned river valley estuaries, due to their higher sedimentation rate.

If an estuary has a restricted opening to the ocean, caused for example by the buildup of offshore barrier islands, it can become a lagoon or even a marsh. A lagoon, sometimes called a salt pond or back bay, is a broad but fairly shallow body of water that is partially separated or restricted from the main ocean by islands or a barrier beach. The Cape Hatteras and Cape Lookout areas of North Carolina, and the Laguna Madre along the Texas coast, are considered to be lagoons.

The presence of a barrier beach at the mouth of an estuary often protects the estuary proper from the full force of ocean waves and storms, thus making many bar-built estuaries places where the water is relatively calm. Some lagoons are almost completely isolated from offshore waters and, as a result, have little or no tide and wide-ranging salinity. In such areas, the currents are caused mainly by wind.

A lagoon that is isolated from the ocean is often vulnerable to the effects of pollution, as there is very little or no tidal mixing and exchange of its water with the ocean to remove or dilute incoming pollutants. With limited river inflow, the water in the lagoon can become very saline, even to the point of precipitating mineable salt deposits. Lagoons with better environmental conditions can be productive areas, and sustain large fish populations. In general, however, lagoons are fragile environments, especially those near populated or industrialized areas where pollution is common.

The third topographic type of estuary is a fjord, which is formed by glacial erosion and therefore is found in glaciated areas such as Alaska,

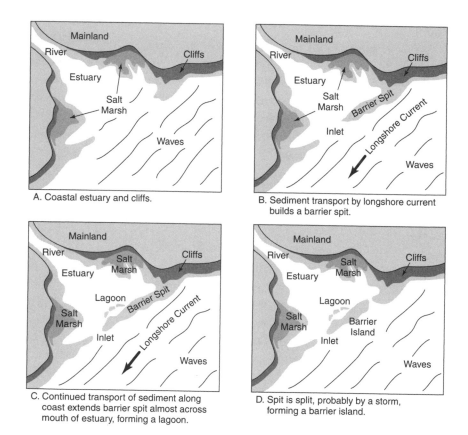

A. Coastal estuary and cliffs.

B. Sediment transport by longshore current builds a barrier spit.

C. Continued transport of sediment along coast extends barrier spit almost across mouth of estuary, forming a lagoon.

D. Spit is split, probably by a storm, forming a barrier island.

Fig. 3-6 The formation of a barrier spit, lagoon, and barrier beach by the longshore movement of sediment. The process is a continuing one that also is influenced by sea-level changes.

Canada, and parts of Puget Sound. The Straits of Juan de Fuca between Washington and Vancouver Island, Canada, is an example of a fjord.

Fjords commonly have a deep basin, with a shallow ridge, or sill, at their seaward end. The water in many fjords is not well-mixed, because the shallow sill limits tidal activity in the deep basin. This lack of mixing often causes the deeper waters of fjords to become stagnant and devoid of oxygen. (The oxygen gets used up during respiration of plants and animals and by the decay of organic matter.)

Less common topographic forms of estuaries are those resulting from faulting and similar tectonic activity. One well-known example is San Francisco Bay, parts of which were formed by movement along major faults in that area.

Water Flow in Estuaries

The water flow in most estuaries is a two-way street. In one direction, fresh water from the adjacent river flows seaward along or near the surface. (It flows near the surface because it is less dense than salt water.) The denser sea water moves landward along the estuary's bottom. The amount and degree of mixing between the two flows is determined by wind, tidal range, shape of the estuary, and relative flow rates and volumes of river water and sea water in the estuary. The interplay of these factors ensures that the movement of water within an estuary will be complex. In general, scientists label estuaries by three basic types of water-mixing scenarios: salt-wedge mixing, partially or poorly mixed water, and well-mixed water.

A salt-wedge estuary develops when the fresh and salt water mix only slightly. This occurs when a large, rapidly flowing river enters an estuary that has a limited tidal range. Under these conditions, the salt water and fresh water remain almost completely separate, and a wedge of salt water develops along the bottom, near the mouth of the estuary. This wedge often moves seaward at low tide or when the river flow is strong, and moves landward at high tide or when the river flow is low. Some well-known examples of salt-wedge estuaries are the mouths of the Hudson River in New York, the Columbia River in Washington and Oregon, and the Mississippi River in Louisiana.

A partially or poorly mixed estuary occurs when the estuary is deep, tidal ranges are moderate, and river flow is high. Estuaries of this type can have properties of both salt-wedge and well-mixed estuaries. Examples are found in Puget Sound, San Francisco Bay, and along many fjords. The water-mixing pattern within a fjord is determined by how much the sill restricts the circulation between the salt water of the ocean and the fresh water in the fjord.

A well-mixed estuary develops when the river flow and tidal range are both moderate. The stronger the tidal flow, the more complete the mixing becomes. Examples of where this type of water mixing occurs include the Chesapeake Bay and Delaware Bay estuaries.

A fourth type of flow, called a reverse estuary, can occur when there is no river flow into the estuary. Some lagoons, in which water moves from the ocean back into the estuary, fall into this category: water evaporates from the lagoon's surface and is replaced by ocean water. Several Gulf Coast estuaries, and some along Baja California, are of this variety.

The mixing patterns described above can vary with seasonal and tidal conditions, and with strong winds. As the river flow into an estuary decreases, the effects of the tide will usually become more important, and

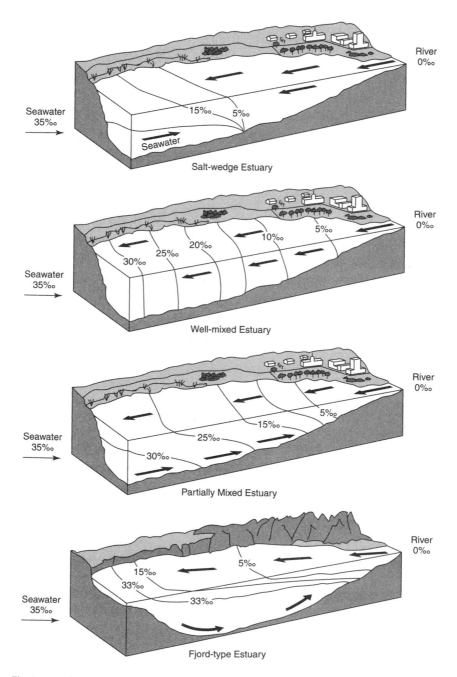

Fig. 3-7 A series of salinity-depth profiles across the three main types of estuaries: a salt-wedge estuary, a well-mixed estuary, and a partially mixed estuary. Also shown is a salinity-depth profile across a fjord. The river water input is on the right, the seawater input on the left. The arrows indicate the main directions of water movement and mixing.

vice versa. Tidal flow in an estuary also causes turbulence and mixing of fresh and salt water. The stronger the tidal flow, the more mixed and thus less stratified the water. Of course, the tidal flow in many estuaries can be very complex, and frequently will differ from the tide in adjacent offshore areas.

THE EFFECTS OF WIND

Wind affects estuaries mainly in two ways, the first of which is to generate waves. Waves usually have a limited impact on small estuaries, but their force can be significant if the estuary is large, or if the prevailing wind blows along the longest part of the estuary. In this instance, the wind direction increases the fetch effect of the wind on the water's surface, and large waves can result. Such waves may stir up the bottom sediments, causing turbidity in the water and making fishing difficult; waves also can restrict boating and cause erosion along the banks of the estuary.

The second wind-generated impact is to reinforce the tides in an estuary. Strong winds that blow for an extended period can cause anomalously high or low tides within an estuary. When this happens, the tides are often called wind or storm tides. Estuaries shaped like funnels can be particularly affected by winds or coastal storms. Water will be forced into the funnel, resulting in an increase in water level.

Onshore winds—hurricane winds are an extreme example—will increase the water level within an estuary, while offshore winds will lower the water level. Though less damaging to property than high water, low water can be catastrophic to the animals and plants living in shallow estuarine waters, which are not used to being exposed to air for long periods.

TIDAL PROCESSES IN ESTUARIES

Tides are what make fishing an estuary different from fishing in any other type of marine environment. Each tide in an estuary can change where and when you can best catch fish; sometimes the tide can even attract unexpected species.

As I mentioned earlier in this chapter, the general character of the tide in an estuary is determined by factors such as the shape and depth of the estuary, its overall size, and the width and length of the opening to the estuary. Sometimes the tidal pattern within an estuary itself will vary as the tidal wave moves up the estuary. Often, the time interval between high and low tide is longer than the time interval between low and high tide. Here's why: the speed of the tide is influenced by water depth, and the crest of the high tide will travel faster than the trough of the low tide.

The Changing Coastline

Estuaries, lagoons, and even beaches are not permanent coastal features. Over time, coastal features often will disappear, either being removed by marine erosion or overcome by marshes trapping sediment and expanding their extent. An estuary can be obliterated as freshwater marshes form inland and saltwater marshes or barrier islands start to close the seaward part of the estuary. Rivers also play a role in this process by depositing large amounts of sediment that may fill up the estuary; sediment can also be carried in from the ocean, and contribute to the filling process. If the estuary is an important navigation channel, such as the Chesapeake Bay is, it may need almost continual dredging to keep it open for shipping traffic.

If the level of the sea were to remain constant or rise slowly (as most scientists predict it will do, due to global climatic changes producing a warmer future temperature and thus melting of glaciers), estuarine destruction will continue as marshes build up and sediment accumulates. The only scenario that would maintain or rejuvenate present estuaries is a rapid rise in sea level, which would keep the growth of the estuary ahead of any sediment accumulation, marsh buildup, and development of offshore bars.

Tides have a dominant role in the interaction between the fresh water input at one end of the estuary with the salt water entering from the seaward side. The strength of the tide, relative to the strength of the river inflow, will determine what type of water flow occurs. The changing tidal conditions can also dramatically influence the variety of fish species found within an estuary. For example, during times of strong river flow, freshwater-tolerant fish may dominate much of the estuary.

Tides also greatly effect the salinity and temperature characteristics of the water in an estuary. At low tide the land surrounding an estuary will influence the heating or cooling of the water within an estuary. Further, evaporation will affect the water more at low tide than it does at high tide. Many estuaries along the East Coast of the United States are funnel-shaped, with large mouths leading up to narrowing channels and tributaries. In these estuaries, the height of the tide usually increases as it moves inland, up the estuary. The tides in many Gulf Coast estuaries tend to be small. Here, the wind raises water levels when it blows onshore and lowers them when it blows off the land.

The mixing of fresh and salt water, by tides or by the wind, can cause a salinity gradient both along the length of the estuary and sometimes through its depth. The fresh and salt water are usually of different temperatures, so a water-temperature gradient may also result. Incoming and outgoing tides can then move these salinity or temperature gradients up and down, which means that fish and other inhabitants of the estuary may also have to move, rather than stay in the estuary and deal with

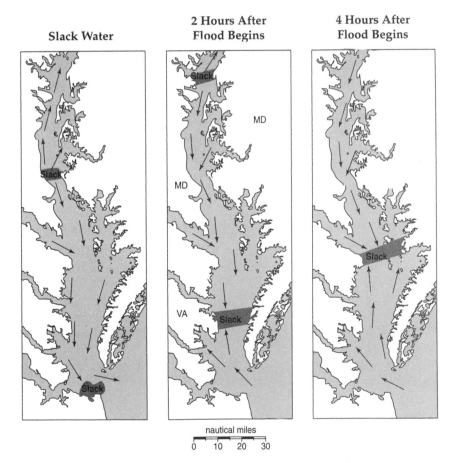

Fig. 3-8 Tidal currents in Chesapeake Bay at slack water at the mouth of the bay, two hours after flood at the mouth of the bay, and four hours after flood at the mouth of the bay. Note how the location of slack tide and the general tidal pattern change along the estuary with time. The arrows indicate current direction.

changing temperature or salinity. Salinity and temperature gradients tend to be more prevalent in estuaries that have relatively large inputs of fresh or salt water, or both. During spring tides, the gradients tend to be moved more by the tide than during times of neap tides.

The gradient pattern of water temperature or salinity within an estuary can change due to strong tides, offshore storms, or seasonally due to variations in river runoff, all of which can drive increased amounts of sea water into the estuary. Because fresh water is less dense than sea water and can, in a manner of speaking, float on the surface of an estuary, there can be a considerable difference in the salinity of the water from the surface to the bottom. This layering, however, may be quickly removed or reduced by the mixing action of wind or waves.

Of the two changing environmental conditions, temperature and salinity, temperature probably has the stronger impact on fish. Salinity itself, however, can prevent dominantly fresh- or saltwater species from even entering an estuary. Some species will move into an estuary to be within a specific salinity range, but even more will move there to be within a specific temperature range. Young fish can be vulnerable to an abrupt change in salinity, such as one caused by increased river runoff following heavy rains. This runoff can cause rapid and abrupt changes in both salinity and temperature. In extreme instances, a large-scale fish-kill can occur.

In addition to influencing temperature and salinity, tides create currents in estuaries. The tidal flow, and resulting currents, will be reinforced in areas where the flow is restricted, such as near or in the estuary's inlet, where the depth shoals, or where there is a change in the direction of the channel.

When fishing in estuaries, keep two points in mind: first, you should always explore and determine (either directly or via reports from friends or the local fishing shop) the tidal conditions and patterns for the area you want to fish; second, the times of high and low tides within an estuary will almost always differ from those of the ocean outside the estuary, as will the times of maximum and minimum currents.

SALT MARSHES AND MANGROVE SWAMPS

Most estuaries are bordered by a vegetative or wetland area. In temperate regions, this area will usually be a salt marsh. In warmer tropical regions, generally between 30°N and 30°S, the dominant vegetation will more likely be mangrove trees, often forming a mangrove swamp.

Estuarine wetlands can be defined as low-lying areas, protected from waves, which are exposed at low tide and covered by sea water at high tide. They are important ecological areas in that they provide habitat for fish, shellfish, and other forms of wildlife. In many instances, wetlands filter out or chemically remove some forms of human and industrial waste, as well as protect inland areas from erosion and damage from storms.

The National Oceanographic and Atmospheric Administration recently determined that there are about 32,000 square miles of wetlands around the estuaries of the continental United States. About 31 square miles of estuaries and wetlands are lost each year in the United States to development or erosion. In some areas, wetlands that had been "destroyed" by farming practices, or by industrial or residential development, are now being reclaimed and converted back to their original state. This is not an easy process, but it does show that the importance of wetlands is being recognized in coastal communities.

Salt marshes are generally found in intertidal areas along the banks of rivers or on the inner sides of barrier islands and can vary in width from a few feet to a mile or more. The width and vertical extent of a salt marsh is determined by the general slope of the land and the tidal range.

Fig. 3-9 An aerial view of a Cape Cod salt marsh. The entire marsh is drained by the single channel in the lower center, and the barrier beach in the lower part of the figure protects the marsh from the ocean.

Salt marshes tend to be less common in steep and rocky areas, and will not develop in areas that are not reached by the tide. They are extremely productive biological areas; some may produce as much as five to ten tons of organic matter per acre, per year. By way of comparison, the organic production per acre, per year from a typical wheat field is about one ton of organic matter.

The high biological productivity of salt marshes provides a rich and important source of food for its inhabitants and for neighboring creatures, which include shellfish, baitfish, game fish, four-legged creatures, and birds. In turn, the typically large populations of various forage species that live in or near the marsh make fishing around, and sometimes in, the marsh itself very productive.

The baitfish that inhabit salt marshes include killifish, mummichogs, and silversides. Anchovies, mullet, sticklebacks, menhaden, herring, and many other species may use the salt marsh as a spawning area, or as a refuge in which to avoid predation by larger fish. These baitfish often attract large numbers of predators, such as fish and birds, and wildlife, such as raccoons and deer. The quiet water and decaying material in estuaries unfortunately also attract many insects, especially mosquitoes.

Mangroves are found mainly in tropical areas, growing with their roots in the water. As a mangrove plant grows, it develops offshoots that grow farther out into the water; eventually these offshoots form a dense, almost junglelike stand that sometimes extends for miles along a coast or in an estuary. The thick, interlaced network of mangrove roots supports the trees, of course, but also is a place where baitfish can find food (mainly from decaying organic matter) and shelter. Mangroves can also form small islands, and grow along the edges of lagoons and small channels or other waterways.

Mangrove swamps can be home for many varieties of baitfish, as well as popular game fish such as tarpon and snook. These swamps occur in parts of southern Florida (the red mangrove is the common species in Florida), in some areas of the Gulf Coast, and throughout the Caribbean region. Eventually, a mangrove plant develops a seed pod, which drops into the water when it's mature. If the conditions are right, the pod will stick into the bottom, develop roots, and grow into a plant, thereby extending the range of the mangrove swamp. Sometimes, the seed pod does not settle near the parent plant but is carried elsewhere, where it will then start growing and begin another mangrove island or swamp.

In sheltered areas, the water under and around the mangrove roots can have a higher salinity than that of most other parts of the estuary. The quality of the mangrove growth usually reflects the environmental condi-

Fig. 3-10 A typical growth of mangroves along the coast of Belize. Note the interlocking network of roots. Once a fish gets into these roots it will be very hard to get it out.

tions, with smaller or stunted growth more typically indicative of stagnant or oxygen-poor waters. Also, you probably won't find many fish in areas where the salinity is high or the oxygen content in the water is low.

SEA GRASS AND TIDAL FLATS

It's common for a sea-grass or tidal-flat environment to be located in the shallow water just seaward of a salt marsh or mangrove swamp. Sea grasses have several important roles in the estuarine environment: their roots and leaves trap sediment and help stabilize the bottom; and their leaves provide growth area and shelter for many organisms, some microscopic. When these leaves die and decay they become a valuable source of food. One organism particularly dependent on sea grass is the bay scallop, which is perhaps the tastiest food harvested from the ocean. In the 1930s there was a major disappearance of sea grasses in the estuaries of the East Coast of the United States, which in turn caused a dramatic decrease in bay scallops. In recent years, many sea-grass beds have returned along the East Coast, and so have the bay scallops, though neither has reached its earlier level of abundance.

There are many species of sea grasses, but the dominant ones in estuaries are eelgrass (*Zostera*) and surf grass in temperate regions, and turtlegrass (*Thalassia*) in tropical areas. Eelgrass usually grows best in quiet waters, whereas surf grass can tolerate rough water. The food and cover provided by these plants make grassy areas attractive habitats for numerous marine species, including many young fish. You'll find these grasses in shallow water, where there are often rapid changes in water temperature and salinity; such changes, in turn, can limit the presence of some marine species. Thus the inhabitants of a sea-grass area can change over the course of a day or a night, as well as with the seasons, due to variations in water temperature and (to a lesser degree) in salinity.

Tidal flats occur where salt-marsh plants do not or cannot grow, probably because the area is exposed at low tide, which will kill salt-marsh plants. Depending in large part on the strength of the currents flowing over them, tidal flats have either sand or mud bottoms. Sand is the common bottom sediment in areas where the currents are strong, such as near the mouth of an estuary. Usually, sand-type sediment is found in deeper parts of the flat; mud typically occurs shallower on the flat.

Even though plants do not grow on tidal flats, the areas still have a high content of organic detritus, which is carried onto the flat by water flushed from the adjacent salt marsh or mangrove swamp. Thus in spite of the apparent absence of plants and animals, tidal flats usually contain abundant benthic life such as algae, and other organisms that live either on, or buried in, the mud or sand. These organisms may include bottom-dwelling creatures such as crabs, worms, clams, snails, oysters, and small shrimps. Baitfish are also common visitors to tidal flats, and their presence will attract larger fish looking for a meal. The abundant supply of food frequently attracts predators such as flounder, striped bass, skates, sharks, and bonefish.

INLETS

The inlet situated at the estuary's mouth connects the estuary and the ocean. In an inlet you often find strong currents, shifting bottoms, and considerable turbulence. For these reasons, an inlet can be an excellent place to fish. The strong currents and turbulence result mainly from the narrow inlet restricting the flow of water in or out of an estuary.

Some inlets can be dangerous areas for boat traffic, especially when tides and winds are strong. In a large estuary, when a falling tide flows into a wind-driven incoming sea, the situation is particularly perilous for boaters trying to exit the estuary. The strong currents in an inlet can quickly redistribute the bottom sediment, and in doing so can shift the

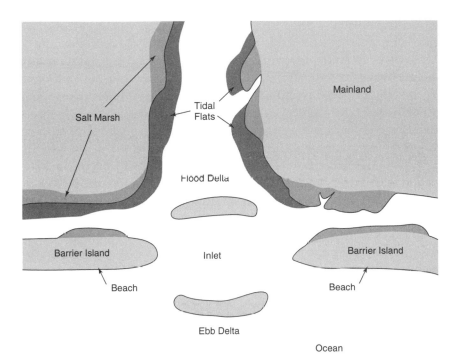

Fig. 3-11 Typical pattern of ebb- and flood-tide deltas near the inlet of an estuary. In general, estuaries are areas where sediment accumulates. High tides and storms can carry sediment from offshore, which quickly settles out and deposits on the bottom as the incoming water flow slows, or when it reaches the outflowing or stationary waters within the estuary. A similar pattern occurs during periods of strong outflowing currents. In this case, the sediment carried from the estuary will settle out just beyond the mouth of the estuary when the current slows. This pattern of sediment movement often forms small deltas, one just inside the estuary, the other at the mouth of the estuary. Often called flood-tide and ebb-tide deltas, the areas are common features to many estuaries, although you may not see them until low tide. Deltas can be hazardous to boaters entering or leaving an estuary.

position of sandbars, making them dangerous obstacles for boaters. All boaters should exercise caution when entering or leaving an unfamiliar inlet.

MARINE LIFE AND FISH IN ESTUARIES

Life can be rigorous for the creatures that inhabit estuaries. They generally use considerable energy adapting to environmental shifts within an estuary, such as the changing water temperature or salinity gradient. Sometimes, they move out of the estuary because of these changing conditions.

On the positive side of estuarine life, a substantial amount of food is usually present because of the typically large supply of nutrients, and the abundance of plants that use these nutrients to produce organic matter. The food base in an estuary is rich and varied, and groups of food chains are linked into a food web that includes any adjacent marshes, as well as the well-mixed and usually nutrient-rich waters of the estuary. The variety of forage in an estuary may explain why many estuarine fish do not limit themselves to just one type of food; it may also explain why estuarine fish can be caught on a wide variety of flies. Another positive is the relatively high oxygen content in the water, which results from the mixing and turbulence between an estuary's two water sources, the adjoining river and the ocean, and the atmosphere.

In some estuaries, an oversupply of nutrients from pollution can lead to excessive plant growth. As these plants decay (a process that uses oxygen) the free oxygen in the water may be reduced or eliminated. Sewage, with its high content of organic matter, can also reduce the oxygen content of the water. If the oxygen content in the water is seriously lowered, or removed altogether, the situation can be lethal to marine organisms.

In modest amounts, pollution from human, industrial, or commercial sources can actually be a valuable source of nutrients in an estuary; however, if the nutrient supply is too high, or the water-mixing rate is too low, the pollution-supplied nutrients can cause considerable environmental problems. One example of this is the recent damage to fish along the coasts of North Carolina, Virginia, and Maryland by the dinoflagellate *Pfiesteria*. The frequent red tides that occur in some coastal regions also are caused by excessive nutrients in the water.

Fish in Estuaries

A wide variety of fish spend all or part of their lives in estuaries. Freshwater fish, such as some species of sunfish and carp, often live in the headwaters of an estuary, where the salinity is close to, or equal to, that of fresh water.

Some fish, often called brackish species, live comfortably in the mixed-salinity (neither fully fresh water, nor fully salt water) areas of estuaries. Examples of such fish include spotted seatrout and white perch. Diadromous fish are species that spend time in the estuary as they migrate either to fresh or salt water. The term catadromous is applied to fish that go from fresh water to spawn in the ocean, such as eels. Species that go from the ocean to fresh water to spawn are called anadromous, of which shad and salmon are examples.

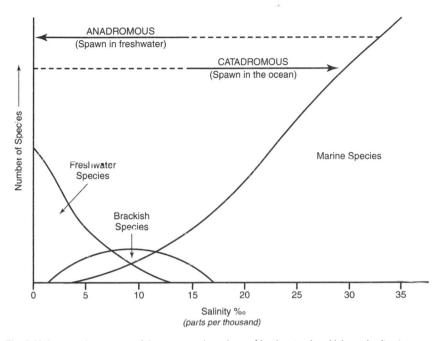

Fig. 3-12 A general summary of the types and numbers of freshwater, brackish, and saltwater species that inhabit an estuary and their distribution with salinity. It is generally thought that most of the animals that now live in estuaries evolved from marine species, who adapted over time to the conditions of the lowered salinity typical of estuaries. This may be seen in the fact that marine species tend to dominate in estuaries.

Many fish, including diadromous fish, use estuaries as nursery areas in which they spend the young portions of their lives and then eventually migrate either to fresh or salt water to live. Examples are freshwater sturgeon and striped bass.

When anglers think of life in an estuary, we generally focus on game fish, but other economically important marine species find homes in estuaries, too. In the Gulf of Mexico, shrimp, menhaden, oysters, and blue crabs are caught in estuaries by commercial fishermen.

Some species of fish are not really dependent on estuaries, but use the areas for specific benefits. For example, these fish may feed in the productive waters of estuaries or bury or hide their eggs in sheltered estuarine areas. Some marine species, such as menhaden, breed near an estuary, and their young then migrate into the estuary to feed. The adjacent marshes and areas of abundant vegetation provide cover in which larval and juvenile species of fish can avoid predators.

Striped bass are one marine species that have successfully adapted to estuarine environments. The fish can live in a wide range of temperature and salinity conditions, and can tolerate quick environmental changes. Stripers spawn fairly far upstream in an estuary and usually spend their first two or three years within, or very near to, the estuary in which they were born.

On the Pacific coast, perhaps the most important estuarine fish are the various species of salmon. These are truly anadromous fish, in that they are born in fresh water, later migrate and spend considerable time in the ocean, and then return to fresh water, usually to the place of birth, to spawn. Salmon are very valuable to the commercial-fishing industry, and are probably the best-studied marine fish. In North America, the Pacific salmon species include the chinook (or king), coho (or silver), pink (humpback), chum, and sockeye. Sea-run cutthroat, steelhead, sea perch, and rockfish are also common to Pacific estuaries.

Marine predators, sometimes large ones, are also drawn to estuaries, primarily because of the rich plant growth and the large number of forage species present. One such predator common to many northern estuaries, both in the Atlantic and Pacific Oceans, is the seal. These mammals are cute and interesting to watch, but they eat a lot of fish and their presence often means that fishing in the area will be poor, as many fish vacate waters inhabited by seals. Anglers who fish the estuaries of the Pacific Northwest may see another mammalian predator—killer whales. Needless to say, their presence will usually drive away most fish, and most anglers.

HUMAN IMPACTS ON ESTUARIES

Many large cities are built on estuaries, and several estuaries in the United States are major harbors used by cargo and oil-tanker vessels. Here, oil spills and similar problems are common occurrences. The urban and commercial development around such harbors often leads to pollution and the destruction of marine habitat. Pollution, and its impact on the estuarine environment, is typically greatest in areas where the population density is highest. Pollution also influences the fish population of an area. Some studies have shown that bottom-dwelling fish near areas of pollution often have various diseases and tumors apparently caused by toxic material in the bottom sediment.

Often, the waters of an estuary are used to cool power plants or for other industrial uses. The discharge water, often many degrees warmer than the estuarine water, can cause environmental problems. Sometimes this warm water can also lead to unique fishing opportunities, such as for striped bass wintering-over in areas of the Northeast.

There is considerable annual damage and loss to the coastal and inshore environment. Government estimates state that the United States has lost more than half its original coastal wetlands (originally about 220 million acres) since our country's inception; at present, a little more than 100 million acres of coastal wetlands remain. (Unfortunately, filling in wetlands was an established way of life several decades ago.) Some states have lost considerable acreage. For example, Florida has lost more than 9 million acres of its coastal wetlands; California has lost more than 90 percent, and Arkansas about 50 percent. Losses in Louisiana and Texas average several square miles of wetland per year. Furthermore, the Everglades in Florida have been severely damaged by the diversion of much of the area's freshwater supply. Damming the rivers of an estuary can also cause environmental problems. For instance, hydroelectric dams on the Columbia River estuary, between Washington and Oregon, prevent salmon from reaching their spawning areas. There are some estuary areas, such as parts of coastal Georgia, that have been impacted minimally by human development.

Because so many species, including many baitfish, breed or spend their early life stages in estuaries, the health of our ocean's estuaries will determine the health of our coastal fisheries. The conclusion is obvious: Without proper safeguards, our remaining healthy estuarine areas could quickly disappear or become irrevocably damaged.

Chapter 4

Nearshore Environments

The nearshore region comprises the shoreline, beach, surf zone, and nearby offshore areas. It's where ocean meets land, often in a dramatic or destructive fashion. Indeed, the physical and biological conditions of the region are constantly changing. Waves that have traveled a thousand or more miles reach the end of their journey and expend considerable energy on the beach, sometimes building it up, other times eroding it. Also, currents move water, bait, and sediment along beaches, and in doing so create favorable habitats for fish.

NEARSHORE FEATURES
The shoreline is the actual boundary between ocean and land. Its position is constantly altered by wind, breaking waves, the rise and fall of the tides, and the processes of erosion and deposition of sediment. A common term used for the area around the shoreline is the shore or shore zone, which includes the shoreline, the landward beaches, and the ocean surf zone.

The surf zone is where waves break and water moves forcefully toward the shoreline. Within this area, the water is highly mixed and well-oxygenated, and a wide variety of food is available to fish.

BEACHES
These are areas of unconsolidated sediment, most often sand but sometimes coarser material such as gravel. The character of a beach—its length, width, steepness, and the like—is controlled by several variables, including the amount and type of sediment present, the general dimensions and energy of the waves that impact the beach, the direction in which the waves approach, the tidal range, the strength and direction of the prevailing winds, and even the climate. Most beaches change either daily with the tide, seasonally with changes in wave patterns, dramatically during

Fig. 4-1 An aerial photo of part of Monomoy Island, which is actually a barrier beach, at the eastern end of Cape Cod, Massachusetts. Note the numerous channels, shoals, and other good fishing areas. Many of the small channels and shoals change in character almost on a daily basis. The area shown in the photo is less than a mile wide.

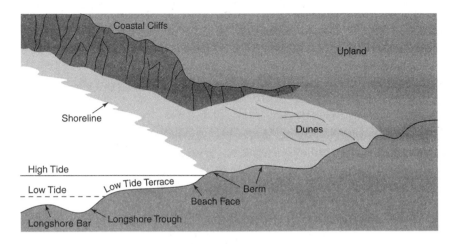

Fig. 4-2 Some specific features of the nearshore environment. On many beaches, there are smooth, flat areas called berms, which are popular spots for sunbathers. Berms are formed by wave action, often during storms. Dunes are mounds of sediment formed and moved by the wind. If colonized by coastal plants they can become stable features and protect the more inshore areas from storm erosion.

and following storms, or gradually over time with the rise and fall of sea level. Human activity such as construction and development leads to beach erosion, although erosion occurs naturally, too.

Beaches that extend parallel to the coast are called barrier beaches. If a barrier beach is separated from the mainland it's called a barrier island, examples of which include Padre Island in Texas, Fire Island in New York, Ocean City in Maryland, and Cape Hatteras and the outer banks in North Carolina. Because of their position on the coast, barrier beaches and islands protect inland areas from damage caused by offshore or coastal storms. They can also be prime areas for surf fishing, and for coastal development.

If you're fishing from a beach, you'll want to know the state of the tide and the character of the incoming waves. These two forces produce most of the structure and fishing opportunities along a beach.

WAVES AND CURRENTS IN THE NEARSHORE REGION

As waves approach shallow water near the shoreline, their characteristics begin to change. When an incoming wave reaches a depth about half its wavelength, the wave begins to "feel" bottom and rapidly grows larger as the wave energy is compressed into shallower water. The wave will eventually break, for one of two reasons: the wave simply becomes too steep to support its weight and the waveform collapses; or the velocity of the water particles at the wave crest exceeds the overall wave velocity. In the latter scenario, the water in the crest overtakes the waveform, making it tumble and surge forward, or break. On a gently sloping beach, waves usually break when the ratio of the height of the wave to the water depth is between 0.8 and 0.6. For example, a 4-foot wave will break at a water depth of between 5 to 6.6 feet. This is a good way to estimate where waves will break while you're fishing in the surf.

There are three types of breaking waves: plunging (or collapsing), spilling, and surging. The distinction between these is not great, and they

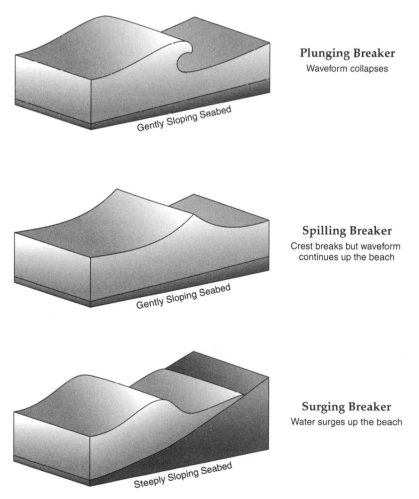

Plunging Breaker
Waveform collapses

Spilling Breaker
Crest breaks but waveform
continues up the beach

Surging Breaker
Water surges up the beach

Fig. 4-3 The three main types of breaking waves: plunging, spilling, and surging.

frequently grade into each other. Spilling waves usually occur over a gently sloping bottom of about 3 degrees or less, and roll forward with a turbulent crest. This type of waveform can continue right up onto the beach. Plunging waves occur over bottoms with a slope between 3 to 10 degrees. They essentially collapse onto the water receding from the beach. You'll find surging waves on steep beaches having a slope of 15 degrees or more. They may continue right up on the beach without appearing to break.

Waves can also be reflected, diffracted, or refracted when they enter shallow water. Each has implications for anglers.

If an incoming wave encounters a steep beach, a cliff, or a seawall, its energy may be reflected back toward the ocean. This reflected energy will carry your bait, lure, or fly seaward, interrupting your drift or presentation. When a wave is *reflected* away from shore it will collide into a subsequent incoming wave, which will cause what is called a standing wave. Here, the water moves up and down at a fixed spot. Wave *diffraction* occurs when a wave moves by some obstruction such as a point of land, a breakwater, or the end of a jetty. The process can cause complex wave patterns around a jetty and in harbor entrances. With *refraction*, the waveform bends. Incoming waves will change their direction if they enter shallow

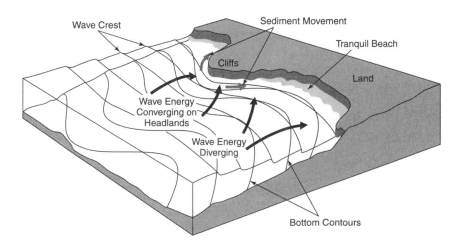

Fig. 4-4 Wave refraction in the nearshore region. As the waves enter shallow water, they "feel" the bottom and are slowed relative to those parts of the wave that are still farther out in deeper water. This results in a bending or refraction of the wave pattern. Wave energy becomes focused, or converges, on topographically high areas. The wave energy spreads out or diverges over open baylike areas.

water at some angle to the beach, as they often do, or if they encounter changes in the nearshore bottom topography. When part of the wave reaches shallow water before the rest of the wave, that part is slowed, causing the entire wave to turn toward shallow water. The wave crests tend to run parallel with the bottom topography or bottom contours, and the wave breaks just about parallel to the coastline, regardless of its original angle of approach. Refraction also can occur around objects in the water, such as rocks or small islands. Refraction of waves can be very important to fishermen, especially when working rocky points or cliffs.

Whether or not refraction of waves occurs depends upon the bottom topography, wavelength, and the direction of approach of the waves to the shoreline. On irregular coastlines, refraction will cause a concentration of wave energy, or a convergence, on topographically high areas such as submerged ridges, headlands, or elevated points. Waves will be relatively higher in such areas. There will also be a dispersion of wave energy, or divergence, over low-lying or open areas such as bays. Here, the waters will generally be calm. Sediment, seaweed, or anything in the water will be moved toward the calmer areas and deposited there. Erosion is greater in convergence areas than in divergence areas. If the processes of erosion and deposition continue undisturbed for many years, the headlands will be eroded and a straight shoreline will eventually develop.

UNDERTOW, LONGSHORE CURRENTS, AND RIP CURRENTS
After waves break, a large volume of water moves into the surf zone and travels toward the beach. Some of the incoming water will return seaward near or along the bottom of the surf zone, forming what is frequently called backwash or undertow. Most surf fishermen are familiar with this—when the waves are big, the returning water can erode the sediment under your feet, and even knock you down; when the waves are smaller, less water returns seaward, and the eroding effect is milder. For their own safety, surf fishermen should always be aware of the type of bottom on which they're standing (fine-grained sand is more easily eroded than coarse-grained sand), the slope of the bottom, and the character of the incoming waves. They also should anticipate the irregular occurrence of especially large waves. Turning your body at an angle to the backwash, or to the incoming breaking waves, will reduce the wave force on your body when you're wading.

Despite refraction, most waves still approach the beach at an angle, so water is transported along the beach and then starts to flow seaward along the slope of the beach. The next wave, however, will push some of this backflowing water up the beach, both up and down the beach, but

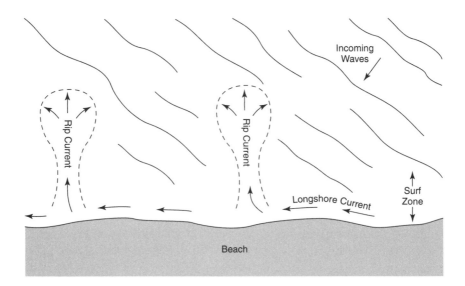

Fig. 4-5 Schematic illustration of nearshore circulation driven by the approach of waves at an angle to the beach. When waves approach the beach at an angle they produce a longshore current that moves water, sediment, and perhaps bait along the beach. Eventually some of the water returns seaward as a narrow and swift flow called a rip current. Generally the head of the rip current, beyond the breaking waves, will be white sediment-laden water.

also along it. This leads to an "along-shore current" or as it is more commonly called, a longshore current.

If you stand and fish in such a longshore current, you should be able to detect the direction in which it's moving with little difficulty, although at times it can be subtle. The longshore current can move sediment, bait, and anything that floats, such as pieces of algae and debris. Sometimes fish feed downstream of these currents. Combined with the breaking waves and the changing tide, longshore currents often build up submerged longshore bars and trough systems parallel to the beach, which often hold fish.

Water is continuously supplied to the longshore current by the incoming waves, but eventually this water must move seaward, which happens when the volume of water in the longshore current overcomes water in the incoming waves. Now the water in the longshore current moves seaward in a strong narrow current called a rip current. The longshore current essentially is "feeding" the rip current. (Rip currents are often inaccurately called rip tides; they have little to do with tides.) Because of their strong seaward flow, rip currents can be dangerous to swimmers or surf fishermen.

Fig. 4-6 The white water beyond the breaking waves is due to rip currents. The picture was taken off the Torrey Pines coast of southern California.

Causes of Beach Erosion

The action of waves on a beach will essentially keep the bottom sediment in a state of movement, the result of which is erosion in one place and deposition of sediment in another. The long-term effect of this erosion and deposition will be to smooth out the shoreline, unless people interfere with the process. Longshore currents will move sediment along the beach, and eventually straighten out the beach by repeated periods of erosion and deposition. The sand being moved by the longshore currents can be trapped by structures along the shoreline, which usually results in deposition of the sand on the upcurrent side of the structure. In many coastal areas, waterfront property owners build jetties or groins to interfere with the longshore currents, thus preventing or reducing erosion along their property.

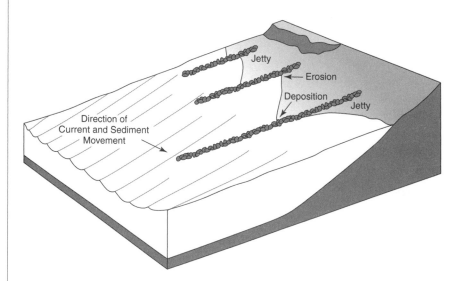

Fig. 4-7 How a beach can be modified by coastal structures. Sand moving along the coast can be trapped, causing deposition in one area and erosion in another. For example, the beaches are much narrower on the sheltered side of the jetty because the sand the beach would have received was intercepted by the jetty.

(A groin is a series of large rocks placed at right angles to the beach and extending out into the sea.) The effectiveness of these groins or jetties varies, but they will almost always cause erosion down the beach, which prompts the adjacent property owner to construct more of the same structures. On the positive side, they can be nice platforms from which to fish. Most attempts to prevent coastal erosion, however, are rarely successful—and if they are, success usually comes at the expense of nearby areas.

Fig. 4-8 A real example of how a jetty can trap sediment, the longshore current predominately runs from the top to the bottom of the figure. The long jetty along the inlet has trapped the sediment moving along the coast as well as the current flow around the inlet area and allowed sediment carried in or out of the estuary to accumulate in various places in the inlet.

Where a rip current sets up depends on factors such as bottom topography, slope of the beach, wave direction, wave height, and the period of the incoming waves. The strong currents often form channels cutting through the longshore bars paralleling the beach. The deep water in the channel will appear darker than the surrounding shallow water, which is one way you can identify a rip current. Also, waves generally do not break over a rip current; instead, you'll see a broad, distinctive chop in the rip current and immediate offshore region, and the normal pattern of breaking waves on either side of the rip current (See Figure 4-6).

Rip and longshore currents are usually strongest during a falling tide because the dropping tide contributes to the water being drained from the beach. These currents can be especially strong when waves are high and the wind is blowing onshore. Under these conditions, unaware swimmers and anglers can be carried seaward, sometimes with fatal results.

You can use rip currents to get your fly or lure farther offshore simply by letting the current take it seaward. This can be a productive tactic, as fish often feed around the edges of the seaward-flowing rip current on bait held in the strong flow. If you're ever caught in a rip current, let the current carry you seaward; don't try to then swim against the current back to shore. If you are wearing waders, get them off as quickly as possible. As the current moves seaward, its strength will diminish. You can swim parallel to the beach until you're free of the current, and then swim to shore. You can use a similar tactic to fight a hooked fish that gets into a rip current: rather than trying to bring in the fish directly against the flow, let it move out of the current.

RIPS AND ROGUE WAVES

When waves and currents meet, they can form a rip, which is an irregular, rough, and sometimes dangerous pattern in the water. (Again, a rip is different from a rip current.) The waves in a rip can be hazardous to small boats, causing them to roll or pitch awkwardly and rapidly. The current itself is caused by a shoaling of the bottom or a constriction in the water flow, such as you'll often see at the mouth of an estuary or in a narrow passage. These shoaling situations, even without waves, can cause problems for boaters, and the increased wave heights and irregularity in their pattern just increases the danger. Of course, because of the water motion in these areas, rips are also excellent places to fish, especially along their edges. The wise fisherman will keep his fly or lure in the rip, while keeping the boat out of the rip.

Sometimes, especially large and dangerous waves can form at the intersection of moderate-size waveforms coming from different direc-

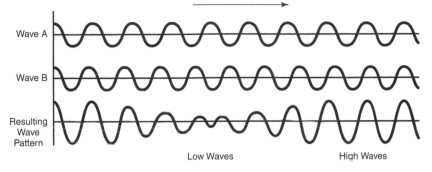

Fig. 4-9 Two or more wave patterns of different wavelengths (wave A and wave B) can interfere with each other, forming a new wave pattern. In some instances, the interference may cause extremely high, or "rogue," waves.

tions. These converging wave patterns interfere with one another, resulting in a reinforcement (or increase) in the wave height in one place, and a reduction (or decrease) in the wave pattern elsewhere. This can cause freak or rogue waves, which seem to come from nowhere and inflict extensive damage to ships at sea. Amazingly, on the average one large ship a day is lost somewhere in the ocean due to such waves.

The process of wave interference also explains why the sea surface may be calm for a while, then quickly have large waves, then be calm again. Experienced surfers and surf anglers are aware of this effect and know that large waves often come in bunches. Statistically, about one wave in twenty-three will be twice the size of the average wave.

CUSPS AND BOWLS

When the wave conditions are relatively uniform, a cuspate pattern may develop along a beach's shoreline. Cusps are a series of crescent-shape prominences, or high areas, separated by intervening low areas called bowls. Some anglers refer to cusps as "points". The high areas often extend into the water and form a small ridge composed of coarse-grained sediment or rocks. Bowls are usually composed of fine-grained sand.

Cusps can occur singly or, more frequently, in a series along the beach, spaced uniformly. The distance between the cusps is related to the height of the waves—the larger the waves, the wider the spacing between the cusps. In areas with strong waves, the spacing between cusps can reach 200 feet or more. Cusps are more common on coarse-grained sand or gravel beaches than on fine-sand beaches, and tend to be less common on long beaches and more prevalent in bays.

Fig. 4-10 A small beach cusp and adjacent bowl area shown at low tide. The bowl is in the foreground. These can be very good areas to fish when the tide is higher (see Chapter 10 for more details).

Cusps and bowls are temporary nearshore features, and are often altered or moved by storms. The waters around them, especially around cusps, can be very productive for fishing.

TIDELINES

Occasionally, you may see seaweed, foam, or wood floating on the water, oriented in a relatively straight line. You're looking at a tideline.

Tidelines can form in various ways, some of which have nothing to do with the tides. They generally indicate where waters of different characteristics, or where waters moving at different speeds or in different directions, are meeting. A common example is when fresh water from a river meets and rides over denser sea water. Any debris in the sea water will be skimmed away by the overriding fresh water, and form a line. These tidelines are common just outside estuaries and inlets.

Tidelines can also form along a tidal current. Debris will accumulate at the juncture between the current and the slower-moving water along the flank of the current. They can also form within an estuary, near its inlet. Here, the tideline sets up between the faster-moving water in the main channel and the slower-moving water along the shore. Tidelines often predict good fishing, as baitfish may be trapped in one of the different water masses causing the tideline. Also, some fish are attracted to, and hold underneath, the floating debris in a tideline.

Chapter 5

Offshore Environments

Seaward from estuaries and nearshore waters is the offshore region. As far as fish and fishing goes, there is no clear-cut boundary between nearshore and offshore waters. Indeed, some so-called offshore fish spend part of their lives in coastal waters. Food is probably the most important factor contributing to the distribution of marine life offshore. It certainly is critical in the deepest parts of the ocean, where much of the available food has to settle through the overlying waters. On the other hand, in some areas the upper offshore layers are mixed by waves, currents, tides, and the wind, and can be biologically productive. This part of the ocean can hold a wide variety of fish, including common nearshore species.

OFFSHORE GEOLOGIC FEATURES

Based on its depth or distance from shore, the floor of the ocean can be divided into two main parts: the continental margin and the ocean basin (or deep sea). The continental margin is adjacent to the continent and includes the marine portion of the coastal region and the continental

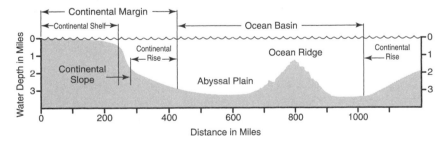

Fig. 5-1 A diagrammatic profile across an ocean that shows the main features of the continental margin and the ocean basin. Note that the vertical scale is shortened by about a factor of fifty when compared to the horizontal scale; in other words, there is a vertical exaggeration of about fifty times.

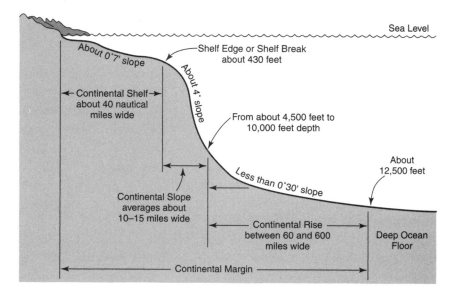

Fig. 5-2 Some of the general characteristics of the continental margin. This figure is not drawn to scale, and the vertical exaggeration is considerable. Also see **Fig. 10-3** for some coastal zone features.

shelf, continental slope, and continental rise. Most recreational fishing occurs over some part of the continental margin.

The continental shelf is the shallow part of the seafloor immediately adjacent to and surrounding the coast. Worldwide, the average width of the shelf is about 40 nautical miles. Geologically, the shelf is considered a flooded part of the continent; prior to the rise in sea level 18,000 years ago, much of the world's continental shelves were above sea level and thus were exposed land. In most coastal areas, the continental shelf is relatively smooth, almost flat or gently sloping, though it may have small hills or ridges and valleys or depressions. An abrupt change in slope occurs at the seaward edge of the continental shelf, at about 430 feet. This is called the shelf break or shelf edge, and it's here that the continental slope begins.

The continental slope extends from the outer part of the continental shelf down to the deep ocean floor. Its slope is fairly gentle, averaging about 4 degrees, which is a decline of about 21 feet, for example, over a distance of 300 feet. Near areas of faulting, such as along parts of the Pacific coast, its slope becomes steeper. In some areas, the seaward trend of the continental slope is interrupted by an intermediate feature, called the continental borderland, before it reaches the deeper parts of the ocean. The

Blake Plateau off the coast of Florida and Georgia is an example of such an area. As the water gets deeper, the grade of the continental slope becomes more gentle and eventually merges with the continental rise.

The seafloor of most of the continental shelf and slope is soft sand, silt, or mud. In general, fewer fish species are found over soft bottoms than over hard or rocky bottoms. Water depth is another factor influencing both the number of species, types of species, and even the size of fish found in a particular area. This relationship becomes a bit more evident when the water depth exceeds 100 feet. As the depth increases, fewer fish will be found, although these fish might be larger than those higher up in the water column. If a seasonal change in water characteristics occurs, if water temperature or the quality or quantity of food present changes, there may also be a seasonal change in the types of fish found along the bottom.

In some places, the outer continental shelf and upper continental slope are cut by submarine canyons. These features may even cross the continental rise and extend out into the deep-ocean basin. The term submarine canyon is used for those canyons with winding, rock-walled, V-shaped cross sections, often with tributary canyons that extend down

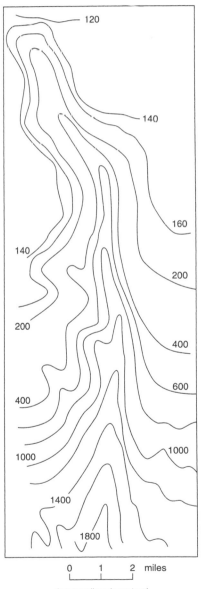

Fig. 5-3 The bathymetry of Lydonia Canyon, a typical submarine canyon on the seaward side of Georges Bank southeast of Boston. Note the generally straight trend of the canyon and how quickly its depth changes. Contours are in meters; 200 meters equals 656 feet.

0   1   2   miles

(contour lines in meters)

The U.S. and Canadian Continental Margin

The northern part of the East Coast of the United States, from the Canadian coast down to New York City, was eroded by glaciers. Evidence of glacial erosion is seen in the numerous depressions, topographic highs, basins, and valleys on the continental shelf here. The irregular topography of the shelf off Nova Scotia and in the Gulf of Maine suggests that the glaciers probably reached out to Georges Bank. Most of Cape Cod, Martha's Vineyard, Nantucket, and Long Island is composed of rocks and various debris carried there by glaciers. Glaciation did not extend beyond Cape Cod and Long Island, which we know because of the abrupt change in the character of the continental shelf south of these areas—the deep basin, channels, and topographic highs common to the north are absent, and the topography is relatively smooth. Generally, glaciated shelves have more natural structure than nonglaciated shelves.

Off coasts where the currents are strong, the continental shelf can be narrow or nearly absent. An excellent example occurs along the coast of southeast Florida, where the Gulf Stream, flowing at speeds up to 6 knots, comes close to the mainland. This current is strong enough to prevent deposition of most sediment, and apparently has prevented the normal development of a shelf. The Gulf Stream is so strong here that, even at depths of several hundred feet, it has scoured and removed much of the bottom sediment.

In the Gulf Coast region another variety of shelf occurs—the delta formed by sediment carried into the Gulf of Mexico by the Mississippi

the continental slope. The dimensions of some submarine canyons are impressive: Monterey Canyon off the coast of central California has a relief of about 14,900 feet, similar to that of the Grand Canyon. Hudson Canyon off New York's Hudson River extends seaward 150 miles into the Atlantic Ocean, then continues another 150 miles as a channel across the continental rise.

Submarine canyons are also found around the Hawaiian Islands. They're popular areas for offshore fishing, both for their structure and because they often funnel up deeper, nutrient-rich water to the surface, which can trigger increased biological productivity and ultimately attract fish. Canyons along the Northeast coast of the United States are espe-

River. A complex coastal and nearshore set of estuarine, barrier island, and lagoon or back-bay environments has formed in this area. The delta is also cut by channels that extend across most of the continental shelf and supply sediment to the deeper parts of the Gulf. The central offshore part of the Gulf of Mexico is a relatively deep and flat basin.

The West Coast of the United States differs considerably from the Gulf of Mexico and the East Coast. The differences reflect the differences in the origin and evolution of these continental margins. Much of the character of the East Coast and Gulf Coast results from sedimentary processes. Along the West Coast, however, tectonic processes such as faulting, earthquakes, and volcanoes predominate. Off California, Oregon, and Washington, there are small northwestward-trending narrow basins. These form what is called a continental borderland. Large fracture zones and several submarine canyons also cross the region. Still farther north, off Canada and eventually Alaska, the more typical shelf topography continues, eventually ending in the deep Aleutian Trench.

In general, the shelves off the West Coast of the United States are unglaciated and relatively narrow. (Some glaciation is evident off the coast of Washington and British Columbia.) The islands of the Pacific Ocean generally have a narrow continental shelf, or none at all. These chainlike islands (the Hawaiian Islands are an excellent example) are volcanic in origin. The surfaces of these shelves sometimes have thick sequences of coral deposits. In southern parts of the U.S. shelf, especially around Florida and the Hawaiian Islands, coral reefs or even atolls may occur.

cially popular areas in which to catch big-game species such as blue marlin, sharks, and various species of tuna.

The other major part of the ocean, the ocean basin, contains the ocean's deepest areas and constitutes about 79 percent of the total area of the seafloor. It is dominated by three components: flat abyssal plains, deep trenches, and mountainous ocean ridges. (Because of its distance from shore and general lack of game fish, the ocean basin is not usually fished by recreational anglers.) The ocean basin is where the process of seafloor spreading occurs, which results in new ocean floor being added at the ocean ridges due to the discharge and eventual cooling of molten lava. The trenches are the deepest parts of the ocean.

A VERTICAL VIEW OF OFFSHORE WATERS

The creatures of the ocean live in one of two realms: the benthic (on the bottom of the ocean) and the pelagic (in the water overlying the bottom). The pelagic realm can be further subdivided into the neritic system (the water overlying the continental shelf) and the oceanic system (the water overlying the deeper and more offshore parts of the ocean). The physical characteristics of these parts of the marine environment are shown in Figure 5-4.

The waters overlying the continental shelf to a depth of about 600 feet (within the neritic system) are well lit, with many changing properties that account for variations in temperature, salinity, nutrients, and dissolved oxygen. The waters overlying the deeper parts of the ocean (the oceanic system) are biologically less productive and have fewer fish per unit area than the waters of the neritic system. With its great depth, the oceanic system has a wide range of living conditions, although there is little variation in water temperature within its different depth zones. In general, the deep sea is an environment with uniform conditions; most species living there can range over considerable distances without experiencing any major environmental changes.

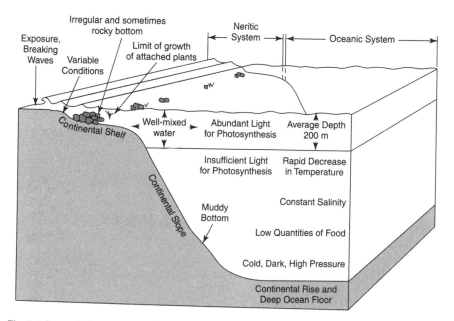

Fig. 5-4 General characteristics of the marine environment. Note the variable conditions typical of the upper part of the ocean compared to the relatively constant conditions in the deeper part.

Of most interest to us, as anglers, is the uppermost zone, which includes the waters over and beyond the continental shelf from the surface to 200 meters or about 600 feet deep. In a manner of speaking, this zone is really an extension of the inshore neritic system, except that it is underlain by the water that comprises the deeper parts of the oceanic system. The uppermost zone of the ocean has many of the environmental changes that also occur in the neritic zone, but is not as biological productive. As elsewhere in the ocean, photosynthesis can occur in the upper lighted layers of the uppermost zone, though in offshore waters the process is limited by the relative lack of nutrients in the water.

Albacore, salmon, bonito, mackerel, dolphin, sharks, marlin and other billfish, and even bluefish are found in this zone, as are several important commercial fish species, such as herring and anchovies, which tend to collect in especially large numbers in areas of upwelling. (We'll examine upwelling in more detail later in this chapter.) There are few places for fish to find shelter in this zone. Some species congregate around or below anything floating in the water, including seaweed, trees, boats, navigational markers, scientific instruments, drilling platforms, or even whales.

The next offshore zone extends from a depth of about 600 to 2,000 feet. The waters here become increasingly darker and the water temperature stays relatively cold; pressure increases, too. Some fish living in this zone move upward at night to feed, following migrating zooplankton, and return to the depths as day begins. Animals that live in these waters either are dependent on food that settles down through the overlying water, or they migrate closer to the surface to feed. Few of these fish, however, are of interest to anglers. I dived to this zone in the research submersible *Alvin* and was startled by the immense numbers of small (2 to 3 inches) lantern fishes or myctophids I saw there. Some schools we passed through were hundreds of feet thick and certainly contained several million fish.

From about 2,000 feet to 12,000 feet the water is colder, darker, and has greater pressure than the overlying water. There are few or no seasonal changes in the physical aspects of this environment, and the water temperature is generally a few degrees above freezing. The only light comes from bioluminescence. Much of the available food has settled down through the overlying waters. Fewer fish, and fewer varieties of fish, are found in the bathypelagic zone than in either the overlying water or along the ocean bottom.

The deepest part of the ocean, which biologists call the abyssopelagic zone, includes all areas deeper than 12,000 feet. This zone covers almost half of Earth's surface, and is larger in area than all of the continents com-

Electronic Fishing Aids

In the last decade or so, electronic devices have been developed that help fishermen find fish or return to specific offshore areas. A Global Positioning System (GPS) or Loran will help you navigate back to good fishing areas, or to your home port. New and sophisticated fish finders will help you find bottom structure and locate fish; some systems even pick up baitfish schools and the thermocline. What was missing, however, was a method to examine large areas of the ocean to find where migrating pelagic fish might be. Offshore fish often concentrate in areas where there is some type of change, either in water temperature, salinity, turbidity, or even water color. To find or predict such changes in nearshore waters is relatively simple, but in the broad expanse of the ocean it can be a formidable task. Recently, several companies and NOAA developed services that offer sea surface temperature data, as determined from satellite measurements. Temperature changes can indicate currents, eddies, and temperature boundaries, as well as areas where flotsam or weed lines might occur; more general temperature data can indicate where the water is sufficiently warm or cool enough for certain fish. Most satellite temperature services will provide information for local areas on at least a daily basis, and transmit it directly by fax. (Many offshore fishing boats have fax capabilities.)

Some services add their own interpretation to the data and pinpoint high-potential fishing areas—by noting, for example, where a temperature change occurs over a favorable bottom feature. You can find ads for these services in many saltwater fishing magazines. One company, Roffer's Ocean Fishing Forecasting Service, looks at twenty factors in making its analysis and offers a money-back guarantee. (You can obtain NOAA satellite data via a computer equipped with the appropriate software.)

Having up-to-date data on water temperature and combining this information with a profile of bottom structure should help you find offshore fish. You can save fuel by having this information, as you won't have to run around as much looking for fish. If you know where the bait is, or can find birds (radar can help here), your chances of finding offshore fish are even better.

bined. It is a dark, very cold (water temperatures are near or even below 32 degrees), high-pressure environment. Many of the creatures that live here either have no eyes, or are blind or almost so. Less is known about this environment than most other parts of the ocean. We do know that life exists in the deepest parts of inner space—when the bathyscaph *Trieste* made the first dive into the deepest part of the ocean, the Marianas Trench, it startled a nearby fish when it touched the bottom at 35,795 feet. Most scientific observations of life in this zone come from underwater photographs or observations from research submersibles, although not many can dive below 12,000 feet.

SURFACE WATERS

The surface waters of the offshore region offer the greatest potential for fishing, and can be divided according to water temperature into two principal zones: warm (or tropical) waters, and temperate (or cold or polar) waters. The warm waters of the ocean are usually defined as where the water temperature stays above 64 degrees Fahrenheit. As much as 80 percent of all known marine fish live in warm ocean water; most of these species stay relatively close to land, often around coral reefs or atolls. Many game fish spend much of their lives in these warm offshore waters, including tuna, billfish, and various sharks. Some species, such as tarpon, bonefish, and permit, are found more commonly in nearshore and estuarine waters, but journey offshore at various times.

Coral reefs are important warm-water environments. Reefs or atolls—reefs are usually submerged, whereas atolls rise above water and have an inner lagoon—are beautiful but fragile environments. Coral reefs grow in tropical areas, where the water temperature is at least 64 degrees. The water must also be clean, have normal salinity, and be relatively shallow; most reefs grow at depths of 100 feet or less.

Reefs are composed of various species of coral and calcareous algae living together in a symbiotic relationship. Together, they build and form a living structure. (Coral are primitive animals that grow attached to the bottom or to other coral; algae are plants and require sunlight, which is why the reefs only grow in shallow water.) Among the more famous reefs are the Great Barrier Reef of Australia, the reefs off Belize, and many islands in the south Pacific Ocean. The only living reef in U.S. waters is found along the Florida Keys.

Coral reefs are important environments for fishing. They provide food and habitat for small fish and baitfish, which in turn attract larger game fish. In recent years, many coral environments have been threatened by storms, pollution and oil spills, damage from ships at anchor, increasing ocean temperatures caused by El Niño or global warming, and illegal removal of coral and fish by collectors. Experts on coral reefs have predicted that 25 percent of the world's coral reefs could be permanently damaged or destroyed within the next decade or two unless remedial action is taken.

Temperate and colder offshore waters generally contain fewer species of fish than warmer waters. The areas do, however, contain many commercially caught fish such as cod, herring, mackerel, pollack, haddock, and flounder. Many of these fish are taken from areas where there is upwelling of deeper nutrient-rich water.

The kelp beds found off the Pacific coast of the United States are unique temperate-water environments. Kelp is a large brown algae that grows attached to the seafloor, often to large rocks, by what is called a holdfast. The plant's long leafs (called fronds) reach from the seafloor to the surface, sometimes 60 to 100 feet up. They can form a junglelike underwater environment. Kelp beds grow in highly productive areas, so a large and usually diverse collection of fish are found around the beds. Off the California coast, kelp species include sheephead, kelp bass, white sea bass, and kelp perch.

WATER TEMPERATURE
Water temperature greatly influences where offshore fish are found. It seems that each species has a preferred temperature range that it tries to hold to, though this range is often not accurately known.

Almost all fish are cold-blooded, so the temperature of the surrounding water influences many aspects of their behavior, including how they feed and breed, and when they migrate and where they go. Cold water will slow down most fish, whereas warmer water will activate them, but only to a point. Beyond a certain temperature, warm water can make fish very lethargic; however, a return to cold water will usually energize them.

A water-temperature difference of a degree or two can determine where some fish may or may not be. Indeed, many fishermen plan their fishing trips on the basis of the surface temperature. For example, billfish are often found only in waters above a certain temperature. Sailfish along southern Florida will move south to warmer water when a cold front passes, whereas increasing temperatures will cause them to move north. Tuna will move north as the temperature warms, and return south as the water cools. Along the Alaskan coast, a change in temperature of a degree or two often will determine the presence or absence of salmon.

Temperature Preference Studies on Tuna

Studies of tuna using acoustical transmitting devices found that the fish often prefer a specific water temperature. Researchers discovered that some tuna stayed above the thermocline, while others preferred a cooler or warmer layer of water. In other studies, tuna demonstrated a knowledge of where they were in the ocean and would return to specific areas over the course of a day, or even from one year to the next. It was also found that most tuna prefer to swim closer to the surface at night than they do during the day. The late Dr. Frank Carey, one of the first to acoustically monitor fish, found that fish such as yellowfin and bluefin tuna made more vertical trips between the surface and the thermocline when traveling in a school, whereas when traveling alone they tended to stay more in the thermocline. Interestingly, many tuna and billfish are able to heat parts of their bodies, especially their brain or their eyes, so that these organs can function adequately when the fish dive deep into the cold water of the thermocline.

EXAMINING THE THERMOCLINE

In offshore waters, we can say that the ocean has three layers: the surface waters, the water column, and the ocean bottom. All three play a role in fishing, but the middle layer, the water column, frequently is not considered by anglers. Within the water column, the thermocline should be considered a type of structure.

Starting somewhere from 30 to 1,600 feet below the surface and sometimes reaching down to 5,000 feet, the thermocline is a zone in which the water temperature changes more rapidly than the water below or above it. The water above the thermocline is usually well-mixed by the wind and currents and therefore has a relatively constant temperature. (Oceanographers call this the mixed layer.) Within the thermocline, however, temperatures can change by two or three degrees within a few feet. Below the thermocline, the water temperature slowly drops as depth increases.

The temperature differences within the thermocline can work as a barrier or boundary to some fish. Many fish won't swim down through it—baitfish and predators may hold atop the thermocline, as if it were a type of structure. Alternatively, some fish may seek out the cooler water in the thermocline.

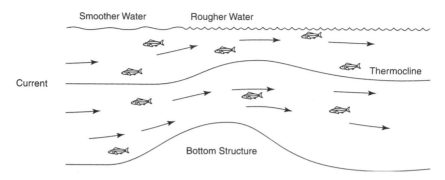

Smoother Water   Rougher Water

Current

Thermocline

Bottom Structure

Fig. 5-5 A tidal current flowing over a bottom structure or shoal area will have its velocity increased, often forming a surface rip. In some situations the position of the thermocline will be modified by the upward-moving water. Note that fish will almost always face in the direction of the moving water.

FRONTS AND EDGES

A front is the transition area between two different bodies of water. One of the better known examples occurs along the boundary of the Gulf Stream and its adjacent waters. Fronts are often turbulent and well-mixed areas in which biological productivity is high. Sometimes the front can be identified by an accumulation of floating materials, such as seaweed and various debris. Other indicators of fronts are a rapid change in temperature or color of the water, a change in the wave pattern, and sometimes even fog.

In a manner of speaking, fronts in the ocean are similar to fronts in the atmosphere. Some ocean fronts will change quickly; others may be stable and remain in place for a considerable time. Ocean fronts can also form downcurrent of islands, reefs, or headlands when these features interfere with current flow. Areas where warm and cold water intersect are called edges.

Fish are often concentrated around fronts and edges. Occasionally, tuna

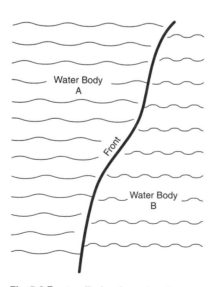

Water Body
A

Front

Water Body
B

Fig. 5-6 Fronts will often form along the contact between waters having different characteristics. Sometimes the front is marked by a surface accumulation of flotsam.

migrate along fronts, as well as forage in them. Swordfish and sperm whales are other creatures known to hang around fronts. Commercial longliners, fishing offshore for swordfish, tend to hang their baits between waters of different temperatures (in other words, along a front) because bait can be concentrated there.

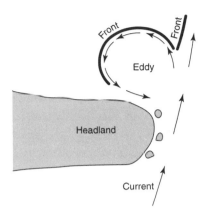

Fig. 5-7 Fronts can also form along the edges of a current or along the edges of small eddies formed by the current.

EDDIES AND RINGS

An eddy is a large circular flow of water that occurs along the edge of a strong ocean current; the water in the eddy moves in a different direction than the water in the adjacent current. Eddies can be more than 100 miles wide and can last as long as two months. In the Pacific, eddies up to 600 miles in diameter have been found. There are many types of eddies, including some that only occur underwater.

Large loops or meanders similar to eddies can pinch off from the Gulf Stream and form rings of water with strong internal currents. These rings, like eddies, can move large masses of water, in the process transporting organisms or pollutants through the ocean. Various tropical fish species are carried into temperate waters via such rings. Eventually the ring breaks down and its water will blend back into the ocean proper. Rings tend to be about 100 to 200 miles wide and may extend deeper than 10,000 feet. Several rings may exist in one oceanic region, and may endure for months or a year or more. Though scientists first identified rings emitting from the Gulf Stream, similar types of rings have been found around the Japanese, or Kuroshio, Current region, the Pacific analog of the Atlantic's Gulf Stream.

Eddies and rings have similarities to weather systems in the atmosphere, only they usually last longer. They can affect large areas of the ocean for periods of weeks to months. During their life they move water, which essentially stays unmixed from the surrounding ocean water, over long distances. Eddies often carry their own population of fish, sometimes moving them far from their original habitat.

Scientists have much to learn about eddies and rings and how they affect other aspects of the ocean, though they clearly impact fish survival and development. For example, if a breeding school of fish or a large num-

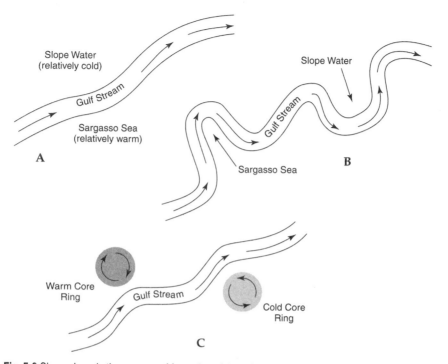

Fig. 5-8 Shown here is the process of formation of rings from the Gulf Stream. A, B, and C are a sequence of events occurring over a period of weeks. Those rings that incorporate Sargasso Sea water and that end up north of the Gulf Stream are called warm core rings because their core temperature is warm relative to the surrounding water. Those found to the south and enclosing water from over the continental slope are cold core rings. As a ring forms and develops, a column of water is captured from one side of the main current and carried to the other side. The water in the ring has salinity, temperature, oxygen content, and other properties from its original water that often are very different from the water in its new surroundings.

ber of juveniles were to become trapped in a ring or eddy, they could eventually be carried away from their normal and favored habitat. When the ring or eddy breaks up and mixes with the surrounding water, the fish may find themselves in an inhospitable environment that could prove fatal. If so, a significant portion of the year's fish population could be wiped out.

OFFSHORE UPWELLING

The process of upwelling—the upward movement of water from some depth to the surface—will cause currents and temperature changes in the surface and near-surface waters. These changes form fronts or edges where baitfish and larger fish often accumulate. As a result, upwelling can be a major factor determining where fish are located offshore.

The classical type of upwelling happens along a coast when the wind blows away the surface water, which then is replaced by deeper, colder, and nutrient-rich water. Turbulence and currents can also result from this process, all leading to good fishing.

Upwelling may also develop when the topography of the seafloor interferes with water movement. This occurs when tidal currents are deflected toward the surface by ridges, shoals, or other bottom features (see Figure 5-5). Sometimes, this upwelling causes irregularities on the sea surface; usually the upwelled cold water occurs in patches or plumes that may change shape over time. The contact or boundary between the cold upwelled water and the warmer surface water is usually very distinct, and the temperature differences between the two waters can be five degrees or more. A color change may be apparent at this contact area: the colder water will be deep blue, contrasting nicely with the green color of the surface water. Such color differences can be seen from the air, by a satellite, and often from a boat. These boundaries are excellent areas in which to find fish. In some places, the cold upwelled water can produce fog when it comes in contact with warm air. This is common along the Pacific coast of the United States and Canada.

Localized upwelling can take place downcurrent from where a point of land intersects an ocean current. The flowing current may pull surface water around the point of land, which causes deeper water to rise up (upwell) to replace the surface water. Upwelling also happens along the leeward side of a shore when the wind moves the nearshore water seaward and it's replaced by deeper water.

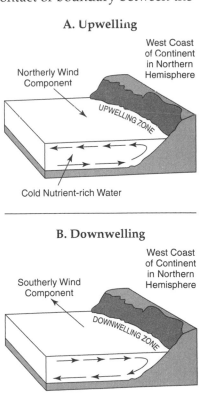

Fig. 5-9 Upwelling or rising of surface waters due to southerly nearshore winds (A), and sinking of surface waters due to northerly nearshore winds (B). These phenomena occur along the western coasts of continents.

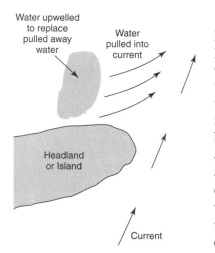

Fig. 5-10 A small area of upwelling can sometimes occur when a current pulls in adjacent water, which may cause deeper water to rise (upwell) to replace it.

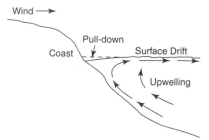

Fig. 5-11 Upwelling can also occur along a leeward shore, as the wind causes a pull-down of the nearshore water.

To put the value of upwelling into perspective, consider that about 50 percent of the world's ocean fish catch comes from areas of upwelling, and these areas make up only 1 percent of the total area of the ocean. The local importance of an upwelling area can be considerable. An example is the anchoveta fishery in an upwelling area along the coast of Peru, which at one time was the largest fishery in the world. During El Niño conditions, upwelling usually ceases and the fishery dramatically declines. In the past, this has caused severe economic problems for Peru, and has resulted in the death of millions of seabirds that feed on the anchoveta.

FLOTSAM

Offshore fish are attracted to debris floating and drifting on the ocean surface. Such flotsam can range from accumulations of seaweed, 55-gallon drums, pieces of wood, tires, and the like. In fact, any floating object can attract offshore fish—even a large turtle. Fish may travel several miles away from the flotsam, but later return. These trips may occur over several weeks, but the fish always return to the same place. One possible reason for this attraction is that the flotsam serves as a marker or stimulus of some kind in the otherwise featureless ocean. For small fish, the flotsam may offer protection from predators, although predators are also attracted to flotsam. Dolphin (also called dorado and mahi-mahi, and one of the prettiest offshore species) are attracted to anything floating in the water. Indeed, anglers find dolphin by first searching for some flotsam, especially if there is bait in the area.

Structure

The presence of structure is obviously a key factor in determining where fish will visit or stay in offshore waters. Structures can include bottom irregularities such as mounds or rocks, larger topographic features such as submarine canyons, wrecks, man-made structures, drilling platforms, and navigational towers. Often such structures interfere with tidal flow or other currents, resulting in surface rips, upwelling, or deflections of the thermocline. They are good places to fish.

When flotsam appears in a long line, we call this a tideline or a flotsam line. A tideline or flotsam line represents a situation in which two different bodies of water have come into contact (see Figure 5-6). Predators may be attracted to this transition area, in which a change in water characteristics or current speed is taking place. Flotsam will also accumulate along the edges of major currents such as the Gulf Stream.

Part II

Ocean Fish

Chapter 6

General Characteristics of Ocean Fish

Fish have been on this planet a lot longer than most animals. The first fish, creatures similar to today's lampreys, appeared in the ocean more than 500 million years ago and were preserved as fossils. Fossils of ocean species more familiar to us were first found in rocks about 460 million years old. (By way of comparison, dinosaurs appeared about 250 million years ago and became extinct about 144 million years ago.) As we'll see in this and subsequent chapters, fish have evolved and adapted very nicely to the complex aquatic environment in which they live.

AT HOME IN THE OCEAN

Although fish are found throughout the ocean, about 80 percent of all marine species live in relatively shallow water, particularly around continents or islands. Ocean fish range in size from a dwarf pygmy goby that can breed when it is less than an inch long to whale sharks that grow to about 65 feet long and weigh more than 25 tons. Indeed, the largest creatures on our planet live in the ocean.

Most fish live suspended in the water, floating, almost defying gravity. They do this with the help of an internal mechanism, usually a bladder (called a swimbladder) that contains gas or oil. By adjusting the amount of gas or oil (both of which are less dense than sea water) in their swimbladder, fish can regulate their buoyancy. Land creatures do not have such a mechanism and instead have strong skeletons and use considerable energy to support their weight; water supports the weight of fish.

An advantage of living in the ocean is that organisms rarely experience rapid environmental changes, such as major or quick shifts in water temperature. On land, air temperature can change by as much as 30 degrees within a few hours, but in the ocean a change in water temperature of just a degree or two over that same time period is rare.

Classification of Fish

Fish belong to the phylum Chordata, as do amphibians, reptiles, birds, and mammals. (Porpoises and whales are mammals, though they're often confused for fish.) All of these are vertebrates, which means they have a backbone that is composed of numerous smaller bones called vertebrae. We don't know how many different species of fish exist, but most ichthyologists believe the number is between 21,000 to 25,000. (The number of fish species exceeds that of all the other vertebrates combined.) More than half of the species of fish, about 58 percent, live exclusively in the ocean, while the remainder either live in fresh and salt water (1 percent) or exclusively in fresh water (41 percent).

Fish are generally divided into three main classes: jawless fish (the Agnatha), which are the lampreys and hagfish; cartilaginous fish (the Chondrichthyes), which include sharks, rays, and chimeras; and bony fish (the Osteichthyes, though some recent classifications have used the term Teleostomi instead of Osteichthyes), which include all remaining fish. (See Appendix 5 for descriptions of fish classes.) New species of fish are continuously being found. Expeditions into remote areas, such as the Amazon River or deep parts of the ocean, frequently reveal new and strange species. During a recent study in the Amazon, for example, more than 200 new fish species were discovered, including an electric fish that mainly feeds on the tails of other electric fish.

There are so many varieties and shapes of fish that it is hard to provide a general description of one. Key aspects are that they live in water, have gills for breathing in water, have fins for moving and balance, have an internal skeleton, and are usually cold-blooded. (See Appendix 5 for more about warm- and cold-blooded fish.) As I mentioned at the beginning of this chapter, the earliest fish appeared in fossils dated to more than 500 million years ago. These early fish seem to have evolved into the present-day fish of the Agnatha category. Fish with jaws and paired fins appeared about 440 million years ago. The combination of jaws and paired fins permitted these fish to eat a wider variety of food and to be better swimmers than their predecessors.

(continued)

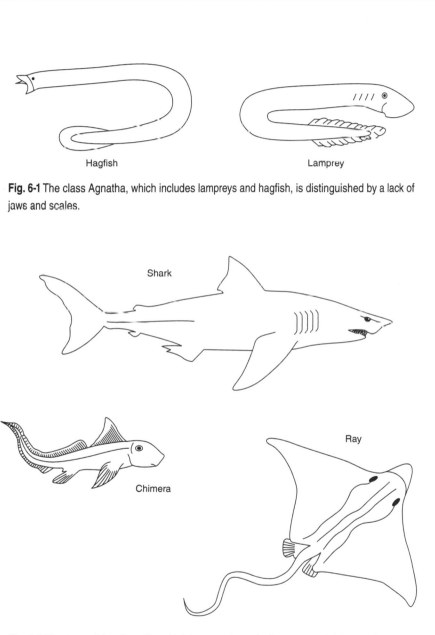

Fig. 6-1 The class Agnatha, which includes lampreys and hagfish, is distinguished by a lack of jaws and scales.

Fig. 6-2 Members of the class Chondrichthyes, such as sharks, rays, and chimeras, have skeletons composed of cartilage rather than real bone.

CLASSIFICATION OF FISH (continued)

The bony fish (Osteichthyes) and the cartilaginous fish (Chondrichthyes) developed independent of each other, each with distinct characterics. Other categories of fish, such as the heavily armored predators Placodermi, dominated the ocean for about 100 million years but eventually became extinct around 350 million years ago. It has been suggested that humans evolved from primitive fishlike organisms. Among the supporting evidence is that during a human embryo's development it goes through a phase wherein it has gill slits, which suggests some common ancestry between humans and fish.

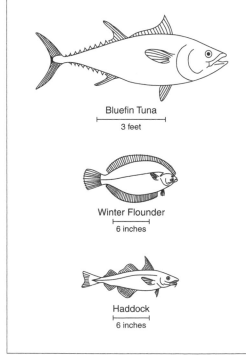

Bluefin Tuna
3 feet

Winter Flounder
6 inches

Haddock
6 inches

Fig. 6-3 The class Osteichthyes, or bony fish, is found in all parts of the ocean and includes most popular game fishes. This class includes by far the largest number of species of the three fish groups.

Life is not perfect in the ocean; for example, if you swim you know that it is much harder to move through water than through air. Because of this, much of a fish's body is composed of muscles that it needs for swimming. Most fish have evolved into streamlined shapes to reduce their drag and friction when moving through water.

A fish's life centers around finding food—and avoiding becoming someone else's meal—and reproducing. There are great, sometimes bizarre,

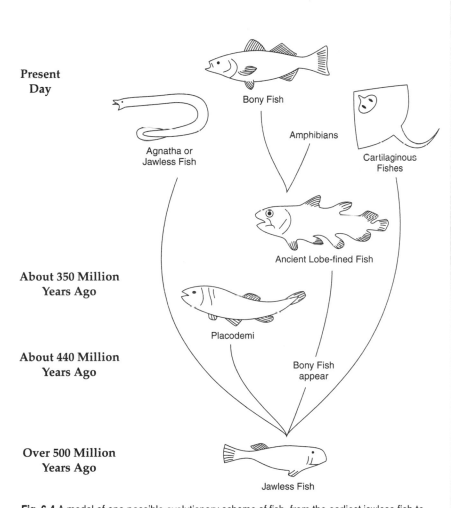

Present Day

Bony Fish

Agnatha or
Jawless Fish

Amphibians

Cartilaginous
Fishes

Ancient Lobe-fined Fish

**About 350 Million
Years Ago**

Placodemi

**About 440 Million
Years Ago**

Bony Fish
appear

**Over 500 Million
Years Ago**

Jawless Fish

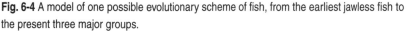

Fig. 6-4 A model of one possible evolutionary scheme of fish, from the earliest jawless fish to the present three major groups.

differences in how fish feed and reproduce. The food web in the ocean is a wonderful but complex system in which most organisms are both predator and prey. Evolution has made the predators very efficient, but their prey has also developed sophisticated ways to survive and endure. The survival of an individual fish depends on factors such as its swimming ability, its camouflage, and the acuteness of its various senses. Also, some fish mate almost daily and with various partners, others only at specific times.

ANATOMICAL ASPECTS OF FISH

Fish tend to have a torpedo-like shape (called fusiform), with many varia-tions. For example, bottom-dwelling fish tend to be flattened, whereas fast-swimming fish have more streamlined shapes. Despite the many variations in shape from species to species, a fish's body will be bilaterally symmetrical, which means that its left and right halves are mirror images; humans have the same anatomical symmetry.

Skeleton

The skeleton of a typical fish has three main parts: the skull, the vertebral column, or backbone, and the bones of the fins and tail. The backbone con-tains numerous bones that protect and enclose the fish's internal organs and provide a frame to which muscles are attached. Because much of a fish's weight is supported by the surrounding water, its skeleton does not have to be as strong and extensive as those of land-dwelling animals; the skeleton of a fish is designed more for swimming than for support. This feature works against a fish when it is lifted out of the water, at which time its essentially unsupported internal organs can be easily damaged. For this reason, anglers should be very careful when handling and holding a fish. It's best not to remove a fish from the water if you plan to release it.

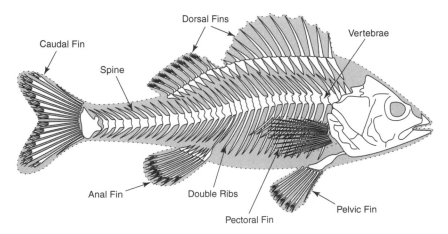

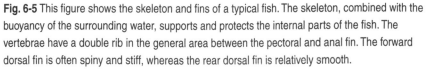

Fig. 6-5 This figure shows the skeleton and fins of a typical fish. The skeleton, combined with the buoyancy of the surrounding water, supports and protects the internal parts of the fish. The vertebrae have a double rib in the general area between the pectoral and anal fin. The forward dorsal fin is often spiny and stiff, whereas the rear dorsal fin is relatively smooth.

Do Fish Feel Pain?

I've been asked this question many times, and it's difficult to offer a conclusive answer. In a search of several ichthyology books, none had an entry for "pain." A more correct question might be: Do fish have nerve endings in their skin and, if so, do they detect and/or transmit pain impulses? I've found that fish with thin skin have a relatively simple skin structure, whereas thicker-skinned fish are more likely to have nerve endings. Also, fish with thin skin (which includes many of the ones we fish for) usually have relatively thick scales. The nerve endings present in fish are pretty simple, and are generally less numerous than those of higher animals such as mammals. Most significantly, it appears that most if not all fish lack the region of the brain that would generate a pain impulse.

Many fish scientists with whom I've spoken believe that fish "fight" mostly because of panic rather than pain. There are several bits of evidence to support this idea. When a fish becomes hooked, say on a fly being gently retrieved, it often will not fight until it is pressured. And then there is the difference in fighting intensity when a fish is hooked in shallow water versus deep water. In shallow water, a fish usually fights fairly hard, probably because its panic response is greater because it has limited space in which to maneuver. In deep water, a hooked fish generally is less threatened and will simply go deep and fight by pulling.

In my research, I've found no good evidence that hooking a fish is painful for the fish. The bottom line is that hooking a fish probably causes less discomfort than an unnecessarily long fight or mishandling the fish after it's landed. In any case, it's probably less traumatic for the fish than is pollution to its environment. Do keep in mind that a debarbed hook is less damaging to a fish, whether or not that fish can actually feel the hook.

Most fish cannot bend in the vertical sense, but they can bend or flex to either side. These fish roll on their side when they want to dive. When a fish rolls near the surface, its tail may break the surface or create an observable swirl. As a result, you might think the fish is feeding at the surface, when it's really just diving from near the surface back toward deeper water.

Skin

A fish's skin is composed of living cells, whereas most other vertebrates have skin that is covered either with dead cells or nonliving hair or feathers. The outermost layer of a fish's skin is protected by mucus material secreted by various glands. This layer aids in swimming by reducing the friction between the fish and the surrounding water, and protects the fish by keeping bacteria and parasites from entering the skin. This mucus can be the source of fishy odors.

Scales

Most fish are covered with scales, which are attached to their bodies like overlapping shingles on a roof. Scales provide protection against attacks and, along with the fish's skin, protection against disease. A few species do not have scales, such as lampreys, hagfish, and some freshwater catfish; some bony fish are only partially covered with scales. Fast-swimming fish generally have finer and smaller scales than slow swimmers or fish that live near the bottom. As a fish grows, so do its scales. In this way, scales have growth rings, similar to the growth rings of trees; the rings will be wide when food is abundant (usually in the summer), and narrow when food is less abundant or when the fish are spawning. By examining, measuring, and counting the rings on a fish's scales it is usually, but not always, possible to determine the fish's age and learn quite a bit about its life history, such as how many times it has spawned.

Fins

These are an important part of a fish's anatomy. The caudal (tail) fin is mainly used for propulsion, while the top dorsal (some fish have their dorsal fin divided into two or more parts) and bottom anal fin work like rudders. The pectoral fin is typically in front of the pelvic fin, and the fish uses both to turn, stop, and maintain position. When swimming fast, many fish will collapse their pectoral and anal fins and fold back their pelvic fins to reduce their drag and increase their streamlining. (The shape of the caudal fin greatly influences a fish's swimming ability and speed. See the sidebar on "aspect ratio" for more on this topic.)

The Lateral Line

Fish and some amphibians have an external sound-detecting organ called the lateral-line system. This line usually starts near the fish's head and extends back to the tail; some fish have several lateral lines. Most species have a fairly visible lateral line or lines: the black stripe along the side of a snook or the irregular pattern along a bonito are good examples. The lateral line is usually visible because of its pores and canals, and is not related to other lateral stripes or color patterns.

Aspect Ratio

The shape of the fish's tail, or caudal, fin greatly influences the speed and thrust it can attain; you feel a fish's thrust in that wonderful pull against your line when you hook up. The mathematical expression for the caudal fin is called the "aspect ratio" and is defined as the height of the fin squared and then divided by the surface area of the fin. In mathematical terms, aspect ratio is (fin height)^2/fin surface area.

A tail with a large surface area relative to its height (thus a low aspect ratio) permits quick acceleration and maneuverability, but its large surface area causes frictional drag and eventually slows down the fish. Fish such as tuna, with caudal fins that have a relatively small surface area compared to the fin's height (high aspect

(continued)

	Caudal Fin Shape	Aspect Ratio	Examples	Comments
	Rounded	About 1	Flounder and many bottom fish	Quick acceleration, good maneuverability, but limited swimming range
	Truncated	About 3	Striped Bass, Salmon	Similar to above
	Forked	About 5	Tarpon, Yellowtail, Herring	Similar to below
	Lunated	7 to 10	Swordfish, Marlin, Tuna	Limited maneuverability, but can swim fast for long periods
	Variable	Variable	Sharks	Fin provides uplift as well as forward motion

Fig. 6-6 The higher the aspect ratio, the faster the fish can swim, but with less maneuverability than a fish with a lower aspect ratio.

ASPECT RATIO (continued)

ratios), do not have much maneuverability but can swim fast for relatively long periods. Tuna are amazing creatures—they can beat their rigid caudal fin up to 30 times per second, and hooked yellowfin tuna have been clocked at more than 40 knots—but they actually can become unstable when making slow turns, and therefore rarely do so. In general, slow-swimming fish tend to use more turning maneuvers than faster-swimming fish.

The caudal fin of many sharks is larger and longer on the upper part than the lower part. This shape can provide lift and move the shark upward, as well as forward, when it swims. Such uplift from the caudal fin, combined with a similar uplift from the pectoral fin, helps sharks overcome not having a buoyancy-regulating swimbladder.

A fish's swimming ability is an important aspect to consider when you're fishing. Slow-moving fish generally do not go far to attack prey, and wait for prey (a fly, lure, bait, or the real thing) to come to them. Fast-swimming fish such as tuna, however, catch their prey by outswimming it; however, such fish can have difficulty catching erratic-moving, highly maneuverable prey because they are not maneuverable themselves. For fishing, you should troll or retrieve fast and straight for fast-swimming fish such as tuna, bonito, albacore, and Spanish mackerel, but not so fast for fish such as striped bass, which have caudal fins with a moderate aspect ratio. Bass and similar fish are not built for long, fast chases, but can maneuver well and strike dramatically.

Mouth

The character of a fish's mouth can offer some clues about how the fish lives and feeds. Predators usually have large and hard mouths with sharp teeth. Most bony fish have small mouths with relatively hard lips, a characteristic that helps the fish feed on a variety of foods. In general, the larger a fish's mouth, the larger the prey that fish can consume. Bottom-feeders often have soft mouths or down-pointing lips. Some fish have barbels, which are fleshy features around the mouth or on the chin; a fish can detect odors, and chemicals or physical features of the ocean bottom, through barbels.

When most fish feed, they extend their lips forward and open their mouth, expanding their mouth cavity and causing water to rapidly flow into it. Food enters the mouth with the incoming water. The fish then closes its mouth and expels the water though its gills, retaining the food. Using this feeding technique, a fish doesn't have to pick out and grab individual pieces of food, but can capture whatever prey is in the incoming water. This ability may be one reason why bony fish thrive in their environment. Fish also use this technique to breath, as it forces a large volume of water to move across the gills.

Internal Organs

The liver is usually a fish's largest internal organ. This is especially so for some sharks, which store lightweight oil in the liver to help maintain buoyancy. During the breeding season, however, a fish's gonads may expand and, sometimes in the case of females, even account for 50 percent or more of the fish's total weight. At other times, the gonads are relatively small and hard to detect. Gonads can either be the orange or yellow granular-like ovaries of females, or the smooth, white testes of males. The swimbladder, another important organ, is found in the abdominal cavity, usually between the overlying backbone and the underlying stomach.

The organ that's likely of most interest to anglers is a fish's brain. Certainly, everyone has wondered what makes a fly or lure attractive to a fish, or how a fish adapts its behavior according to the information it receives from its vision and other senses. At our present level of scientific knowledge and technology, we can only observe a fish's behavior and how it responds to different situations and stimuli. It may be a long time, if ever, before we learn what actually goes on in a fish's head. We do know that, compared to other vertebrates, a fish's brain is small and poorly developed, particularly the cerebrum, where thought and reasoning occur for humans.

Digestive System

Fish have a digestive system like most other vertebrates: food enters from the mouth and after digestion exits via the anus. From the mouth, food goes into a large opening called the pharynx and then into the esophagus, which can expand to hold most things that a fish can swallow. The actual digestive process starts in the stomach. The shape of a fish's stomach generally depends on what it eats; predatory fish tend to have elongated stomachs, while plant eaters tend to have a saclike stomach. (Some fish lack a stomach, and their esophagus is directly connected to their intestines.) After the food leaves the stomach, the digestive process will con-

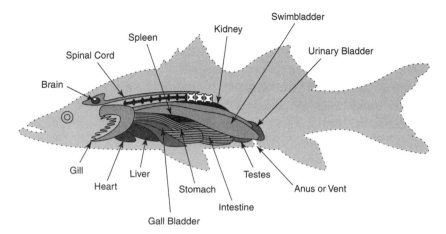

Fig. 6-7 The general internal organs and structure of a typical fish. Most of the important organs are enclosed by the double ribs of the vertebrae (see **Fig. 6-5**). The fish shown is a male.

tinue in the intestines. Nutrients, vitamins, and other digestive by-products are absorbed into the blood and moved by the fish's circulatory system.

Circulation and Blood

The circulation system of most fish is relatively simple. Blood moves from the heart to the gills, where oxygen is absorbed and carbon dioxide is released. The blood then carries the oxygen to other parts of the body. When the blood reaches an organ, an exchange of oxygen or waste products can occur through a thin-walled capillary system. Thus the blood flows from the heart through arteries to capillaries (within the various organs), then to veins and back to the heart.

Muscles

The shape of a fish's fins and its muscle mass clearly influence where it can live and how it feeds. Fish that spend a lot of time swimming tend to have a higher percentage of muscle in their body mass than those that do not swim much. Muscles constitute a major portion of a fish's body weight, ranging from about 40 percent of its total weight for a fish of average activity, to as much as 75 percent for very active fish, such as tuna. These muscles are the fish fillets we eat.

Fish have red (slow) muscle and white (fast) muscle; a few species also have pink muscle. For table fare, most anglers prefer white muscle. Red muscle gets its color from the high amounts of hemoglobin contained in its blood and tissues, and is generally used for cruising or regular, continuous swimming. White muscle, which has a relatively low amount of blood and the oxygen-binding pigment hemoglobin, makes up the largest part of the fish's flesh, and is used when a sudden but short burst of speed is required. The chemical energy within the white muscle, however, can quickly be used up, leading to fatigue. Fish with a modest amount (20 percent or so) of red muscle can swim at higher speeds for longer periods than those with no red muscle, and are usually better fighters; examples include bonito, bluefish, and tuna. Fish with only white muscle generally quit fighting soon after being hooked—they simply run out of energy.

If you fight a fish a long time and plan to release it, there is a chance it could die a few hours later due to overexertion. During a hard fight, a fish will exhaust its energy stores and start to produce lactate (or lactate acid). This buildup of lactate can cause internal poisoning, which will kill the fish.

Gills

The gills are the key part of a fish's circulation system. Fish use their gills to obtain oxygen from the surrounding water, and to release waste products such as carbon dioxide. The diffusion of oxygen from the surrounding water into the fish, via its gills, is critical for the fish's survival. Gills contain delicate, thin membranes through which oxygen and carbon dioxide can enter or leave the blood supply. Inside the fish, the gills are protected by gillrakers, which filter out particles in the water, including food, before anything can reach and damage the sensitive gills. Any damage to the gills, such as that from a hook, can cause a fish to bleed to death. Externally, bony fish have a cover over their gills that is called the operculum, which both protects the gills and facilitates water motion across them.

When a fish is out of the water its gills will collapse, dry out, and cease taking in oxygen—and the fish will die. Some fish living in waters where the oxygen content is very low have developed an ability to gulp air from the atmosphere. For example, tarpon can breath air from the surface, which they do when the oxygen content of the water is low, when the temperature is high—or just because they want to.

SHAPE, SWIMBLADDERS, AND SWIMMING

The shape and external features of most fish are really very simple, in large part due to the uniqueness of the marine environment. Because sea water is relatively dense, almost 1,000 times more dense than air, most fish are close to being, but are not quite, buoyant. A buoyant fish can use more of its energy to swim rather than to work against the pull of gravity. Water, however, is also about 100 times more viscous than air. (Viscosity is a measure of a substance's resistance to flow—for example, syrup is more viscous than water.) In other words, water is relatively sticky and dense compared to air. For a fish to move through the water, it must actually push the water out of its way. For example, compare the resistance you feel as you move your hand through the air compared to when you swish it through water. Fish, therefore, need a mechanism whereby they can adjust their buoyancy (or density) and an engine to propel them through the water.

Fish achieve and regulate their buoyancy with an internal organ called the swimbladder, which contains gas or oily fluids. By altering the volume of this organ by eliminating or adding air or oil, a fish can adjust its buoyancy so that it can easily move up or down. For a fish to balance or eliminate its weight in water, making it weightless, its swimbladder only has to occupy about 5 percent of its total volume.

The location of the swimbladder of most fish is somewhat behind their center of gravity, so they must actively maintain their posture in the water. A hooked fish, however, often becomes exhausted during the fight and cannot maintain its posture; in this situation, it may roll over or go "belly up." If the fish is quickly pulled to the surface from deep water, its swimbladder may be damaged, or it may extend out of the fish's mouth or push other organs out of its mouth. If the fish is to be released, do not puncture the swimbladder in the hope of helping the fish. By quickly getting the fish back under the water, you'll increase the pressure on the swimbladder, which will force it to shrink.

Most fish move up and down in the water as part of their daily activity, such as for feeding. Many fish also go closer to the surface at dark, and return toward the bottom as the sun rises. These vertical movements would be difficult if it was necessary for the fish to be precisely neutrally buoyant, as it can take hours for a fish to adjust the gas content in its swimbladder to reach exact neutral buoyancy. As a result, fish generally make short vertical movements; to do so they expend some energy by swimming and maintaining their position as the swimbladder adjusts.

Sharks and rays do not have swimbladder organs and thus are heavier than sea water. Some sharks and other fish can improve or even regulate their buoyancy by storing fats and oils (which weigh less than water) within their bodies, frequently in their livers. Fish that live on the bottom rarely need or have swimbladders.

The swimbladder is mainly what reflects sound back to a boat's echo sounder. In general, the larger the swimbladder, the more intense the returning echo will be. Sometimes, it's even possible to identify the type of fish by the character of the returning echo. The swimbladder can also be used as a receiver and transmitter of sound. (More on this in the discussion of fish's ability to hear in the next chapter.) Some fish transmit sound by vibrating their swimbladder using internal muscles and, in doing so, they produce grunts, growls, or even barking noises. These noises are usually made during feeding, reproduction, or at times of danger.

Some tuna and other fast-swimming and active fish either have small swimbladders or lack the organ altogether. These fish must constantly swim or else they will sink. On the other hand, if such large and fast predators had large swimbladders it would be difficult for them to move rapidly up and down through the water while chasing prey. The change in pressure with changing depth could rupture their swimbladders, if they had one. Large tuna have small swimbladders and large pectoral fins, enabling them to cruise at low speeds; both features contribute to a meaningful energy savings.

Most fish are good swimmers. Some, such as tuna and swordfish, are exceptional: they can achieve short bursts of speed or accelerate to more than 40 mph. Swordfish can reach an amazing 60 mph, which is fast enough to catch just about anything in the ocean. Striped bass can do about 12 mph, and barracuda about 27 mph. A fish's swimming speed is mainly due to its shape, its size, and the power of its swimming thrust. The more muscles and more streamlined the fish, the better and faster it can swim.

For a fish to swim efficiently, the prime challenge is to overcome the resistance of sea water. Anything moving through water creates turbulence, which in turn produces a frictional drag that slows the moving object. The amount of turbulence (and thus frictional drag) is controlled by the speed of the object and its shape. The more streamlined the fish's body, the less frictional drag it will experience.

Fast-swimming fish have evolved some specific adaptations to reduce their frictional drag; some even have small depressions into which their fins can fit when they're swimming at high speeds. Another streamlining adaptation is the "slime" coating on many fish, which reduces their surface drag in the water. The ability of fish to easily and swiftly move through water has not escaped the view of engineers and designers of submarines, boats, and even airplanes, all of which incorporate some streamlining in their design.

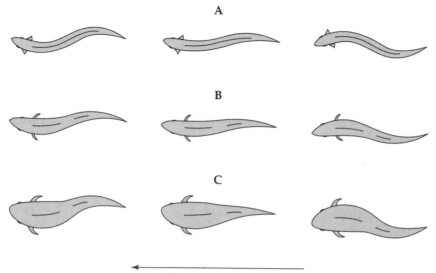

A

B

C

Direction of Movement

Fig. 6-8 Some of the ways that fish can swim. (A) This type of swimming pattern (usually slow) is typical of long flexible fish such as eels and some sharks and bony fish. The whole body of the fish produces an undulatory wave for its movement. (B) This pattern is intermediate to (A) and (C) and shows a less distinct undulatory wave that has most of its amplitude toward the tail, or caudal, fin. (C) This is the swimming pattern of most fast-swimming fish, such as tuna and billfish. The fish are very streamlined and the rapid movement of their large tails provides their speed.

In general, most fish move through the water by making rhythmic undulatory (or S-shaped) motions of their body and fins, or by beating their tail, or caudal, fin. Essentially the fish's body, plus its dorsal (top), ventral, or pelvic (bottom), and tail fins produce a series of waves moving from front to back, thrusting the fish forward. Other fins help the fish stop, hover, and maintain precise movements. The more intense these undulatory waves are in a period of time, the more power the fish will develop and the faster it can swim. Fast-swimming fish generally have more rigid bodies than slow-swimming fish and depend on their tail fins to propel them through the water.

GROWTH RATES OF FISH

Most fish continue to grow throughout their life, though not at the same rate over their lifetime. Growth usually is greatest in the early phases of life and lessens as the fish ages. Lifelong growth is not typical of other

How Fish Use Oxygen

Like all living creatures, fish need energy to survive. They obtain energy from the food they eat, and they use this energy to swim; to locate, capture, and consume food; to reproduce; to grow; and to maintain internal body functions. Food is organic material, which is converted by the fish's metabolic processes into energy. This metabolic process requires oxygen.

A fish's activity, its weight, and the temperature of its environment all influence how much oxygen the fish needs. The link between activity and oxygen consumption is obvious—a swimming fish needs more energy and thus more oxygen than a resting fish. A fast-swimming fish can quickly use up its oxygen supply, incur an oxygen debt, and produce lactic acid (similar to what happens if you run too hard). This can ultimately kill the fish. For this reason, if you plan to release a fish, land it and free it quickly—don't fight it for an extensive time. An over-fought fish, although it may look healthy when released, could die in a few hours either from lactic-acid buildup or because it's so weakened that it cannot escape a predator.

As a general rule, larger fish need more oxygen than smaller fish; however, smaller fish use more oxygen per pound of body weight than larger fish. Fish living in warm water have a higher oxygen consumption rate than those living in cold water. After feeding, fish will show an increase in their oxygen consumption rate—they need the extra oxygen to digest their food.

species—mammals and birds, for example, will stop growing once they reach sexual maturity.

Key factors influencing the growth rate of fish are the water temperature and the availability of food. There usually is a temperature range in which a fish will grow fastest, assuming that it has an adequate food supply. That's why there can be a difference in size among fish of a similar age within the same species. Frequently, there is a size difference between males and females; for example, most large striped bass are females. In addition, the males of many coastal species reach sexual maturity before the females; the striped bass again is an example.

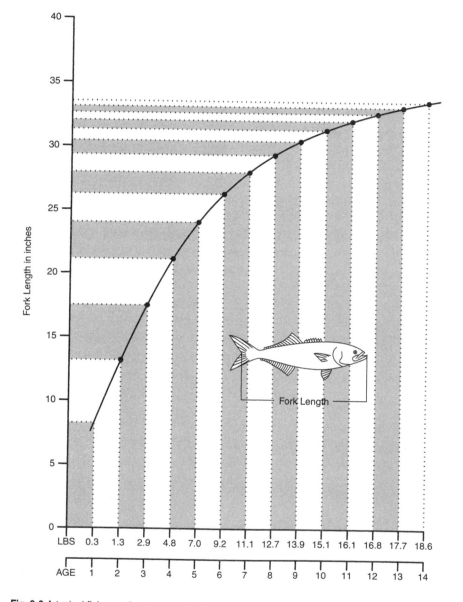

Fig. 6-9 A typical fish growth-rate curve, in this instance for bluefish. Growth, usually represented by weight or length, is usually plotted against age. For many commercial and recreational fish species, much of this data comes either from tagging programs or from capture. (Data from Massachusetts Division of Marine Fisheries.)

Fish living in a warm climate can differ in size compared to those of the same species living in a cold climate. Although ones from either habitat may eventually reach the same size, those living in warmer climates will grow more quickly. This temperature-growth relationship is not surprising, as warm temperatures generally increase a fish's metabolism and its food consumption. Fish that live in the tropics generally have rapid initial growth, but are often smaller than fish from temperate regions. There are many exceptions to this point—tarpon, sharks, barracuda, sailfish, and marlin, for example. Fish that live in deep water far from shore generally grow very slowly and can live to considerable ages.

A fish's age is usually established by examining its scales or otoliths. Counting rings on otoliths or scales is not foolproof, however, as you cannot always be sure that each ring really represents a year. In the tropics, where there is little climatic change between seasons, a ring may be missing or indistinct. Such otolith and scale data typically show rapid growth when a fish is young, then tapered-off growth as the fish gets older, generally after it reaches sexual maturity; a fish often directs much of its energy toward reproduction rather than growth.

Determining growth rates of fish in the ocean is a challenging task. Much of the data comes from fish-tagging programs. Fish are marked or tagged, measured, and then released into the ocean. Upon recapture, their growth rate can be estimated if the fish are measured. Fish can also be grown in a controlled environment such as an aquarium, and their growth measured over time. A statistical approach involves noting the length-frequency distribution of caught fish. Here, individual fish sampled from a population are measured, and the frequency (number of fish) of each length caught is plotted. The lengths will generally fall into distinct groupings, with individual peaks indicating separate age or year classes. The differences in weight and length of adjacent groups will represent the growth from one year to another.

How long can a fish live? The answer varies with the species. Few fish live longer than about 20 years, though some carp may live to be 50 years or more. A recent publication noted that a small Australian fish called the orange roughy may not mature until it's 32 years old, and that radioactive dating of some have indicated an age of no less than 77 to 149 years! The fact that fish continue to grow as they age, of course, fuels a fisherman's desire to catch larger fish of a particular species—an aspect of our sport that might not exist if fish stopped growing at a particular age. In reality, few fish actually die of old age in the competitive world of nature and due to fishing pressure from humans.

Internal Regulation of Salt and Water

One of the major problems that fish face in their environment, regardless of whether they are marine or freshwater species, is that the concentration of salts in their internal fluids differs from that in the surrounding water (or external fluid). For a fish to survive, it must maintain a precise concentration of water and salts in its tissues, organs, cells, and body fluids. A difference in salt concentration between the water surrounding the fish and the fluid inside the fish causes an osmotic pressure.

Osmotic pressure can be defined as the force required to prevent water from moving or diffusing across a semipermeable membrane, such as the wall of a cell. It develops when fluids having different concentrations of salt are on either side of this semipermeable membrane. Osmosis is the term for the actual movement of fluid from one solution to the other through a membrane. For marine fish, the difference between its internal salinity (about 1.5 percent) and that of the surrounding sea water (35 parts per thousand or 3.5 percent) will cause such an osmotic pressure. This will force water (but not the dissolved salts) to move across the membrane, going from the less-concentrated solution to the more-concentrated solution. If a marine fish didn't have a regulatory system to control this flow of water, it actually could become dehydrated by the loss of its body fluids to the ocean. Marine fish solve this problem by drinking sea water and discharging a small amount of concentrated urine to compensate for the water loss. The excess salt in the sea water the fish drinks is excreted back to the ocean through special cells (called chloride cells) located in the fish's gills. For a freshwater fish, the problem is somewhat reversed: its internal fluids are saltier (about 0.6 percent) than the surrounding fresh water and it can gain water and thus dilute its internal fluids. Freshwater fish regulate their internal osmotic pressure by not drinking water and producing large amounts of dilute urine. They also absorb salt through special cells in their gills. Some fish, of course, can live either in fresh or salt water; to do this they must literally switch regulatory systems as they move between the two environments. Fish that live entirely in either fresh water or salt water have little ability to adjust to major changes in salinity and usually will not survive such changes.

All organisms must work against osmotic pressure to maintain the composition of their internal fluids. For marine organisms, there is a rather amazing chemical similarity in the composition of the salts in their body fluids to that of sea water, which is lacking in their fresh-water brothers and sisters. Because of this similarity, marine organisms need not use as much energy as freshwater organisms to keep the chemistry of their body fluids in balance and thus can put some of this energy into their growth—which helps explain why marine species are generally larger than freshwater species.

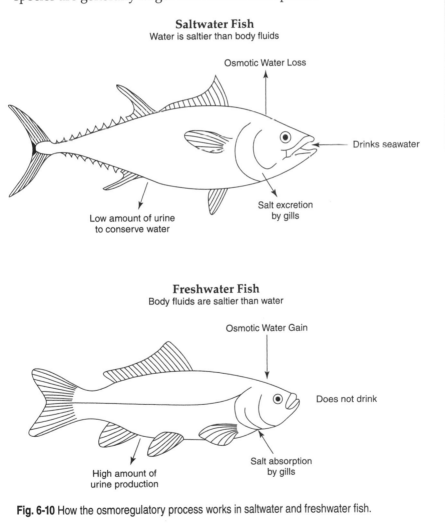

Fig. 6-10 How the osmoregulatory process works in saltwater and freshwater fish.

FISH MORTALITY

Fish can die due to a physical aspect of the environment, a biological cause, or by being harvested. It is often difficult to separate the biological from the environmental impact. The death of most fish in the ocean goes unobserved, so unless fish are killed by fishing harvest, we just don't know the causes of mortality for many species.

Changes in the physical environment of the ocean, such as variations in water temperature or current flow, can be lethal, especially when the fish are in the larval or egg stage. Strong currents can carry drifting eggs, larvae, and very young fish that are barely able to swim out of their best growing area, whereas weak currents may allow the eggs or larvae to sink below their normal growing area into colder, deeper, and less favorable waters. Such variations in currents can cause fluctuations in the survival rate of many species of ocean-breeding fish, including cod and bluefish.

In nearshore regions, environmental changes in temperature or salinity (due to rainfall or river inflow) are common and can affect the survival of eggs, larvae, and young fish, as well as the availability of the food they eat. These factors, either directly or indirectly, can lead to weakened fish that are more vulnerable to predation, starvation, or disease.

Biological reasons for the death of fish, including some diseases, are often related to the environment, such as starvation due to some environmental change or problem that diminished the food supply. There is considerable scientific evidence showing that the lack of food, especially during the early stages of a fish's life, is a prime cause of death.

Upwelling of oxygen-poor or oxygen-depleted water can cause extensive fish-kills. This can happen when the wind and weather are calm, reducing wave action and water mixing. If the bottom waters have a depleted oxygen content and are subsequently brought to the surface when the wind picks up, the lack of oxygen in these waters can be lethal to fish. Fish-kills can also occur during a so-called red tide, which is a sudden growth, or bloom, of dinoflagellates (microscopic phytoplankton). This algae growth can be so intense that it actually discolors the water, often making the surface appear red. (The process has nothing to do with the tide.) These dinoflagellates produce toxins that can kill fish and harm humans who eat organisms that have fed on the dinoflagellates. There is an increasing incidence of red tides in the ocean, and many biologists believe this is due to an increasing supply of nutrients, from pollution, in nearshore waters.

Of course, predation by other fish is a big, if not major, contributor to fish mortality. Fish weakened by an environmental impact or disease are usually most vulnerable to predation. Essentially all fish, with the exception of those on top of the food chain, are both bait and predators. And the organisms at the top of the food chain—tuna, for example—are food for humans and were prey for other animals when they were in their larval or juvenile stages.

SIZE

Most fishermen describe their catch by its length, and the weight if a scale is available. For scientists studying fish, or who are trying to manage fish stocks, accurate lengths and weights are necessary. Of the two, a fish's length is probably more important as the relationship between length and age is more reliable than the relationship between weight and age.

There are several ways to measure a fish's length. The first (preferred by fishermen because it yields the largest measure) is called the "total length" and is measured from the fish's snout or nose to the end of its tail. The problem with using this measurement is that the shape of the tail can vary and its tip could be worn or partially missing. Fishery scientists tend to prefer the "fork length," which is measured from the snout to the fork in the tail. A third measurement, preferred by taxonomists, works best on laboratory or preserved samples of fish and is the "standard length." The standard length is measured from the snout to the end of the fish's vertebrate column or the base of the caudal fin. The first two types of measurements can be made fairly quickly, an important factor if the fish is to be released.

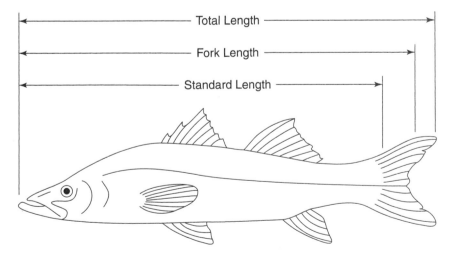

Fig. 6-11 Some of the most frequently used ways to measure a fish's length.

COLOR AND CAMOUFLAGE

Fish commonly avoid predation by using their colors and patterns to develop some form of camouflage. Camouflaged fish can blend in with the background, disguise themselves, or somehow just confuse a predator. Fish also use their color to communicate, both with their own and other species. Specific colors or changes in color can indicate warnings, recognition, sexual signals, or threats. Some fish change color if frightened, or when they become aggressive.

A fish's use of color for camouflage mainly works by reducing the fish's contrast with its background, whether the background is the white sand of a tidal flat, the vivid colors of a coral reef, or the blue-black depths of the ocean. Nearly all fish have evolved some type of color or color pattern that resembles their surroundings.

Cryptic Coloration

A basic method by which fish avoid detection is to adjust or change their color to match the background. This process, called cryptic coloration, is often used by bottom-living fish such as flounder. Most flounders have the ability to quickly change their color, and even the pattern of their colors, to match the sediment they live on or in. Laboratory experiments with one species of flounder showed that the fish could change its markings to match varied backgrounds within an amazing eight seconds. When placed on a checkerboard, some flounders change their color patterns to match their position on the board. Changing color is a very complex process, involving reflex actions induced by the fish's vision, hormones, or by a light-sensitive organ on their brain called the pineal body, and other intricate biological reactions and responses.

Countershading

Many fish have a simple color pattern that consists of a light or whitish underside (their belly), and silvery sides that grade into a darker top (their back), which is often iridescent green or blue. Seen by a predator from above, the dark top blends into the dark of the depths. Looking upward, the white and silver undersides will blend into the lighted surface of the ocean. From the side the fish will appear flat. This pattern is called countershading and is a convincing method of camouflage. Countershading almost seems to be a uniform for fish. If you turned a countershaded fish upside down in the water, it would clearly stand out compared to how it looks in its normal swimming position.

Among countershaded fish are many sharks, flying fish, marlin, herring, barracudas, mackerel, jacks, and silversides. Interestingly, a few

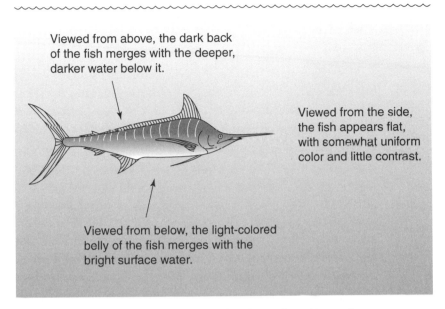

Viewed from above, the dark back of the fish merges with the deeper, darker water below it.

Viewed from the side, the fish appears flat, with somewhat uniform color and little contrast.

Viewed from below, the light-colored belly of the fish merges with the bright surface water.

Fig. 6-12 The camouflage concept of countershading: illustrated on a blue marlin.

species of African catfish swim upside down and most (but not all) are countershaded, but this time in reverse—their undersides are dark.

In addition to countershading, many fish that live near the surface where the waters are well-lit have a silver band along their flank. This band can act like a mirror and reflect back, to a predator, the colors of the ocean, which confuses the threatening predator.

Scales also can reflect light, helping fish blend in with the background. This type of coloration is especially effective for schooling fish such as silversides and herring. Bonefish have a system of numerous and closely overlying scales that effectively scatters and reflects light, making bonefish on a shallow tidal flat one of the most difficult of all fish to detect.

Disruptive Coloration
In this method of camouflage, the fish has some irregular markings or color patches that draw attention away from the actual shape of the fish. Such a fish often is easier to see against a drab or colorless background, but in its normal environment (usually among the vivid colors typical of tropical coral regions) its patches break up the general outline of the fish. Fish with vertical stripes or bars extending down their sides display disruptive coloration. These fish often live around plants, and the vertical

patterns on their body blend in with the branches or main trunk of the plant. Some fish have lateral or horizontal lines along their bodies; bonito and striped bass are examples. It's not clear how, or even if, these lateral lines confuse predators, other than make it hard for a predator to focus on one fish in a school of similarly lined fish.

Red Coloration

A surprising number of fish have red patches, spots, fins, or stripes. This may seem contradictory for a fish trying to be inconspicuous, as red is such a visible color on land. Red in the ocean is the least visible color and essentially is filtered out of the water as a color by a depth of 10 feet or so. Any fish with red colors living below that depth may be difficult to see.

Eyes

Eyes are usually visible features on a fish and frequently attract predators. Indeed, predators often attack their prey at the eyes. The attractiveness of eyes to predators may be one reason why flies such as Clouser Minnows and other flies and lures with pronounced eyes are so effective.

Some species have evolved spots or markings on parts of their bodies that resemble eyes. This form of camouflage diverts a predator away from a vulnerable part of the fish (its head) toward a less vulnerable part (its tail), or just makes it easier for the fish to escape. Many fish have evolved ways of disguising their actual eyes, such as by having stripes or color patterns around the eyes.

The eyes of some fish, particularly those living amid coral reefs, are emphasized by color. The reasons why aren't clear, but perhaps recognition or some other type of communication is more important to these fish than camouflage. Interestingly, fish that school generally have larger eyes than solitary or rarely schooling fish. The point seems to be that schooling fish can use various schooling procedures and maneuvers to avoid predation, and therefore do not need inconspicuous or false eyes.

Schooling and Camouflage

The behavior and appearance of fish in a school is a form of camouflage. A predator will have difficulty choosing one fish out of the large number of similar prey. Many of the fish that school are silver and are usually thin. When a school makes quick turns and maneuvers to avoid an attack, individual fish may literally disappear for a second or so in the flash and blur from the light reflecting off the fish's scales. An individual fish that appears different or does not move with its neighbors often will be the fish attacked by the predator. This may explain why flies and lures are still effective when large numbers of bait are present.

A school of fish can make a spectacular maneuver: when they rapidly move in all directions, they can literally cause an explosion of reflected light (likened to a bomb blast, and called a "flash explosion") and then quickly regroup. As a result, the predator is confused, and the bait can easily escape. Amazingly, the schooling baitfish rarely collide during this maneuver, probably thanks to their lateral line. In experiments, fish whose lateral lines had been severed sometimes collided when making such "explosions."

If you examine your collection of lures and flies you'll probably see that those meant to resemble a swimming fish generally have some sort of countershading pattern. It's clear that this type of camouflage works well in the marine environment—if it didn't, it wouldn't be so common among so many fish from so many different environments. But is it really necessary for a fly or lure to have such a pattern? The answer is probably yes, if your lure is meant to look realistic; however, baitfish with poor camouflage are rare in the ocean for good reason—they have been eaten.

Some lures (not flies, yet) have actual pictures of baitfish printed on their sides. Is such realism worth striving for? Until one knows what a fish actually sees and what stimulates it to eat, this approach may be excessive, although the lures probably sell. On the other hand, if the camouflage pattern on the lure or fly was poor or nonexistent might not the fly be more easily detected and perhaps attacked by a predator? I have flies that always seem to catch fish, but don't resemble anything living. Still, at times these flies are irresistible to fish.

Chapter 7

Fish Senses

All animals rely on their various senses—vision, hearing, and smell, in particular—to orient, defend, and feed themselves. The creatures living in the ocean have developed unique ways of using these senses, ways much different than those of land animals. Using their senses, fish are sensitive to subtle changes in the movement of the water, to temperature and salinity changes, to light and sound, and to other, less obvious, influences. Sound travels faster and usually farther in water than through air, so many fish are sensitive to vibrations and have excellent hearing. On the other hand, the ocean is relatively opaque, making it difficult for fish to see, so they must either adapt to the low-light conditions or get by with senses other than vision. Also, light is rapidly absorbed by water, and colors quickly change with depth and distance. Wind, which carries odors on land, moves about ten times faster than ocean currents,

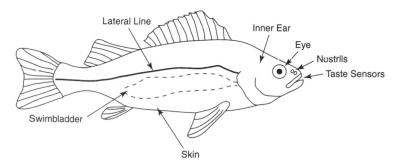

Fig. 7-1 Similar to most advanced organisms, fish can see, hear, taste, feel, and smell. Because these abilities must work in water, fish have sophisticated and unique sensory organs. The main sensory systems of a typical fish are: the inner ear (sometimes connected to the swimbladder) and the lateral line, used to detect sound and vibrations; the nostrils (nares), used to smell; the eyes, for vision; taste buds, which are sometimes located in the fish's mouth or attached to its lip; and skin, which is the main source of its sense of touch.

which carry odors in the ocean. The ocean also has none of the many landmarks or visible signs that are so common on land.

Scientists and anglers have much to learn about the sensing abilities of fish. Even with our limited insight, when we compare the sensory abilities of fish to our own, theirs are often more impressive. For anglers, knowledge of the senses of fish and how they work, and their limitations, can help increase fishing success.

THE SENSE OF SMELL

Smelling is one of the best-developed and most important abilities of fish. A fish's sense of smell is far more acute than that of humans and most animals. For example, we know that dogs have an excellent sense of smell; some breeds are more than a hundred times more sensitive to scent than humans, and can detect smells in the order of one-part odor to one-million-parts air. Some fish, however, can detect odors or chemicals in the parts-per-*billion* range or more, which is more than a thousand times better than most dogs and close to a million times better than humans.

Using its sense of smell, a fish can differentiate between categories of chemicals, as well as between specific compounds within these categories. For instance, fish not only can detect amino acids (a type of organic compound), but can respond differently to specific types of amino acids. Fish detect chemicals in water by using their senses of smell *and* taste. Sometimes it's not clear which sense is at work.

The Smelling Process

Most fish have small nostrils (called nares) on each side of their snout, just in front of their eyes. Many fish, even those with an excellent sense of smell, have nostrils that are inconspicuous or not visible. (A fish doesn't breathe through its nostrils like many other creatures, but rather uses them exclusively for smell.) Sharks tend to have relatively visible nostrils, a feature that's earned them the reputation of being extremely dependent on their sense of smell. Actually, sharks do have a well-developed sense of smell, and this sense is important to their survival, but not necessarily any more so than it is for other species of fish.

The smell "sensor" within the nares is called the olfactory organ, which contains numerous odor-sensing cells. For fish to smell, water must move rapidly over these cells. This can happen as the fish swims or faces into the current to force water into the nares, or as small hairlike cilia within the nares move water over the sensory cells. Many game fish species have two nostrils on each side of their head—one for incoming

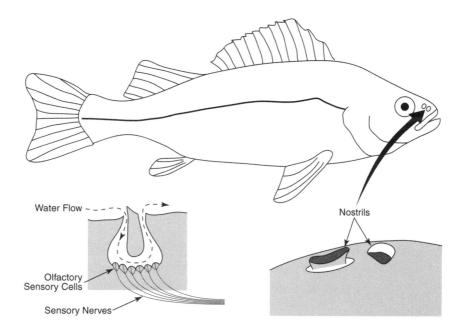

Fig. 7-2 A simplified view of the pathway of water moving into and over a fish's olfactory sensory cells. The information received by the fish's olfactory sensory cells is forwarded to the fish's brain via the sensory nerves. A fish's breathing and other movements will help move water through its nostrils and over its sensory cells.

water, one for outgoing—which facilitate a greater water flow over their olfactory cells. Fish with such double nostrils generally have an especially excellent sense of smell.

The Value of a Sense of Smell

Fish often depend heavily on smell, such as when the water is too turbid or dark for their vision to be effective. In general, fish that feed in dim light or at night have a well-developed sense of smell. Open-ocean predators and daytime feeders often have a limited sense of smell, and may depend more on sight or some other sense to find food. Bottom-dwelling species, which live in a low-light environment, often have acute sensing abilities. Fish with a good sense of smell—anglers often call such fish "nose sensitive"—generally prefer natural baits over artificial lures. Many fish use their sense of smell to find and identify food, then use their sense of vision to locate food and their sense of taste to determine if the food is edible.

Some fish can detect scent emitted by other members of their species, an ability that may be important in schooling behavior. Several species of fish communicate with other members of their species via chemical odors. For example, these fish may emit pheromones (a type of chemical compound) that can attract members of the opposite sex for mating or influence other types of fish behavior. When fish feed, they often excrete urine and feces, and the odors in these waste products may lead other fish to the food source. Some species of fish emit odors that indicate danger when they are attacked, injured, or frightened. Minnows release an odor when attacked or injured that causes other minnows to flee or disperse. When the skin of certain species of fish is damaged and torn (as by a predator), a scent is released from the injured cells, which will cause an alarm or a fright reaction among nearby fish. These fish may flee for cover, rapidly swim away, stop swimming and freeze, or close ranks and tighten up the school. As a fishing tactic, some anglers cripple or wound live bait and toss it in the water, with the expectation that its irregular movements will attract predators. This assumption is probably correct, but the wounded fish may also release odors that tell other fish to stay away.

A few fish species, such as Pacific salmon, migrate literally hundreds to thousands of miles to reproduce, often returning to the stream in which they were born. The last part of this journey is strongly influenced by the fish detecting and recognizing the odor of their natal stream. Scientists have confirmed the importance of smell in this process by marking the waters in a hatchery with a specific chemical and then releasing the fish, which migrated to the ocean. After the fish spent a year or more in the ocean and were due to spawn, scientists added the same chemical to a different stream along the fish's migration path. The hatchery fish imprinted with the specific chemical went up this stream thinking it was their birth stream.

Experiments on Scent
Many experiments have demonstrated how the sense of smell helps fish to find food, avoid predators, or orient themselves. For example, studies have shown that tuna become aggressive and begin displaying feeding behavior when extracts from their normal prey are placed in their laboratory tank. As you might expect, a fish's response to food odors (in the laboratory and perhaps also in the ocean) is generally more intense if the fish is hungry, whereas a recently fed fish is usually less interested in food odors.

Experiments have shown that a chemical commonly found in oils from human skin is offensive, even repulsive, to some fish. The offending chemical has been identified as an amino acid called L-serine, which is more prevalent in light-skinned people than in dark-complexioned individuals. Other common chemicals also seem to repel fish. These include gasoline and oil products, sunscreens, nicotine, and insect repellent. Imagine getting your outboard engine primed and running for a fishing trip, putting on some sunscreen and bug repellent, lighting a cigarette—and later wondering why your lures or flies do not attract fish. The experience will be even more frustrating when your tanned, nonsmoking spouse or friend easily outfishes you. Chemical odors can be absorbed by fishing line, leaders, and flies and lures; nylon-based monofilament fishing line can absorb odors from oil and gas products. Such imprinting, which cannot be removed, probably will reduce your fishing success.

It makes sense to keep your hands free of the offensive odors mentioned above when you're fishing. Washing your hands in sea water and, perhaps, rubbing your hands against bait or in fish oil are ways to prevent transferring offensive odors to your lures or flies. Human saliva seems to contain chemicals that either mask the L-serine odor or are attractive to fish, so you might want to try spitting on your lures. Probably anything that reduces or neutralizes the natural L-serine scent from your skin will lessen your chances of "offending" fish.

Other chemicals may attract fish. These can include juices and liquids from natural baits (worms, baitfish, and the like), fish extracts and oils, sugar, dairy products such as milk and cheese, and human saliva. Fish oils or special brews that can be applied to lures, especially to plastic lures, are commonly sold today; there is evidence that they may work. The International Game Fish Association (IGFA), however, has ruled that the application of a natural or artificial scent to your lure or fly is not acceptable, if you want to submit a fish for IGFA-record consideration.

I once tried soaking a fly in fish oil to see if it made any difference to the fish. I found no increase in my catch rate, but it was not a very sophisticated experiment. If you want to try this with one of your lures or flies, I strongly suggest that you first tie the fly to the leader before putting it in the fish oil; otherwise, the line may become "greasy" and the knot might not hold.

There is a caveat here: different fish may respond differently to a specific odor; some fish might even like L-serine or (less likely) gasoline. Surprisingly, many fish do not seem bothered by the exhaust from boat engines (maybe because a good portion of the odor goes into the air and not into the water). This variability in response to odors adds to the adventure of fishing—if we had a chemical that attracted all fish, fishing would not be much of a sport. Not to worry: Because the response to odor is generally different among different species, most scientists feel that the possibility of developing a universal fish attractant is unlikely. Even proven chemical attractants may only work at specific times, tides, or seasons.

Fishing Tips Involving Smell

Chumming and bait-fishing are good ways to capitalize on fish's excellent sense of smell. Placing pieces of bait or a slurry of ground-up bait in the water can create a "scent track" in the water near your boat. Fish, if attracted to the scent track, will follow it back to its source—your boat. A key to making this technique work is keeping the scent track continuous, which requires continual chumming, even when you're fighting or landing a fish. Also, the scent track must be established in moving water so the scent is dispersed. Mix the chum with sand to reach deeper water.

Another way to capitalize on the scenting ability of fish is to add a piece of bait to an artificial lure. Live and fresh bait produce better scent than frozen bait or chum. People who fish for bonefish know this trick and frequently add a piece of shrimp to their lures. Most big game fish are visual feeders, but scent can be the initial attractant. Fish need time to detect a scent, and a slow-moving lure or fly may give them time to do so, whereas a rapidly retrieved lure or fly often will not.

THE SENSE OF TASTE

Many fish have a sense of taste, but scientists have not studied this ability as intensively as they have other fish senses. Most fish have taste sensors within their mouth; however, species such as catfish have external sensors or taste buds, called barbels, on their lips.

As I mentioned earlier, in many cases it's difficult to know which sense a fish is using, smell or taste. A few species, again catfish and some sea robins, clearly use their sense of taste in their search for food. Sea robins have many taste sensors in their three pairs of pectoral fins, which they use to "walk" on or dig into the ocean floor.

Fish often use their sense of taste to test the quality of food they're chewing. Some researchers believe that fish can discriminate between the tastes of sweet, salty, acidic, and bitter substances. Experiments have shown that fish will reject rotten or poisoned food; either the texture of the food or its taste may cause that rejection. Taste can also influence how a fish reacts when it takes a fly, which may be one of the reasons a fly is quickly rejected if the fish is not immediately hooked.

In summary, it's clear that the sense of smell and taste play important roles in a fish's search for food, in some types of migration, in the reproduction process, and in various types of communication between fish. Still, much remains to be learned about how fish detect and react to certain chemical stimuli and how these processes might influence our fishing methods.

THE SENSE OF VISION

The question of what fish actually see has been, and still is, a challenging one for marine scientists. Despite numerous studies on the character and structure of fish's eyes, it's not known what image their brain is actually seeing. Scientific knowledge about a fish's sense of vision comes from two main sources: physical examination of various parts of their eyes; and studies of how fish respond in the laboratory and in the field to various images, colors, or other sight stimuli. Most of these laboratory and field studies, however, have been done on freshwater species. Also, different species may exhibit different physical and behavioral responses during scientific studies, so generalizations about fish vision should be treated with caution.

General Aspects of Vision

Fish species, during their hundreds of millions of years of existence, have developed sophisticated systems of vision with which they distinguish prey, find companions, and detect obstacles or movements by other creatures. These systems enable fish to see in low-light conditions, in dirty or murky water, and sometimes even over long distances. Studies have shown that the eyes and retinas of most fish provide good contrast detection, motion perception, and the ability to obtain a clearly focused image. In general, most fish are nearsighted, though some sharks are thought to be farsighted.

Fish do not have necks, of course, and therefore cannot turn their heads independent of their bodies. Indeed, they would not be very efficient swimmers if they had to constantly turn their head to see what was off to the side or above or below or behind them. They compensate for this physiological limitation in two ways. First, their eyes usually protrude out from the sides of their head, and each eye can move independently. Second, they can rotate their eyes without moving their head; thus, each eye has an almost 180-degree view of the fish's surroundings, and can scan up and down. This adaptation gives most fish a wide lateral field of vision. The eyes of some fish are positioned so that they have a expanded field of vision up or down—the direction is related to whether they feed at the surface or on the bottom.

This visual system is not perfect, as fish have some blind spots immediately in front of and behind them. Depending on the spacing of their eyes, some fish have a small blind area immediately in front of their nose, so a fly presented there actually might not be seen. The blind spots can be somewhat reduced or even eliminated by the fish as it moves its head side to side while swimming. Because both eyes work together, fish can very accurately see objects directly in front of them. At some fixed point in front of a fish, both eyes can pick up an object. At this point, they have binocular vision. It's not necessary, however, to put a fly directly in front of a fish, as it can easily detect the fly if it's presented to either side.

Although vision is an important sense for most animals, for some fish it is less important than their sense of smell or the use of their lateral line. Many fish use their sense of smell or

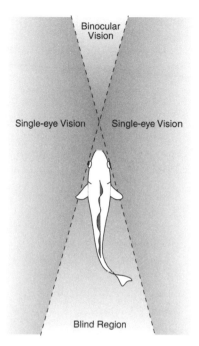

Fig. 7-3 The various views that most fish have, a combination of binocular vision, where both eyes see, and monocular vision, where only one eye is involved.

hearing to initially detect or find their food, and then use their eyesight to guide them on the final attack. Some movement of the prey is usually necessary to trigger or provoke the final attack, since most predatory fish are very curious and will examine anything that crosses through their field of vision. Scientific studies in aquariums have shown that predatory fish get agitated and excited by movement.

Eye Structure

The structure of a fish's eye is similar to that of a human eye. One difference is that we have an adjustable iris or diaphragm that controls the amount of light that enters our eye and reaches the retina. Most fish have fixed or only slightly adjustable irises and therefore cannot regulate the amount of incoming light that reaches their retinas. Also, many fish either do not have eyelids or, if they do, have poorly developed ones. Without eyelids, light intensity can be a problem for fish, as they cannot squint or

Polarizing Vision

Many fish have the ability to sense polarized light, though it's not completely clear why they have this ability. Light in the ocean can be polarized when it is reflected off some surfaces. (Polarized light vibrates only in one plane; ordinary light vibrates in all directions perpendicular to its direction of travel. Birds and insects also have polarizing vision; humans do not.) One speculation is that fish use their polarizing vision during migration. A fish with polarizing vision could orient itself to the sun and navigate, even on cloudy days. Fish such as salmon may use this ability in their migrations. Because many objects polarize light, including fish scales, there can be a biological advantage in recognizing such objects, especially when they are sources of food. In general, fish that have polarizing vision can enhance the contrast between nearly transparent prey and their surroundings. Flies that reflect light may be more attractive to such fish. Some marine species (squid are an excellent example) have polarizing vision that allows them to see creatures such as plankton, which are often transparent under normal light. Another speculation is that fish with polarizing vision may be able to detect objects farther away, perhaps as much as three times farther away, than fish without such an ability. If this assumption is correct, it could explain why some fish are able to feed under poor light conditions.

adjust their irises to shut out or reduce strong light. Of course, fish can avoid strong light by going deeper, where light intensity is diminished. Also, some fish have special adaptations to their eyes that control incoming light. Sharks and a few species of bony fish have eyelids composed of fatty material. Bonefish, for example, have a fatty tissue with a small opening over their pupils that restricts the amount of entering light. Many fish have pigments in their eyes that become active as light intensity increases; this pigment shades and protects the light-sensitive cells of the retina.

The absence of eyelids on fish has led to the erroneous conclusion that fish do not sleep. Without eyelids, the thinking goes, how can fish close their eyes? Fish actually may spend considerable time sleeping, or at least being in a quiet, energy-saving, resting state, just floating in the water.

This behavior, however, is generally not thought to be sleep in our sense of the word.

Eye Size

Many types of schooling fish and most large fish, particularly predators, have large eyes. (Smaller or less distinct eyes are more common among fish that rarely or never school.) Evidence shows that predators often key in on the eyes of prey, and apparently because of this many prey species have developed camouflage or various color schemes to hide their eyes. This point hasn't been lost on anglers—many successful lures and flies have eyes of some sort, including those that imitate shrimp, crabs, crayfish, lobster, or other similar vertebrates, as well as small baitfish patterns.

As you might expect, fish that feed under low-light conditions, such as at dawn or dusk or in somewhat deep and dark water, usually have larger eyes than those fish that live in bright, shallow water. Fish that are not dependent on their vision for feeding usually have relatively small eyes, a group that includes bottom-feeders that use their other senses to find food. Fish that live in deep parts of the ocean, into which no light penetrates, either have no eyes or very small ones. Most of these fish have a well-developed lateral line system with which they can detect movement by other creatures. Deep-sea fish that do have eyes often have an amazing amount of sensory cells in their retinas. A human retina may contain about 200 million sensory cells per square inch, whereas some deep-sea fish may have as many as 10,000 to 16,000 million such cells per square inch. The sensitivity of the eyes of these fish clearly exceeds that of any other animal.

Color and Night Vision

A fish's eye has two basic types of light-receptor cells: rod cells, which respond to black and white; and cone cells, which respond to color. Rods are more sensitive to light than cones, while cones produce better-defined images. The number of cone cells contained in the eyes of fish varies among species, which means that color vision varies among species. Scientists generally believe that most fish have some degree of color vision, although some species may only be sensitive to one or two colors. For example, deep-sea fish that live in relative darkness tend to see dim blue colors best. Species that depend on sight to find food and are active during the day generally have the highest ratios of cone to rod cells. Nocturnal fish generally have more rods than cones, since rods are more sensitive to light. Fish that live in freshwater or coastal waters tend to have an equally-balanced number of rods and cones.

Snell's Window

When a fish, or a diver, looks up at the smooth surface of the ocean, it sees a large round window, the diameter of which is about twice the observer's depth in the water. This window, called Snell's window, does not give a fish a complete view of the outside world. The phenomena of Snell's window occurs because of refraction and something called the "critical angle." Beyond this critical angle, the light (or the fish's vision) does not penetrate or leave the water but instead is reflected back into the water. The critical angle for water is about 48.6 degrees, but it will be less when the water's surface is rough. What this means is that a fish looking up, toward the ocean surface, gets a somewhat compressed view of the outside world. Instead of having a 180-degree view from one horizon to another, it will only see out through a circle formed by a cone of about 97.2 degrees (or twice the critical angle of 48.6 degrees) above each eye. For a fish, anything beyond this 97.2 degree path (48.6 degrees to either side) would be seen as something reflected from the bottom or simply something in the water.

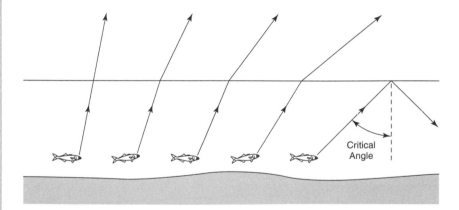

Fig. 7-4 This illustration shows the concept of the critical angle due to refraction. Light from an image is refracted at the ocean surface. With an increasing angle from the vertical, the refraction will eventually reach a point—the critical angle (about 48.6°), where all the light will be reflected back into the ocean. A fish looking at the surface at an angle greater than 48.6° will not see out, but will see reflections from the bottom or the water below the fish.

Saying it another way, light rays from the atmosphere reaching the water surface within Snell's window will be refracted and reach the fish's eyes; light rays falling outside of the window will be reflected away. From the fish's perspective, it can see anything above the surface within its 97.2-degree sight window (less if the water surface is rough). At greater angles, the fish will see the bottom reflected off the water's surface. For a fish looking out of the ocean through Snell's window (within the critical angle), refraction works somewhat in its favor, expanding its limited outside field of view (see Figure 7-5). Under ideal conditions of calm water and a bright sky, a fish might be able to see objects that are about 20 degrees above the horizon, but no less, as the rays in the air are bent down toward the horizon once they leave the water. While fishing on clear and calm days, an angler should try to stay below that 20-degree angle to reduce the chances of being detected—especially if fishing on shallow tidal flats. Even then, a moving rod or cast line could be detected by a fish once it enters the

(continued)

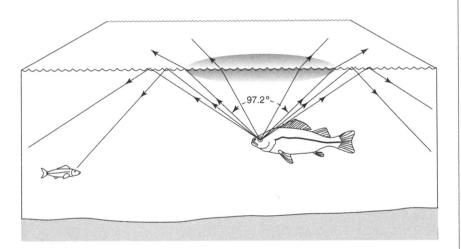

Fig. 7-5 Snell's window. The shaded area shows the window of vision for a fish (or a skin diver) looking up at the surface. In the water anything beyond this window will be reflected back off the water's surface. The person or fish looking out, however, will have a wider view since the light that escapes through Snell's window will be refracted down toward the horizon or sea surface.

SNELL'S WINDOW *(continued)*

fish's area of visibility. Also, Snell's window will not restrict a
fish's vision horizontally—fish can see your legs if you're wading,
or the shadow of your boat on the ocean bottom. Fortunately for
anglers, wave action and surface turbulence usually reduce Snell's
window, further limiting the fish's outside vision. Rough water
will also present focusing problems for fish and sometimes even
causes bright flashes of light that will affect the fish's vision.

If you are casting a surface fly or lure to a specific fish, and it
lands outside of the fish's Snell's window, it will not be seen by
the fish. You might conclude that the fish is feeding selectively,
whereas in truth you have made a bad cast. Always keep in mind
that fish have learned about light at the surface and tend to be
very cautious when near the surface of the ocean and usually are
easily spooked by any overhead movements.

In low light, fish generally use only their rod cells and thus are
mainly seeing objects in black and white. Although rod cells are very
sensitive to light, they produce relatively poorly-defined images. As the
level of light increases, fish start to use their cone cells, and their color-
sensing ability increases. This transition, which involves pigments that
shade the light-sensitive rods cells, can take an hour or more. A similar
transition occurs at sunset when fish change from using their cone cells
to their rod cells. Because the change between rod and cone cells takes
time, some fish do not achieve their sensitive night vision until well after
dark. Likewise, their best color perception will occur some time after sunrise. The quicker a fish can adjust to the changing light, the quicker it can
find food (or a fly or lure) and feed in changing light conditions.

The period of transition at sunrise and sunset may be one of the
best times to catch fish. Maybe you've been in a situation in which fish
activity increased, often dramatically, at dawn or at dusk. This may be
due to the excellent vision-adjusting ability of your target species—
striped bass are a good example of fish that have such an ability. At dusk,
baitfish lose some of their color and camouflage protection, including their ability to reflect ocean colors back at predators, so this may
also trigger predators to feed more actively during the light-transition
period.

Fishing Tips Concerning Color

Anglers probably think color is more of a motivating factor in attracting fish than it actually is. In many instances, a fish's main use of its color vision is to increase the contrast of prey against different types of backgrounds. Therefore, duplicating the colors of a baitfish in a fly or lure may be less important than simulating the shape of the bait and ensuring good contrast between your fly and the background. Contrast is especially important at low-light levels, such as at dusk and just before dawn. Sometimes, good contrast should be avoided, such as when you're fishing for bonefish on tidal flats. Here, the conventional fishing wisdom is that you will do best by using a fly that is similar in color to the bottom.

The question of what color fly to use is a subject of considerable debate and controversy among fishermen. Remember that the color red quickly disappears and becomes gray, and then black, within 10 to 20 feet of the surface or from a fish—yet the color may provide good contrast in low-light conditions and many anglers have success using red lures after dark. Most baitfish have some silver in their body, so your fly probably should, too. White is a good color for flies used in deep water. Dark colors, especially blacks, grays, and purples, generally work well at night, since they produce a better silhouette than brighter flies. In general, the brighter the day, the lighter your fly or lure should be; a dark lure may stand out too much on a very bright day. Yellow often is an effective color to use in turbid water. Many anglers favor using green in their flies and lures, because green will hold its color through most fishable depths.

It's a good idea to use a larger fly or lure when the water is rough, since rough water reduces visibility. Further, a surface or near-surface fly or lure usually presents good contrast against the ocean's surface. Many of these lures have darkened undersides to increase their contrast. Most fish and baitfish, however, have a light or silver belly, which reduces their contrast and makes them less visible. For this reason, some lure-makers and fly-tiers prefer to imitate the real thing rather than increase contrast. There probably are advantages to both approaches.

Fluorescent colors, especially chartreuse, are visible for considerable distances under water and are used in many successful lures and flies. The effectiveness of these lures is somewhat surprising because fluorescent colors are not found in nature. These colors are best seen when energized by ultraviolet light. Humans do not see ultraviolet light, but some fish do, which may explain why they see fluorescent colors especially well.

As all anglers know only too well, there are times when no color seems to work. On these days try dark, try light, try something in the middle, or try fishing in another area. Ultraviolet light is more common on cloudy days, so fluorescent colors will be more visible at this time, and flies or lures with fluorescent colors should work better under these conditions. Finally, flies or lures with flashy materials or surfaces may be good attractors, but the flash, or too much of it, could also be threatening to the fish you are trying to attract.

Fishing Tips Concerning Night Vision
The fact that fish lack color vision at night may seem contradictory to your own fishing experiences, during which you found that colored lures were more successful after dark. You were not necessarily mistaken. Although fish may only see black and white at night, contrast is still very important. A good nighttime fly, it stands to reason, should contrast with the night sky. It's often best to use a dark fly on a dark night, and a light-colored pattern when the moon is bright. The reason is that a dark fly is less transparent and thus creates a better silhouette against a dark sky.

Some colors, especially black and frequently red, work well on dark nights. (Noise-making flies or lures, including ones that push water, are also effective at night.) Contrast is important during the day, too, at which time it might be best to use a light-colored fly, as a dark pattern could produce too much contrast. Furthermore, one way of capitalizing on the fact that some fish can see polarized light is to use flies that reflect light. A reflective fly might work better at night, too—it's worth a try.

At night, the flash of bright light on the water—fireworks, a passing car, or even lightning—can have an adverse effect on fish, since their eyes are adjusted to night conditions. In fact, a bright light can disorient or panic fish. After a flash of light, fish may have to spend a period of time readjusting to the normal dark conditions, and during this interval their night vision will be reduced and they probably will not feed.

Artificial light left on for extended periods of time, such as a light on a pier, often attracts bait- and game fish—stripers, snook, and tarpon, for example. In this situation, the fish will have adjusted to the continuously shining light. Many fish ambush bait by hiding in the shaded water, whereas their prey is easily detectable when in the lighted area. If a fish is hiding in the shade, it usually will be facing toward the light.

SOME RESEARCH ON FISH AND COLOR
Detailed studies on how fish respond to light and color have been conducted on only a few species (usually freshwater fish) and mainly in laboratory situations. Research has shown that freshwater largemouth bass have excellent color vision and can distinguish between various shades of the same color. Bass, including striped bass, can detect color during the day but usually not at night, when they (like most other fish) are using their light-sensitive but only black-and-white rod-cell vision.

Colin Kageyama's *What Fish See* takes an in-depth look at color and what fish see, focusing on freshwater fish such as steelhead. Dr. Kageyama's studies clearly show how various colors appear very different under different water and light conditions.

Research published by Levine and others in 1980 showed that for a color pattern to be conspicuous to fish, its components should differ from each other, as well as from the color and brightness of the background. Their work showed that the most conspicuous pattern should have some combination of black and white, which will be relatively visible regardless of the type of light conditions. Other color combinations may also be visible to fish, but not so clearly under all conditions.

In his book *The Scientific Angler*, Paul Johnson describes laboratory research that tested whether largemouth bass can detect nylon monofilament line. These tests, done in laboratory aquariums, showed that the bass could easily detect 8-pound test monofilament line, and that colored line was much more easily picked up than clear colorless or slightly green monofilament.

Research conducted in a real-world fishing setting (not in an aquarium) by Drs. Fred Janzow and Rudolph Miller from Oklahoma State University attempted to determine if largemouth bass could detect particular colors of line. The scientists made the color of the line the main variable by using the same lures and rods and by switching between anglers to reduce the differences in fishing skill. After two years of what must have been fun work, the researchers found that clear and blue-green monofilament were more productive than brighter lines. Fluorescent lines were especially visible to fish, and are probably not a good choice for fishing.

It's difficult to be conclusive in such experiments. For example, the researchers thought that the reason for their conclusion about line color may have been that the light coming from the typical food of bass (shad minnows) was the same as the blue-green light from the line, so the color of the line did not alarm the fish. An interesting saltwater analogy comes from anglers who fish near jetties or in the surf zone and believe that a greenish-tinted line works best. They feel that the turbulence (which often appears to be green) of the water caused by the breaking waves makes a green line less visible to fish.

THE SENSE OF HEARING

The ocean is a noisy place, especially below the surface. Sounds come from surface waves, ship engines and propellers, underwater earthquakes and volcanoes, raindrops falling on the surface, fish swimming through the water, whales singing, animals feeding or reproducing, or literally

Fluorocarbon versus Monofilament

The high visibility of conventional monofilament fishing line has led to an increased use by many anglers of an alternative, especially for fly-fishing leaders or shock tippets—fluorocarbon line. Visibility of line in water is determined by how close the line's index of refraction is to the 1.33 refractive index of water; the closer it is to this number, the less visible the line. Fluorocarbon line has a refractive index of 1.42, while conventional, nylon-based monofilament has an index of around 1.55. This difference, although small, makes for a considerable visibility decrease in fishing situations.

Fluorocarbon line has several other positive features. It's denser than conventional monofilament and therefore sinks faster, and because of its increased density it is also more resistant to abrasion. Also, nylon monofilament absorbs water, and fluorocarbon does not. This means the fluorocarbon line will maintain its breaking strength in water, whereas nylon monofilament can lose 10 to 15 percent of its strength when wet. Fluorocarbon line also holds up much better to ultraviolet rays, showing no changes after considerable exposure to direct UV light, while conventional monofilament can loose over 30 percent of its strength and change color after only a modest exposure to UV light.

On the negative side, fluorocarbon line is too stiff to be effectively used as actual fishing line and can be difficult to knot. It is, however, good leader material, both for commercial fishermen and for fly or light-tackle enthusiasts. You should carefully test any knot tied in fluorocarbon line, especially when joining lines of different diameters. I lost some nice fish before I learned to be more careful about tying knots with fluorocarbon line.

The main reason why fluorocarbon is not more popular among anglers is that it costs considerably more than conventional monofilament line. It may be worth the price when you're fishing for species that have good vision, such as tuna, little tunny, and bonito. Most major fishing-line manufacturers offer fluorocarbon line, and competition and/or improved production methods should make it less stiff and lower the price in the future.

anything that moves or creates a vibration or turbulence in the water—including the motion of your lure. The coastal region is particularly noisy due to the turbulence created by breaking waves. One of the many problems scientists have in studying sound in the ocean and how it affects fish is that there are so many different sounds, coming from so many different sources (including from the fish themselves), that it's difficult to judge exactly which sound causes what reactions among fish.

Sea water is almost a thousand times denser than air, and because of this, sound travels better, farther, and faster through the water of the ocean than through the atmosphere. For instance, the speed of sound in the ocean is about a mile a second, or almost five times faster than its speed in the atmosphere. In either environment, sound decreases in intensity as it travels away from its source. Water, however, is a very good medium for sound propagation; some sounds can travel for considerable distances in the ocean, whereas the same sound made in the atmosphere might quickly become inaudible.

A discontinuity in one of the physical characteristics of water, such as an abrupt change in temperature with depth, can form an interface that will reflect sound and in doing so increase the distance that the sound can travel. For example, there are "sound channels" in the ocean, and sound made in these channels can travel literally thousands of miles. Interestingly, water is a much more friendly environment for sound than for light, which is rapidly attenuated in water. Fish, because of the wide range of noise in their environment and the importance of sound to their survival, have developed unique systems for detecting sound in the ocean.

A sound made in the ocean has two effects. The first, called "particle displacement," causes a back-and-forth motion of particles in the water. The particle displacement effect, often called the "near field," is more important close to the source of the sound. Sounds in the near field, which can be about 20 to 30 feet from the source, are detected by a fish's inner ear or by its lateral line.

The second effect, called "sound pressure," is a change in water pressure that resembles a sinusoidal or sine wave moving through the water. This effect, often called the "far field," is more important farther away from the source of the sound. Far-field sounds are detected by the fish's inner ear and, if it has one, by its swimbladder, which often works as an amplifier or resonator in combination with the inner ear.

The Inner Ear

Looking at fish, it is easy to assume that they are not very sensitive to sound, since they do not have obvious ears or even auditory openings

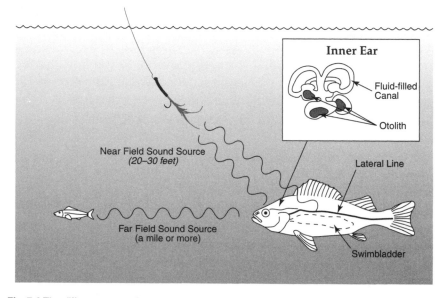

Fig. 7-6 The different ways a fish can detect near-field and far-field sound. The far-field sound is received by the inner ear, the near-field sound by both the inner ear and the lateral line. The inner ear contains several fluid-filled canals, some of which have relatively heavy ear stones, or otoliths. Simply put, sound pressure causes both the fluid in the canals and the otoliths to vibrate, but the heavier otoliths will vibrate at a different rate. These vibrations cause a nerve impulse that reaches the fish's brain and indicates the sound detected.

through which sound may carry. They do have ears (actually only one), but it is an inner ear enclosed within their head. A fish does not need external ears because its body tissue is about the same density as water and any sound in the water can easily pass through its body to its inner ear. The inner ear system is mainly used for detecting high-frequency vibrations, though fish also use it to determine their orientation relative to the Earth's gravitational field—in other words, to maintain their balance.

The inner ear has several fluid-filled canals, some of which contain relatively heavy ear stones, or otoliths. (The term otolith comes from a Greek word meaning "ear stone.") A fish's otolith is composed of calcium carbonate and frequently has growth rings similar to those seen on tree rings or fish scales. These rings can be used to determine the age of a fish. Otoliths vary so much in size and shape among species that they often can be used to identify the fish species from which they came.

The inner ear is often linked to an internal organ that can amplify sound, such as the swimbladder. Swimbladders are filled with gas that can be compressed by sound waves, which usually will make them more sensitive to sound than the inner ear. Fish with especially sensitive hearing, such as tarpon, have closely connected inner ears and swimbladders. Fish that do not have a swimbladder, or do not have their swimbladder in close connection with their inner ear, generally are less responsive to high-frequency sound and respond to a smaller range of sound frequencies.

The same as humans, fish are essentially deaf to sounds having a frequency above 20,000 cycles per second (so-called supersonic sounds). Most fish hear relatively low frequency sound of around 1,000 cycles per second, and are relatively insensitive to sound above 3,000 cycles per second. Certainly, some fish are more sensitive to sound than others. Recent research has shown that shad and herring species can detect high-pitched signals considerably beyond what humans can hear.

The Lateral Line
A fish's lateral line picks up nearby or near-field (within 20 to 30 feet or so) low-frequency sound caused by water movement and turbulence, which can be caused by currents or breaking waves, by movements or activity of other animals, or by movements of the fish itself. The lateral-line system is extremely accurate when the sound is within 5 feet or so. The ability to sense sound through the lateral-line system is sometimes referred to by scientists as a "distant touch" sense. Fish living in relatively quiet waters usually have a simpler lateral-line system than those living in more turbulent water. Deep-sea fish usually have well-developed lateral-line systems.

A fish can use information from its lateral line in several ways, but especially to detect nearby moving prey or predators, and to avoid running into objects at night or in the darkness of turbid or deep water. These abilities are highly efficient because the lateral-line system is very sensitive to low-frequency sound vibrations. In some instances, the fish itself will cause a water vibration, by swimming, and then use the rebounding sound information caused by its own movement and received by its lateral-line system to detect nearby objects (including lures) in the water.

A fish also uses its lateral-line system to determine the direction and distance to the source of a sound, sometimes with startling accuracy, and to orient itself in a current or position itself among waves. Experiments have shown that certain fish can detect and catch prey within 10 to 20 feet by using their lateral-line system.

Schooling fish can use their lateral-line systems to maintain their positions relative to adjacent fish. The sounds from adjacent swimming fish, or just the general noise made by a school, can help individual fish

Lateral Line

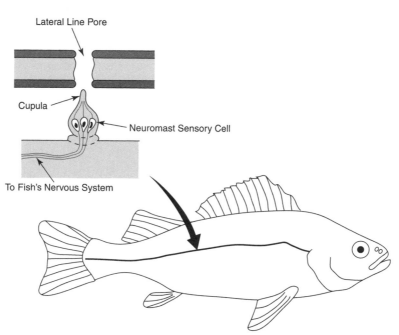

Fig. 7-7 The lateral line, which detects near-field sound, contains a row of small pores. Within the pores are specialized sensory cells, called neuromasts, that contain sensory hairs that are imbedded in a jellylike capsule called the cupula. When water motion or turbulence reaches the lateral-line system, the cupula are moved and bent. This movement deflects the sensory hairs, producing a signal to the fish's nervous system.

maintain their tight-knit pattern in the school, especially when visibility is poor. To test the importance of the lateral line in schooling, scientists conducted experiments using "blindfolded" schooling fish. These fish had no difficulty maintaining their schooling pattern with adjacent fish by using their lateral-line systems. If, however, the nerve endings of the lateral-line systems of selected fish were cut, they were unable to school with other fish. Scientists also recently found that the lateral-line systems of some fish may be sensitive to certain types of chemicals in the water. Additionally, certain fish use their lateral-line systems to generate and receive electrical signals, apparently for communication and for identification of the opposite sex.

In a few species, the lateral-line organ is also part of an electrical sensory system. Sea water is a good conductor of electricity and some fish, particularly sharks and rays, use their electrical sensory system to detect the electrical field generated by their prey (from the activity of the prey's muscles). Fish may also use these electrical sensory systems for long-distance navigation, whereby the fish navigates by detecting subtle changes in the voltage gradients induced by ocean currents flowing through Earth's electrical field. Eels are especially sensitive to electrical fields. One study indicated that, amazingly, they could detect the field generated by a one-volt battery whose poles were separated by more than 3,000 miles.

Fish and Sound
Although the study of sounds made by fish is really just beginning, it seems probable that sound-making is a common phenomena among many marine species. Fish can make sounds in a variety of ways, such as by grinding or snapping their teeth, by vibrating their swimbladder, by using their muscles, or by moving parts of their skeleton. Individual fish may also make sounds when courting or mating, or as just part of their normal behavior.

In general, fish are usually very sensitive to and cautious about unfamiliar sounds, even in deep water. For example, sound transmitted into the water through a boat's hull as a careless angler drops something on the deck may spook any fish in the vicinity. Boat engines or noisy wading can have the same effect. Some anglers put marine carpeting or similar sound-dampening material on their boat decks to reduce noise. Some of the newer flats boats are designed to reduce the thump caused by waves hitting the hull.

Bob Cox, a British fisherman and author of an interesting book entitled *Uptide and Boatcasting*, feels that casting from a party boat is really the way to fish. By casting he means tossing bait rigged with heavy sinkers. He makes a subtle point about how an anchored boat (30 feet or so in length) in a current can influence where the fish will go. Based on his experience, Cox believes that an anchored boat produces sounds that cause moving fish to divert away from the boat and pass to either side. He writes, "A boat at anchor is like a giant double bass. The hull is the sound box and the anchor rope held tight by the pull of the tide is the string." He further says that "the rip of the tide and the slapping of the waves against the hull are transmitted down the rope to the seabed along with any noise the anglers on board may make." He then suggests that you will always do better by casting upcurrent (before the fish are spooked by the boat) or far to the side of the boat, where the spooked fish have moved. It's not evident if a similar effect could occur with a boat smaller than Cox's 30-footer. It's an interesting idea, and although it's not backed up by any real proof, it seems logical.

Updates on Sound in the Ocean

Marine scientists have long studied the various types of sounds in the ocean, but it wasn't until recently that they became aware of the quantity and source of some of these sounds. New technologies, and the improved relationship between the United States and Russia, are showing that the ocean is really very noisy. For example, sensitive ocean-bottom seismographs now routinely detect numerous rumblings from earthquakes, sometimes literally occurring in swarms, as well as volcanic activity along the mid-ocean ridges. Many marine organisms, especially whales and porpoises, are known to be noise-makers. Some whales apparently can compose and transmit complex sound patterns. Some of these whale "songs" have become parts of recordings by Judy Collins, Neil Diamond, and others. The songs of some whales, humpback whales in particular, are especially interesting. Some of their songs can last more than ten minutes, before being repeated. Humpbacks within one locale will have similar "choruses" in their songs that differ from those living in other areas.

It really wasn't until 1993, when the U.S. Navy released data collected from its Integrated Undersea Surveillance System (IUSS), that

Sometimes fish get used to noises, such as boat engines, and show little response to such sounds. Some fishermen feel that a change in the speed of an engine, or starting up an engine, will spook fish. Some offshore anglers believe that game fish such as tuna and sailfish are actually attracted to the noise and vibrations coming from a moving boat. Nevertheless, a cautious angler would do well to keep noise to a minimum.

Scientists have limited data on the ability of fish to discriminate between different sound intensities or sound frequencies. But it seems as if some fish have the ability to analyze the structure of a sound and identify its source, direction, and distance. In doing so, the fish can determine if the sound is coming from a predator or from prey, a piece of information that can be very important in the ocean, where a fish's vision is limited. Wounded or hooked fish often make a distinctive vibration that quickly attracts predators to the scene. Something about these vibrations, perhaps their frequency or intensity, signals the fish's distress to others—

scientists got new insights into just how much sound was in the ocean. For years, the Navy had maintained a network of underwater-listening devices, primarily to detect foreign submarines. This data was recently released to civilian scientists, and its impact is considerable. Now, instead of just being able to hear a few whales alongside a research vessel, marine scientists can monitor sounds from a large population of animals across an entire ocean. The challenge will be to separate the sounds, relate them to specific species or geological processes, and, finally, to interpret their significance.

Previous research has shown that whales, porpoises, and some species of fish use sound to detect food, to navigate, and, perhaps, to communicate with other members of their species. Some Navy scientists who had prior access to the IUSS data said they were able to identify individual whales by their sound and follow their migration across large parts of the ocean. One blue whale was reportedly followed for forty-three days as it roamed the North Atlantic. Among the early results from the IUSS data are that whale sounds can travel in the ocean over distances of 1,000 miles or more. The availability of the Navy data may become the marine biologists "acoustic Rosetta stone" to understand how marine animals communicate.

how else could a predator select just the wounded or injured fish from among the many in a school? Baitfish often detect sounds coming from predators, and by making their own specific sound or alarm they may alert schoolmates of the threat. Fish can also be attracted to the sounds made by other fish chewing and eating. In this way, sound can work for you if you can imitate a baitfish swimming, eating, or in distress, and thus arouse a larger fish's curiosity.

A few marine animals have the ability to produce and use sound, like sonar, to detect objects in the water, including food. This ability, called echolocation, is very well-developed in porpoises (which are mammals, not fish) and is demonstrated by the high-frequency sound clicks they make. Their ability to locate objects as small as an inch is legendary, and is often a highlight of marine shows. Some fish have similar sound-making ability, but none to my knowledge use it to hunt; rather, the sound is used in various methods of communication, including looking for mates and indicating danger.

Fishing Tips Concerning Sound

First and foremost, be quiet when you're fishing—fish can hear very well. Remember that a fish often hears its food before actually seeing it. For this reason, many types of fishing lures and flies, especially poppers, are designed to create sound or turbulence in the water in imitation of injured prey, thereby attracting a predator. On the other hand, if you drop even a small fly very close to most species of fish you may frighten them. If the fish are in a school, scaring one may ultimately spook the entire school.

Some lures and flies contain small rattles that may also draw in fish. These types of flies can work within the near field of the lateral-line system, and in the far field covered by the fish's inner ear. At times, such as when water visibility is limited, a lure or a fly that sends out a continuous or steady noise, such as a swimming plug, will do a good job of attracting fish. Popping flies, which usually make a loud but intermittent noise, often draw fish from a distance. Flies that push or move water, such as the Tabory Snake fly, are often very effective, especially at night.

THE SENSE OF TOUCH

Fish also have a sense of touch, which works mainly through their skin. It's also possible that fish may use their mouths as a touch sensor. The sense of touch can be important in various behavioral activities; for example, some contact is common among many species when they mate. As I first began writing this book, however, I saw no obvious way that a fish's sense of touch could influence fishing—until I talked with Dr. Bill Krueger, an ichthyologist from the University of Rhode Island. He mentioned, for example, how a fly line presented across the back of a rolling tarpon often will scatter the entire school within seconds. The bottom line is simply that there is a lot to be learned about the various fish senses, including the sense of touch.

Chapter 8

Fish Behavior

The study of the behavior of fish usually follows two main approaches: either investigating the internal reasons for the fish's behavior; or looking at its behavior in the broader context of the fish's life history, its ecology, or other factors. I'll take the latter and broader approach, as it yields information on fish behavior that is more applicable to fishing situations.

A common and traditional method for studying fish behavior is to observe fish in the laboratory, usually an aquarium. These studies work best on small fish that are not hindered by the restrictions of an enclosed tank. Large fish can become stressed when placed into an aquarium, so many marine sport fish are not easily studied in a laboratory, although they may be observed in their larval or juvenile stages.

One of the easiest ways to determine the distribution and behavioral aspects of fish is to obtain, keep, and study records of the fish caught by commercial and recreational fishermen. More specific data can be obtained through tagging programs. A knowledge of fish behavior can be useful in many types of ocean fishing. For example, the migration patterns of fish determine where they will be found, and when they will be there. Knowing behavior patterns such as schooling, feeding, responses to specific aspects of the environment, and the like will increase your chances of fishing success. (See Appendix 6 for more about fish behavior and adaptation to environment.)

DISTRIBUTION, SCHOOLING, AND SHOALING

Fish in the ocean can be distributed in one of three basic patterns: even, random, or clumped. Even or random distribution patterns are rare in the ocean, whereas clumped patterns are very common. In other words, fish tend to group—when you find one fish, there's a good possibility that more are nearby. It will be a good fishing day if you can find one of these groups.

Fig. 8-1 How the fish in a school tend to be oriented, showing their typical polarity in that they are all facing in the same direction.

Schools

A school is typically comprised of a single species of fish, of similar size and age, moving about almost as a single unit. Fish in a school are usually "polarized," which means they generally face the same way and are fairly close to the fish nearest them. Schools do not have a specific leader, although their movements seem to be synchronized—the school moves together, usually in the same direction. The precise movement by the school as a whole, without collisions or apparent indecision on the part of the fish, is one of nature's wonders. How each fish in the school knows when and in which direction to maneuver is not fully understood by scientists. Certainly the behavior involves the use of vision, and responses to sounds and vibrations from other fish in the school. A fish also uses its lateral line, with which it detects turbulence and vibrations, to maintain a pattern of movement or spacing relative to its schoolmates. It's possible that sensory aspects other than their vision and their lateral line are also involved. Since the schooling activity is, to some degree, dependent on vision, most schools will either break up or spread out at night.

Shoals

Some fish travel in large or spaced groups, in which each fish behaves somewhat independently of the others. This type of grouping is called a shoal. A shoal of fish stays together for social reasons, whereas a school of fish can be considered as a synchronized and polarized shoal. The term "shoal" is more commonly used in Europe, whereas in the United States the term school is often used both for schooling and shoaling fish. Although schools generally form a circular pattern, shoals may occur as lines, circles (the daisy chain of tarpon, for example), or just irregular patterns.

Fish can shift from schooling to shoaling behavior, and vice versa, in an easy and regular manner—even in a matter of seconds, depending on factors such as the presence of predators or the availability of food. Schooling fish sometimes form shoals or large groups at night, keeping close to each other but staying inactive.

Shoaling is a fairly common behavior for ocean fish. Examples of game fish that shoal include bluefish, striped bass, bonito, little tunny, bonefish, tarpon, and even bottom fish such as fluke. These groups may contain many fish—in the hundreds, and often thousands—distributed over a large area, frequently near bottom structure or close to or in a tidal rip. During migrations, numerous shoals may join up to create a group that can extend for miles—or hundreds of miles. There may be seasonal or environmental factors that influence the size and makeup of a school or shoal; the availability of food may be one of these factors.

Shoaling

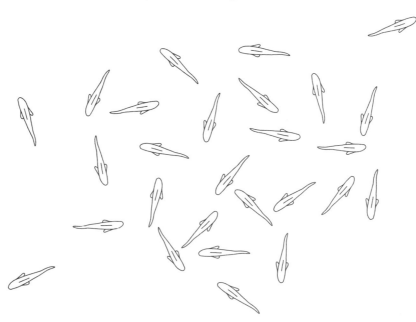

Fig. 8-2 An overhead view of shoaling fish (only a small number of fish are shown).

Fish Tagging

Tagging techniques have been used to study many marine game fish, and considerable basic data have been obtained through such studies. Tags can range from fairly simple devices attached through a fish's muscle, to sophisticated electronic devices that transmit information to scientists tracking or listening to the tagged fish. A simple tagging device might be a thin tube or button that is numbered and contains a message asking that the finder return the tag (the fish can be released or retagged) with information on the location of the catch, and the length and weight of the fish. Usually some sort of reward, such as a hat or a certificate, is given to the returnee. (Interestingly, some fish seem to be captured more than others. The August 1997 issue of *Sport Fishing* magazine told of a 50-pound yellowtail that had been caught, tagged, and released an amazing six times in a two-month period off the coast of New Zealand.)

Newer types of tags are expensive and contain sophisticated electronics and thus provide much more information than the simple tagging devices. These new instruments transmit an electronic signal that can be received by a surface ship. Scientists in the boat can monitor the fish's position and depth, as well as specific aspects of the environment, such as water temperature. Some devices are placed inside the fish and monitor internal aspects such as the fish's breathing or heart rate, its temperature, or even movements of its mouth as it feeds. The beauty of these electronic tags is that they provide

Fish in shoals, although they appear to be separate and independent, may exhibit common behavior. Bluefish and, to a lesser degree, bonito are good examples—one moment they are all over the surface hitting bait, then almost instantly, as if following some signal, they disappear, only to reappear a few minutes later. Usually this pattern will repeat itself many times, perhaps until the fish have had enough to eat.

Many commercially caught fish collect in shoals, which increases the probability that they will be harvested in large numbers. Once detected, all the fish in a school or shoal can be easily captured by commercial fishermen using nets, which leaves little or no breeding stock behind. Many schooling species have suffered from intense fishing pressure, and sev-

detailed and specific information about a fish's behavior as it moves about in natural conditions. Using these devices, scientists have gained new and sometimes remarkable insights into the feeding and migration patterns of swordfish, tuna, sharks, salmon, and other marine species.

Tagging studies can have limitations. One is that the tagged fish usually come mainly from areas that are actively fished. Popular fishing areas therefore will be over-represented in the resulting statistics. Nevertheless, tagging can provide some valuable basic data on fish behavior, and as an important side benefit it allows recreational fishermen to become involved in and aware of fish distribution and management.

As of the late 1990s, some sophisticated tagging programs were underway. One has been to look at bluefin tuna that winter off the coast of Cape Hatteras, North Carolina. The program, sponsored by the National Marine Fisheries Service and North Carolina sport fishermen, employed a tag called an archival tag, which contains a minicomputer that can store data for several years on water temperature, depth (as determined by water pressure), light, and the internal temperature of fish. The tag also has an accurate clock, so that the fish's depth can be determined at various times and at various light conditions. The light detector can be used to determine sunrise and sunset, which in turn can yield an approximation of longitude; latitude can be estimated by the time interval between sunrise and sunset. This information can be combined with the water temperature data to determine the migration pattern of the tuna.

eral species are in considerable danger of being overfished. These include anchovies, herring, mackerel, menhaden, sardines, cod, and tuna.

Why Do Fish School and Shoal?
This is an interesting question. Among the main possibilities are to improve their opportunity for reproduction, to reduce their risk of being preyed upon, and to increase the probability of finding food. Food is easier to find when many fish are searching for it. In addition, if one fish in the school or shoal finds a meal, other fish can steal or share it. Furthermore, some scientists have suggested that the tight spacing of the fish in a school gives them a hydrodynamic advantage for swimming (similar to

Fig. 8-3 A school of sand eels, packed tightly due to the nearby presence of striped bass. The individual fish are about 3 inches long.

a school of geese flying in a V pattern) and reduces the energy expended by individual fish, but this idea has not been confirmed.

Probably the main reason that fish school or shoal is to avoid predation. For fish in a school or shoal, the idea of safety in numbers is a reality—by being in a large group, an individual fish reduces its chances of detection and capture by a predator. Prey species frequently form into a tighter shoal or a school when a predator appears. More than two thousand species of fish exhibit this behavior pattern, which shows that schooling and shoaling must be beneficial to the survival of these species.

Some anglers believe that a large, tightly packed school may create the appearance of a large fish that could scare away predators. It's not difficult for a predator to find the school, but once it does the predator will have trouble picking out an individual fish to attack—the rapid and uniform movement of the school confounds the predator. The large numbers of fish constantly changing direction, and the changing shape of the school, creates a confusing pattern for the predator and may even deter an attack. Flashes of light (light reflected off the fish's scales) coming from a large number of moving and turning fish can also confuse predators. The effectiveness of this flashing light as a defense is reduced at dawn and dusk, which may explain why some predators seem to be more aggressive and successful in attacking prey during low-light conditions. Similarly, predators may attack from below a school, where they are relatively hidden, rather than from near the top, where the school is better illuminated.

If a predator does attack, the entire school will often move together out of its way, again presenting a confusing pattern. In doing so, the school of baitfish often breaks into two groups that swim around the predator and regroup afterward. A tight school of baitfish can literally explode away from an area as a predator attacks. Fishermen may see bait flying in different directions above the surface of the water, followed by the splash of an attacking fish. This "explosion" presents a confusing pattern of light flashes and movement to the attacking fish. Often the school will immediately re-form after the explosion, before the predator can pick out an individual prey. In addition to these various evasive maneuvers, a school or shoal also has quite an effective lookout network, which makes it hard for a predator to initiate a sneak attack.

Conversely, for predators a school or shoal presents an opportunity for a substantial meal. Some predators, such as jacks, may form schools of their own when attacking a school of bait and try to divide it into smaller and more easily harvested groups and then feed on individual fish—a divide and conquer approach. Sometimes, an attack is so furious that the predators drive bait up onto a beach or to the surface, where attacking birds further disorient and pick off the bait. Tuna, because of their good eyesight and excellent sense of smell, can be especially effective at finding and attacking a school of bait. A large bait school will produce a scent trail of fish oil, materials from their slime, and natural waste products. Tuna can detect these scents, and follow them back to the school. Indeed,

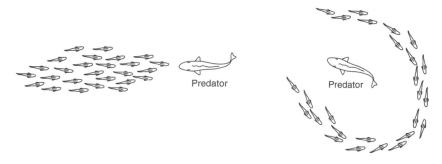

Fig. 8-4 A school of fish being approached by a predator, and a typical evasive pattern they might take.

Fig. 8-5 Tuna will sometimes swim in a pattern resembling a parabola when hunting prey. Such a pattern is a very efficient way to find, encircle, and catch prey. The tuna drive the prey between the ends of the parabola and then surround and eat them.

bluefin tuna have been observed to form up and swim in a parabolic pattern when searching for food.

Another strategy used by predator fish is to attack during low-light periods, when they cannot be seen as easily and the school is relatively dispersed. Some predators simply follow a school and take wounded fish or those that make an error in judgment and stray away from the group. Indeed, most casualties from a school or shoal are fish that have wandered from the main group. Predators such as tuna, sailfish, and marlin are often successful in their attacks on schools because they can overcome some of the school's defenses. For example, by quickly swimming through a school, they can stun some of the fish with their tails or bills and then easily eat the individual prey before it recovers.

Multispecies Groups

Schools or shoals are not always limited to just one species of fish—it's common to see two or more species, sometimes even mammals, in the same group. One example is the joint occurrence of porpoises and yellowfin tuna. Here, the tuna may be capitalizing on the porpoises' ability to locate food through echolocation.

Studies of the size distribution of fish in shoals generally show that the larger fish will be near the bottom of the shoal and the smaller fish near the top. The fish usually maintain this pattern even if the shoal is composed of more than one species. Many fishermen are aware of this distribution and will try to let their fly or lure sink through the upper layers of a shoal in an attempt to catch the larger fish below. The exact reasons for such distribution are unclear, though it seems that most fish prefer swimming near fish of their own size. When a shoal or school of mixed species of fish comes under attack, the fish often separate into groups containing the same species, and then form groups of similar-size fish. In this manner, the fish can gain the full advantage of facing a predator as members of a homogeneous school.

Fishing Opportunities

Schooling or shoaling fish are usually easy for anglers to detect, either by a fish finder, by observing flocks of birds hovering and diving over the school, or by seeing the fish themselves breaking the surface. A good approach is to work the edge of a school or shoal, rather than casting into the middle, where the chances of spooking the entire group are high. You should also try to cast ahead of a moving school, which may mean waiting to see the direction in which the fish are moving.

Compared to isolated fish, which are very alert, fish in a group competing for food seem to be less cautious. You've probably had experiences in which a single fish followed your fly but did not strike. If another fish or two were to show up, however, the group would become competitive and one would frequently strike.

Individual fish in a school or shoal that appear different from their schoolmates often become singled out by predators and attacked. Laboratory studies have shown that minnows doctored with artificial colors will be attacked more readily than naturally colored ones. Likewise, fish in a school or shoal that behave differently or make "mistakes" when trying to avoid a predator become easy prey. This may explain why a fly placed in or near a school of bait will successfully attract a predator, despite the large numbers of real bait present. It also raises the question, Does your fly really need to imitate natural bait to interest a predator?

FISH MIGRATION

Many species of ocean fish migrate, apparently for three main reasons: for reproduction, in the search for food, or due to changing environmental conditions. (A migration is defined as a predictable and essentially continuous and direct movement between two places during a specific time.) Some migrations are very impressive. For example, the North Atlantic bluefin tuna feeds near Norway and breeds off Florida, and makes the 7,000 mile trip in about three months. In the Pacific Ocean, albacore may travel from the central part of that ocean to the Japanese coast or the West Coast of the United States.

How do fish navigate or find their way when making such long trips? It appears that they use several methods. Some species of tuna and albacore in the North Pacific follow a specific isotherm or water temperature. Albacore, for example, track the temperature value of 14 degrees Celsius (about 57 degrees Fahrenheit) north in the summer and south in the winter. Some fish, especially those living in or near coastal waters, may be more sensitive to salinity variations, or may follow ocean currents. Chemical aspects in the water, such as specific odors, certainly are navigational keys for migrating salmon.

Many fish migrate simply to follow their food, or to search for prey after consuming the local bait. Striped bass migrate to follow one of their main sources of food—herring, which migrate up the Atlantic coast in the spring and south in the fall as the water cools. Some fish use the sun for navigation, following it as sort of a reference point. Experiments with freshwater fish showed that when removed from an area they could find their way back when the sun was shining, but not if the sky was overcast.

Certain fish may, like birds, follow the earth's geomagnetic field as they migrate. Some whales, especially those traveling along the California coast, clearly seem to be following the geography of the coast as they migrate.

Fish can make errors when navigating during their migration, and this may be beneficial. An example is salmon choosing the wrong stream for breeding—the benefit is that a new breeding area is established. As more is learned about how migratory fish respond to changes in oceanographic parameters, such as temperature and salinity, it eventually may be possible to predict the fishing potential of a region weeks to months before the migrating fish actually arrive.

VERTICAL MIGRATIONS

Many fish will make trips from the surface to deeper water, and eventually return. These movements are called vertical migrations and usually have some degree of periodicity, such as being related to the changing light conditions that occur at sunrise and sunset. A common vertical migration is when a fish goes toward the surface at dusk, and toward the bottom at dawn. Frequently, such movement is driven by the availability of food, and because low-light periods are the safest time to feed. For example, fish migrating to the surface at dusk may find it easier to avoid

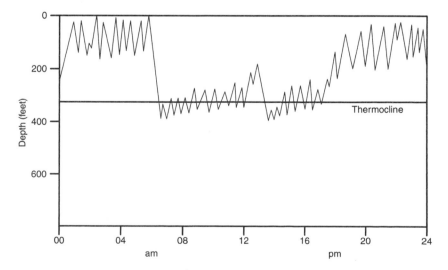

Fig. 8-6 A typical pattern of vertical travel that a tuna might follow over the course of a day. Tuna tend to stay closer to the thermocline during the day and closer to the surface during the night.

predators at that time, and are safer in deeper and darker water during the day. The vertical migration of fish can be interrupted by a bright full moon, which may discourage fish from going toward the surface. Also, short upward vertical migrations often occur during the rare instance of a solar eclipse: the darkness from the eclipse of the sun will initiate a vertical migration of fish toward the surface, and fish will return to the depths as the sun begins to reappear. Vertical migrations can cover impressive distances. For example, some swordfish and tuna have been known to make vertical migrations of 1,000 feet or more. Usually these fish move to the surface at night and go deep during the day.

REPRODUCTION

Reproduction methods can vary from the discharge of extremely large numbers of eggs and sperm into the water, to internal fertilization, to elaborate courtships leading to nest-building and parenthood. Most fertilization by marine fish is external; internal fertilization does occur, however, among some species of sharks.

It's important for scientists, and anglers, to understand fish reproduction and its success or failure, as many ocean species are overfished and are decreasing at an alarming rate. Sharks are an especially vulnerable species because they only produce a few eggs or live young. Bony fish, although also vulnerable to overfishing and environment pressures, usually have a numbers advantage when it comes to reproduction. Most female bony fish release hundreds of thousands of eggs into the water, and the male fish fertilizes them by releasing milt. This process need not be as haphazard as it may appear, as the breeding fish are often schooling and large amounts of milt and eggs are present in an area at the same time, increasing the possibility of fertilization. When samples are taken from such a situation, most of the eggs are usually fertilized. In many respects, this method is less complicated than the reproductive process of land animals, which have to get their sperm directly to the eggs.

Most fish breed on some sort of cycle—some monthly, some yearly, some once and then they die (salmon, for example), and some intermittently after they reach sexual maturity. The latter group, which includes some species of sturgeon and striped bass, can live for a relatively long time, perhaps because of their infrequent breeding. Fish that live in the tropics may spawn year-round, but those living in more temperate climates tend to breed just once a year, usually in the spring. Fish generally breed when conditions are most favorable for the survival of their young, such as when appropriate environmental conditions prevail or when food is available. Breeding may be triggered by changes in temperature, length of daylight, presence of the opposite sex, or appropriate tides or currents.

There is a wide range in age as to when fish become sexually mature. Some species are sexually mature almost at birth, whereas other species take years to reach maturity. For many marine fish, the female will reach a larger size than the male—a good example is the striped bass. The male is frequently larger, however, among fish that are territorial during their breeding, such as salmon. In general, it is often difficult to externally distinguish between the sexes.

Fecundity and Fertility

The term fecundity is often used as a measure of the reproductive potential of fish, and is defined as the number of eggs that a female fish has in her ovaries. Fecundity usually increases as the female grows. A small codfish, for example, may produce only one or two hundred thousand eggs, but the same fish can produce more than 10 million eggs when it's larger.

Fertility refers to the number of individuals produced as a result of reproduction, and is a better measure of reproductive success; however, it's more difficult to measure, as most young fish disperse soon after birth. After fertilization, eggs either sink to the bottom or float, and following a period of time develop into a planktonic (floating) larval form. Because most fish eggs hatch in the water, temperature is an especially critical factor determining the survival of young. Salinity is usually less important, except when there is a large inflow of fresh water, which can kill off an entire hatch of eggs. As plankton, the young fish are very vulnerable, and can be rapidly decimated by predators, or carried by currents into unfavorable or deadly environments.

Fish eggs in the relatively uniform open ocean are usually less vulnerable to environmental changes than those eggs deposited in nearshore waters, where environmental changes tend to be more frequent due to influences such as river discharge of fresh and warm or cold water, and pollution. For this reason, many species that breed in shallow or coastal waters discharge eggs that sink or stick to the bottom, whereas floating eggs are more common in offshore waters. Larvae are usually about one-tenth of an inch or so, and generally have a yolk sac that provides nourishment for a short time. After that, they must quickly find a source of food. Of course, they may become a source of food for other organisms, too.

The larval period, which can last from weeks to months, is followed by the juvenile period. In this stage, the fish undergo rapid growth and come to resemble miniature adults. A fish is deemed an adult when it has the ability to reproduce.

Reproductive success is strongly determined by the survival of fish in their early life stages, as eggs and larvae. The main causes of larval death are predation and starvation, though water temperature and environmental events such as weather and year-to-year variations in wind and currents can also be factors. Most fish do not survive through the early part of their life cycle. Mortality rates for floating fish eggs can be as high as 99.999 percent (only one out of 100,000 survives), which explains why so many eggs are initially produced by females. The timing of the egg-laying can also be very important. For example, suitable and abundant food must be available, or all the offspring will die. Since larvae are both predator and prey, there is a survival advantage to growing big quickly so they can eat larger food and avoid predators.

Pollution can have many effects on breeding fish. British scientists recently discovered that some male fish collected from a river polluted with sewage contained eggs in their testes. Something in the water was apparently acting as a sex hormone, and the initial suspect was an industrial pollutant. Other scientists in the United States and Britain detected similar problems but, to their surprise, they found that the natural hormones in the urine of women (contained in sewage) seemed to provoke the changes in the fish's reproductive processes. The lesson is that even natural substances can have serious and sometimes unanticipated environmental consequences on fish.

Year Class
The fish born in a given year are referred to as the "year class." For example, the 1996 year class would be the fish born in 1996. A year class can be followed, through tagging and other methods, as it grows and reaches maturity and breeds. Small year classes yield reduced breeding stock, which subsequently yield smaller year classes when they breed; however, it's difficult if not almost impossible, according to some experts, to make an accurate prediction about the number of future adult fish based on data from the larval stock. More sophisticated models of the breeding, survival, and growth of year classes are needed and must include oceanographic and biological variables, many of which are not yet known or understood. Be wary when you hear that the stock of a particular ocean fish species has returned to its historic population—this sort of predicition is very tricky business. For many species, especially those living in the tropics, little information concerning their life history and interaction is adequate or even available to make predacations about the health of a certain population of fish.

Cycles in Abundance

Many species of fish seem to have long-term cycles in their abundance. Bluefish, along the Atlantic coast of the United States, are an example of a species that seems to be extremely abundant for many years and then shows a major, and apparently unexplainable, decrease in their numbers. There have been numerous attempts by fishery scientists to learn the reasons for such fluctuations in the abundance of bluefish and other species of fish. For some species, the variations in abundance showed a correlation with water temperature, climatic or weather changes, or some other long-term environmental factor. Many of the fluctuations in fish stocks (including bluefish), however, do not appear to be linked to environmental aspects, at least not to an obvious environmental influence. The answer might be to look at not just one single species of fish, but rather to consider all the related fish, the competition among fish species, the availability of food and breeding space, and predation, as well as the fish's various and complex interactions with the marine environment.

FEEDING BEHAVIOR

When it comes to feeding, fish are very adaptable and use a wide variety of methods to obtain food. Most fish have a specific and favorite method of feeding, although they will eat whatever food is most available to them. Fish usually feed on more than one prey, and they can change their method of feeding if conditions and the available food necessitate such a change. Some fish feed almost continuously, others just at certain times, such as at dusk or sunrise. Some large predators, such as the white shark, may have only one large meal every month or so, although they are always looking for prey. Regardless of how, what, or when they feed, fish are closely linked to other organisms in their environment through a complex food web (as explained in Chapter 1).

Fish are not neat eaters. Most species swallow their food whole, apparently without tasting it. Many fish have a preferred way of swallowing their food, either tail-first, head-first, or just taking a bite out of the middle. Many game fish seem to gorge themselves, and when these fish are caught they may regurgitate an amazing amount of food; often, they spit up only one kind of bait.

Feeding Styles

Fish have a variety of feeding styles, and can be broadly categorized as predators, grazers, filter feeders, suckers, and parasites. Predation, or one fish eating another, is a necessary part of the life processes in the ocean. As in many environments, the weakest and sickliest individuals have the least chance of survival, while the strongest and fittest have the best chance of living. Many fish will eat younger or smaller members of their own species, if given the opportunity.

Predators usually have specialized teeth to grab, hold, and chew their prey. Some have exceptionally sharp teeth, such as sharks and bluefish. Other predators, like barracudas, have needlelike teeth to grab their quarry. Striped bass have small teeth which grasp their prey before it is swallowed.

Grazers usually feed on plankton or bottom organisms and take their food in small bites (sometimes they are called nibblers). Filter feeders, or strainers, filter sea water to remove small pieces of food, such as phytoplankton and zooplankton. Examples of filter feeders range from menhaden and herring to large basking sharks. Their food is removed from the water on rakelike appendages in front of their gills, appropriately called gill rakers. Suckers suck in bottom sediment and remove any food it may contain. Carp and sturgeons are examples of fish that feed in such a manner. Parasites are represented by lampreys and hagfish.

Factors that Stimulate Feeding

Fish can be stimulated into feeding by the season, time of day, amount of light, when the fish last ate, how hungry it is, the availability of food, and the fish sensing or seeing food. Time of day is an especially important factor, as some fish only feed at certain times. This, in part, may be driven by the acuity of one or more of its senses. For example, fish that feed mainly by sight usually feed actively during daylight hours. Fish that depend more on their sense of smell or taste tend to be night feeders. Some species do not feed when they are breeding. Others may stop or reduce their feeding when there are certain environmental or weather conditions, such as the passing of a high-pressure area; however, little is known about the effects of weather or water temperature on feeding activity.

Changes in the intensity of light in the water, which often occur at dawn and dusk, can motivate some fish to feed. Striped bass, especially when they are not migrating, commonly feed in this pattern. With the change in light there may be other, less subtle variations in the environment, such as a change in water temperature, that could also trigger feeding. Sometimes fish are very exact about their food, feeding only on a specific species, and sometimes only on prey of a specific size at a given time.

Marine biologists, by observation and experimentation, have developed some hypotheses about fish feeding. One hypothesis, called "optimal foraging," says that a fish should try to eat the best or most food available, but spend the least amount of energy doing so. This means a fish would be better off eating larger prey, rather than a bunch of little ones, if its total expenditure of energy upon catching and digesting the little ones exceeds that for catching the large meal. Experiments on feeding fish have shown that when fish are hungry (or when food is scarce) they will go for any prey regardless of its size; however, when food is abundant, they will select the prey that is easiest to catch but which also provides the most energy (usually the largest prey available).

When predators have to search for and chase their prey, they expend quite a bit of energy; therefore, some predators just position themselves in favorable areas and wait for food to come to them. This helps to explain why so-called dominant fish (often the largest in an area) often stay in what seems to be the best feeding areas, such as near the edge of fast-moving water. Likewise, fish might not pursue microscopic algae or small zooplankton if they will expend more energy catching them than they can gain from the digestive process. (In general, animal flesh has about twice the caloric value, and four times or more the protein content, of algae.)

Feeding frenzies may have an important influence on what fish eat. Fish such as tuna, carp, and bluefish tend to get very picky about their food after a blitz or big feed; less acceptable food usually is more palatable when fish are hungry. In general, small fish will eat more (on a weight basis) than larger fish of the same species. This is because the smaller fish usually have a higher metabolism.

Many fish can go for long periods without eating, depending on their stored body fats and glycogen, from which they draw energy. Some fish, when the opportunity occurs, eat such a large quantity of food that it can support them for days or even a week. Then there are fish that must eat almost continuously, which includes high-energy fish such as bonito. A fish's appetite, so to speak, is largely determined by its metabolism, which is influenced by the water temperature. In general, the warmer the water, the more food a fish will need, although there is an optimum temperature level above which a fish's metabolism will decrease. In colder water, fish generally eat less than they would in warmer water.

As you might imagine, it's hard to study how fish feed in the ocean, so most studies on this subject are done in the laboratory. Feeding experiments on aquarium fish often indicate that when food (such as live bait) is abundant, most fish will choose the larger-size variety. Alternatively, when the food supply is low, they will go for any size available, even very small bait. Some experiments have shown that hungry fish initially tend to eat very fast, compared to their less-starved brothers and sisters, but after feeding both will have consumed the same amount. This may just indicate the amount of food that the fish's stomach can hold.

During experiments in aquariums in which fish were given various feeding choices when predators (or models of predators) were nearby, the test fish seemed very aware of the predators and tried to stay as far away from them as possible. The distance of avoidance, however, often decreased if the fish were very hungry. In other words, a fish's fear of predation seemed to be diminished by its degree of hunger. Some experiments gave the researchers the impression that the fish were able to weigh the risk of being eaten against the opportunity of getting a good meal. Whether this impression is correct is unclear to me—but there is evidence that many fish can change their behavior if the threat of predation is present. For example, a fish might go to a protected area to feed, or reduce its rate of feeding, if there are predators nearby.

Fishing Tips

Fish have certain expectations when they are feeding or searching for food. One is that they usually prefer their prey to be moving. Numerous laboratory experiments with predators and baitfish show that motionless prey often is left alone, but if it starts to move it's attacked almost instantly. Likewise, most predators expect their prey to swim *away* from them, not at them. A baitfish (or your fly or lure) swimming at a predator may actually spook or frighten the fish. A better approach is to have your offering come from the fish's side and move into its field of vision. Simply said, do not cast directly at your target—cast beyond it or to the side, and then maneuver your lure so the fish can see it, moving the lure away like escaping prey.

Fish often position themselves near or in a current, where moving water can carry food to them. Your lure or fly should also move with the current, starting upcurrent from the fish. The same approach applies to bottom fishing or trolling. For bottom fishing, you often will do better starting upcurrent and drifting the bait downstream. Trollers should keep their lures in front of a group or an individual fish.

Using Multiple Lures

Because fish are competitive feeders, anglers might benefit from using teaser or dropper rigs, or multiple flies. Some anglers may find the idea of dropper rigs or multiple flies to be unacceptable or unsporting. But logic says that if one fly is good, two should be better. Also, using more than one fly, or a fly as a dropper from a lure, will increase your chances of finding the one lure that the fish will take. Multiple flies may also simulate a predator/prey situation in which the fish sees larger prey chasing small prey. Often, a hungry or aggressive fish will find this attractive and will go after one of the flies. Multiple hookups are not uncommon.

Basically, fish will be cautious about, or even flee from, anything outside their normal feeding expectations. The closer you can come to duplicating the natural manner in which fish find food, the better your chances are of hooking up. When a fish refuses your offering, even though everything seems perfect, some aspect of your presentation may be unnatural. The key is to make your offering appear as a natural and easy meal, just what the fish is looking for.

A FISH'S BIOLOGICAL CLOCK

The same as many other animals, most fish have some awareness of time. When animals are isolated from clues about time (no light or dark periods, or changes in the tide) most continue to follow a distinct activity pattern that usually approximates a 24-hour, or solar cycle. This is sometimes called an internal or biological clock.

Scientists know little about how this internal clock works or what organs might be involved, but it often guides the basic activities of fish, such as when they rest or feed. Some animals seem to be able to anticipate and respond to changes in their environment before they occur, an ability that may be related to their internal clock. Saltwater fish also frequently follow a second clock—the tide. For example, fish that live or hunt on shallow tidal flats seem to know when to leave the area before the tide changes so that they don't become stranded by a falling tide. Nearshore species tend to follow the tidal or lunar clock in their feeding patterns, whereas offshore species often are guided by a solar clock, as tidal differences are less obvious in offshore waters. For those fish following a solar clock, the most important times for feeding are dawn and dusk. (Many land animals, such as birds, also show increased activity at dawn and dusk.)

The feeding patterns of fish often have some degree of predictability, especially over the short term. You might catch fish in one area on a certain part of the tide, though this may change over time. An early morning high tide may yield productive fishing one day, whereas the second high tide that day, occurring twelve hours later, may be totally unproductive. This may be caused by the fish following their lunar and solar clock—the related feeding response first is in phase, then later goes out of phase. My experience is that dawn and dusk are the best times to fish in the ocean, and if an appropriate tide occurs at those times, the fishing will really be active. Of course, the ocean is a constantly changing environment, and eventually the fish and the bait will move on from a given area.

One of the great challenges of fishing is to learn the patterns of fish and how they feed in the area you fish. Probably the best way to do this is to keep a daily record of your fishing, logging the quality of fishing, the time of your catches, the state of the tide and/or currents, which flies worked, the weather conditions, and the like. Comparing your notes with those of other observant anglers will increase your data base and help you understand some aspects of fish behavior.

PREDATOR/PREY RELATIONSHIPS

Most marine fish are both prey and predator. Because of the risk of predation, fish have developed a wide variety of behaviors and defense mechanisms to avoid becoming a meal. These include evasive and confusing swimming patterns associated with schooling, various color and camouflage schemes that hide or disguise a fish's appearance, vertical migrations to avoid predators, and various anatomical features, such as spines that will ward off attacks. Similarly, a fish can use its keen sense of hearing, smell, and sight to avoid predation.

Predator/prey relationships in the ocean must be in balance. Slight changes in this relationship due to environmental changes, overfishing, or the introduction of new species in an area can have a considerable impact on the survival of a species within a particular part of the ocean. (Predators may have an overall advantage in this competition, as they can usually chose among a variety of food.) Humans can upset the predator/prey balance by overfishing a certain species, especially by taking large numbers of the breeding stock of a species. Striped bass, herring, redfish, and cod are examples of fish that have suffered from overfishing. In some instances, a prey species is overfished, resulting in the decline of a predatory species. For example, the overharvest of herring in the Berents Sea led to a dramatic decrease in cod stocks.

SYMBIOTIC RELATIONSHIPS

The term symbiosis applies to two or more species living near each other and not engaged in a predator/prey relationship. There are three types of symbioses: mutualism, commensalism, and parasitism.

Mutualism is the term used when benefits exist for each interacting organism. An example is when one species of fish grooms or cleans another by removing parasites, and gets a free meal in the bargain. Another is when fish shoal or school together—they all benefit from, among other things, reducing their chance of predation.

Commensalism is the term used when two organisms interact and one benefits from the relationship but no harm comes to the other. One example is a small fish living in the protective shell of a larger organism. Many species of sharks have a commensal relationship with remoras, which you'll see "stuck" to the shark's skin. The remora benefits from sharing some of the shark's food. Remoras may also do some grooming of their hosts, a small payment for being carried around.

Parasitism is a relationship where one organism benefits at the expense of another. Examples include worms that dwell in the internal organs of animals and cause damage or eventually death. Most fish, if not all, are hosts to some parasites, but few fish are parasites themselves. The lamprey is an exception.

Tuna and porpoises seem to have a symbiotic relationship, as they often school together. It is not clear if one species is following the other, or which is benefiting, though the tuna may be capitalizing on the porpoises' ability to find food using their sonar. In one respect, the relationship has been bad for both species. Commercial tuna fishermen set their nets around the easy-to-find porpoises, which swim and jump above the schools of tuna. As a result, both species can be caught in the nets. In the past, more than 100,000 porpoises (and sometimes dolphins) were being unnecessarily killed each year. Public concern and pressure eventually led to legislation that has reduced this mortality.

ARE FISH INTELLIGENT?

This is a difficult question to answer, for many reasons. Certainly, one is that the definition of intelligence, at least in the context of the study of fish behavior, can vary with the user of the term. Fish generally have poorly developed brains and lack a cerebrum, which in humans is where thought and reasoning occur. Fish do have sophisticated senses, however, with which they can discriminate prey and companions, detect danger, and stay alert to environmental influences. These senses work at a high level of efficiency in a very challenging environment. Fish often must make split-second, life-deciding choices, and they generally seem capable of succeeding in these situations. They are also aware of tides and other natural processes and conditions in the ocean, such as changing water temperatures or shoaling bottoms.

Instinctive and Acquired Behavior

One of the interesting aspects of the study of animal behavior is examining what is inborn, or instinctive, behavior and what is learned, or acquired, behavior. A learned behavior is some conduct or action that a fish acquires from its parents, other fish, or even from a predator. An instinctive behavior is often a complex, inborn response characteristic of an individual species. The method by which a species of fish reproduces, for instance, is a form of instinctive behavior. Sometimes instinctive and learned behaviors occur together, such as when salmon learn the odor that characterizes their birthplace and retain this memory for many years, until they return to their birth area to spawn.

Many fish learn from experience. Fish that have had an encounter with a predator generally are better prepared to avoid predation later on. For some fish, the experience of a victory over, or defeat by, another fish affects how they behave in a subsequent situation. Experiments in aquariums have shown that fish that lose one fight are statistically more likely to lose their next bout, too. Even under laboratory conditions, when there are no other fish present, a single fish has the potential to learn—a solitary fish may see its reflection in the glass of the aquarium, and learn to mimic its own behavior.

Laboratory experiments have shown that some fish can be conditioned to respond to certain stimuli, such as to recognize a specific color or respond to certain smells or sounds. Training often involves a reward such as food, or punishment such as a mild electric shock. Fish kept in a pond and fed at a certain place following the ring of a bell quickly learn to come back to that place whenever the bell is rung.

This ability to recognize a stimulus and make a response is fairly common among animals, and is neither indicative of a high level of intelligence, nor a lack of it. A better indicator of intelligence would be to judge how long it takes an animal to be conditioned to make an appropriate response. Some fish seem incapable of learning anything; other species can learn by having a certain experience once. One study showed that carp hooked once were "hook-wise" for months afterward. Some fish are caught in fish traps and never escape; others make the traps their home and swim in and out at will.

In experiments on color discrimination, most fish learned to identify colors more quickly when the colored objects were moving. Fish can also be stubborn and eat only one type of food at certain times. It would seem that these fish are making learned decisions. Fish also seem to learn more quickly in groups. Indeed, fish often follow a leader, such as a single fish in a group that can solve a maze and find the food hidden at the end. Or if a "trained" fish is added to a group, the untrained fish will often follow their experienced colleague to the reward (the hidden food in a maze, for example).

Does Memory Indicate Intelligence?

One indication of intelligence is an animal's ability to remember information or, in human terms, for it to have a good memory. An example is the ability of a salmon to remember the odor from the exact place it was born in a stream, and then return to that place several years later, after living in the open ocean.

This task is more impressive than it first appears. Not only will the odor from the fish's birthplace be diluted as the fish goes downstream, but subtle changes in the structure of the stream and its odors will certainly occur in the years prior to the fish's migration. When the fish return to their natal stream, after five years or so, they will have to respond to a sequence of odors, which will become stronger as the fish proceed upstream. It's possible that salmon use other remembered clues, such as the character of the stream bottom, or even land topography, to find their way home. Clearly, salmon have remarkable memories.

In their 1977 book *Ichthyology*, K. F. Lagler and his associates wrote about fish behavior and suggested that apprehension and a conceptual use or understanding of space relations are attributes of insight and thus intelligence. The authors describe the apprehension, insight, and remarkable memory exhibited by the frillfin goby, abilities that the researchers suspect many other fish species also have. These particular gobies live in tidal regions and, when the water recedes with the tide, are isolated into small, separate tide pools. At low tide the gobies jump from one pool to adjacent water-filled pools with amazing accuracy—a miss would mean death. The gobies apparently do not see the adjacent pools when they jump, but presumably learned the geography of the area when the tide was higher and the area was fully submerged.

In the study reported by Lagler et al., gobies from one area were transferred to a distant tidal region and put in isolated pools at low tide. They refused to jump from these pools, and if prodded into jumping they had little success finding an adjacent water-filled pool. If they were allowed to spend twelve hours in the area and experience a high tide, however, they were able to successfully jump into other water-filled pools. Forty days later, after having just one high-tide experience, these fish were still able to jump successfully into adjacent pools. The fish certainly were making insightful decisions, and showed appropriate apprehension when presented with a difficult and possibly life-threatening situation.

Are fish intelligent? As we've seen, there is much evidence to suggest that some are. Perhaps an analogy with birds is appropriate: there are chickens (clearly dumb) and there are parrots (clearly intelligent). Some fish cannot find their way out of a simple fish trap; others can easily navigate in and out of the trap at will. One fact is evident: fish are well-suited to their environment, and are often more than formidable adversaries for anglers.

Part III:

Ocean Fishing

Chapter 9

Fishing Estuarine Waters

For fish, an estuary is a great place to visit, browse, or make a home in. Food is abundant and varied, and the waters are usually well-mixed and therefore well-oxygenated. The downsides for estuarine fish are pollution and its potential damaging effects, and the presence of many predators, including fishermen.

For an angler, an estuary can be a quiet and pleasant area to fish, often one in which he can be completely alone. You can fish estuaries by walking along the shore, by wading, or by boat; usually a small boat or even a canoe is adequate. Another benefit is that you may be able to fish in an estuary even when the weather and wind conditions over the open ocean make fishing there difficult or impossible.

SCOUTING AN ESTUARY

To fish successfully in an estuary requires a knowledge of many things, but especially the bottom topography and the tides in the area. Unless you are lucky and have friends who will share this information, you will have to learn much of it yourself. To get the needed insights, you might have to spend considerable time on the water and do a lot of walking. But you can save time, and energy, by getting a good topographic map of the adjacent land and a nautical chart of the estuary.

The U.S. Geological Survey (USGS) produces topographic maps (frequently called quadrangle maps) for much of the United States. The land features on these maps are very detailed, but any body of water shown is just a featureless blue color; however, you can find land elevations and hills and valleys, which in turn reflect high or low regions, if they extend into the sea. The maps also show rivers and marsh areas. Road maps may also be of some help, especially if they show town beaches, boat ramps, or other access areas.

Nautical charts from the National Oceanic and Atmospheric Administration (NOAA) are produced mainly for navigational use, but they may also show high and low areas, wrecks, and sometimes large boulders. These charts display the shape of the coastline, buoys, navigational channels, water depth, and some details about the character of the bottom, such as if an area is rocky, or covered with gravel or shells or mud or sand; the charts also show the location of marshes and grassy areas.

Probably the best visual resources for estuarine and coastal fishing are aerial photographs, particularly those taken as false-color infrared pictures, which often show considerable detail of the bottom topography, including bars, depressions, changes in bottom character, and the like. You can find out about the availability of aerial photos at a local or state government office. Municipalities often collect such photos to aid in assessing local property taxes. Some internet sites provide quality photos of coastal waters; for example, see http://coast.mit.edu/ for a collection of offshore and estuarine photographs of Massachusetts waters that clearly show shallow structure and other features useful for fishing.

Another source of coastal information may be the Sea Grant Program in coastal states. These programs are usually located in the marine-science department (or related office) of your state university. All Sea Grant Programs have an extension or outreach program that frequently provides, usually free, much useful information about local fishing possibilities. Of course, the very best place for coastal fishing information is often your local fishing shop—especially for basic local tide data.

What to Look for
Once you get information about the topography of an estuary, a key thing to look for is narrow areas where the flow of water will be constricted and thus flow faster; inlets are an excellent example. Bars and spits as well as topographical highs, such as ridges, are also places where the current speeds up. Sometimes, just a slight rise in the bottom topography will increase the speed of a current enough to trap or confuse bait, attract predators, and create a good fishing spot. Similarly, a small depression can provide a holding place for fish. These changes can be subtle and barely perceptible, even with an echo sounder, but once found you can take advantage of them as long as the conditions are favorable.

Also look for changing bottom sediment. Fish are attracted to the junction between one type of bottom and another—between a rocky and a sandy bottom, for instance. Bottom areas covered with mussel or oyster beds indicate the presence of well-circulating water and sufficient food to sustain the mussels or oysters. These conditions are also attractive to many species of fish, striped bass in particular. Holes or depressions often hold large fish, for two reasons: the fish can hide and ambush

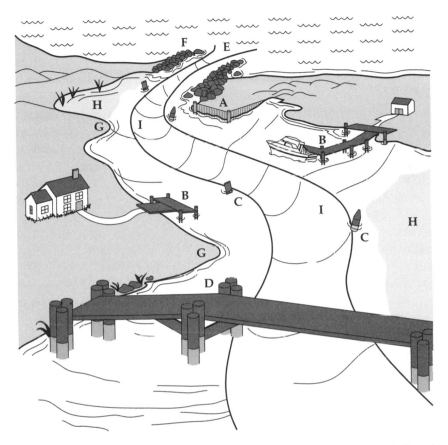

Fig. 9-1 Some of the structures that can be found in a typical estuary. **A**, seawall; **B**, dock; **C**, navigational buoy; **D**, bridge pilings; **E**, inlet; **F**, jetties; **G**, points; **H**, flats; and **I**, slope edge.

smaller fish from the depression, and they can stay out of the full force of the current and thus conserve energy. An estuary is full of many structures and areas of strong currents that can attract and hold big fish.

ON FOOT OR BY BOAT?

Wading is one of the easiest ways to fish estuarine waters, though it limits your range. You can cover more water in a small boat, canoe, or kayak, but again there are limitations—you might not be able to find a launch area, for example. Float tubes, common fly-fishing vessels in lakes and rivers, can be dangerous to use in estuaries or any marine area in which there are tides and currents; I would not encourage their use in marine environments.

Of course, you can be flexible while wading. On foot, you can find areas sheltered from the wind, and you can be stealthy. The latter is important when you're fishing in shallow water—a careful wader can be much quieter than an angler in a boat, even when the boat is being pushed by a pushpole.

On the other hand, beside the obvious depth limitation and limited casting range you'll have while wading, another problem is finding areas where you can legally and safely access the water. Waterfront access for fishermen is limited in many coastal communities. One way around this is to use a boat to get to where you want to wade, which can put you in rarely fished water. Be careful, however, when jumping out of an anchored boat—the water may be deeper than it actually appears. Remember the discussion about this in Chapter 1: refraction will make the water appear shallower than it actually is. For example, if the water looks to be 3 feet deep it probably is actually 4 feet deep. Also be sure that the bottom is not soft muck, and that it can support your weight. Finally, wherever you wade, know the tide and its range in the region, so that you do not get trapped or isolated from your boat or the shore by a rising tide.

In many estuaries, night-fishing is popular, especially as the water warms during the hot days of the summer; however, there are dangers to fishing at night. The bottom might be composed of soft mud in places, and these generally are found where the currents are slow or nonexistent. Strong currents remove the finer-size mud particles from an area, leaving sand and cobbles behind, whereas in areas where there are no currents, or only weak currents, the fine mud particles settle out of the water and accumulate on the bottom.

A careful angler should always check out a new fishing area in daylight, and preferably at low tide. One goal should be to learn where any soft spots are. These often are a darker brown or black, whereas a sand bottom tends to be yellow or a lighter color. In tropical areas, the mud may be composed of lighter-colored carbonate material called marl. Topographically high areas, such as ridges and bars, usually are composed of sand or cobbles. Relatively dark bottoms can indicate deep areas or a boulder-strewn area, which may be good for fishing but dangerous for wading.

Obviously, the major reason to scout an area before fishing it is to identify potential fishing areas, such as ridges, rocks, channels, or other structures that might hold fish as the tide rises, but do not forget about your own safety. (I usually wear a personal flotation inflatable device when I'm fishing in unfamiliar waters, or when I'm fishing at night or alone in my boat.)

Another potential problem for those wading in estuaries or marsh areas is the occasional abrupt, narrow, and deep man-made or natural channels or ditches. In the 1930s, ditches were cut in some marshes as part of a federal program to improve the drainage and thus reduce or eliminate the mosquito population. Whatever their origin, these channels or ditches often have soft mud bottoms and are not easy to discern at night. Stepping unexpectedly into one of these channels or ditches can ruin your day or night. On the other hand, these channels or ditches often can be good places to fish, especially around their mouths and as they drain during a falling tide.

Even if you plan to fish an area by boat, it's prudent to scout it out earlier, preferably in the daytime and at low tide. In doing so, you can identify bottom structures and dangers to navigation, such as rocks and buried objects.

When fishing or scouting an estuary you really are at a disadvantage if you do not use polarizing sunglasses. The lenses of these glasses eliminate much of the light reflected from the surface of the water and allow you to see deeper into the water. Polarizing glasses also filter out ultraviolet radiation, which can cause several varieties of eye problems, including cataracts. If you wear bifocals, I strongly urge you to get polarizing bifocals; it will make tying knots much easier.

Polarizing lenses come in various tints, and your choice of lenses may be decided by where you fish. Darker colors such as amber are recommended for flats fishing, whereas gray is preferred by anglers who fish offshore. If the light level is low, such as on overcast days, lighter lenses often are best. When you're buying polarizing glasses, it's not the time to look for a bargain—buy a good pair, perhaps even a pair with side shields. The difference in vision on the water when you wear polarizing glasses has to be experienced—writing about it doesn't do it justice. Also wear a broad-billed hat with a dark underside. It will reduce the light and glare reflected back to your face from the water.

CURRENTS

In an estuary, currents are usually strongest and most common near an estuary's mouth, or wherever the water flow is constricted. When fishing in an estuary, I'm often most successful by letting my fly drift with the current, imitating a disoriented baitfish. Strikes typically come at the boundary between fast-flowing and quiet water, or where the line tightens and the lure or fly starts to rise in the water column.

In an estuary, the species of fish present, and their location, may change as the tidal current changes. Remember that the time of the maxi-

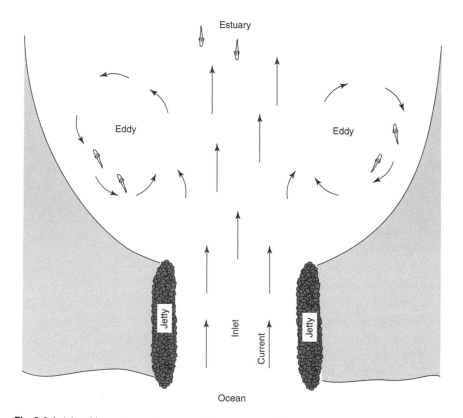

Fig. 9-2 A rising tide creates a strong current in an estuary inlet. When this fast-moving water reaches the relatively still waters within the estuary it can be broken up into small eddies along the main flow.

mum tidal current and the time of high or low tide do not always correspond—this is the rule in most estuaries. (See Chapter 2, pages 40–44).

The current flow in a channel, such as an estuary's inlet, usually follows a typical pattern. If the channel is fairly straight, the strongest flow will be in the middle of the channel, and the slowest flow along the shore or jetty. If the channel has bends, the stronger currents will be found along the outer part of the curve, the concave side, whereas the weakest currents will occur along the convex side of the shore. This type of current pattern is similar to the water flow in a river. Countercurrents and small eddies frequently occur along the sides of the main current; these may be more common where the inlet opens up, or around obstructions. One more point: in general, the velocity of a tidal current near the bottom is only about two-thirds of the surface velocity.

Most fish do not stay in the strongest part of a fast-moving current, although this is where you might catch them. Like most organisms, fish want to conserve their energy; therefore, they perform life functions such as feeding in a manner that's as easy and expends as little energy as possible. That's why fish hold at the edge of a current, behind a boulder, or in the lee of structure, rather than in the middle of the current where they would have to swim rapidly and continuously, using a lot of energy to maintain their position. Fish, however, expect that their food will be easier to catch in turbulent currents, and this is where they strike if something tasty appears.

The various areas in which fish hold can change as the currents change. If you catch fish near the edge of a current, try to anticipate how the fish might change its position when the current changes.

Fish can be attracted to an area where the current speed suddenly changes. This can occur when the water flow is restricted by a narrow channel, a bank or bridge, shoaling of the bottom, or as the water passes through an inlet or jetty system. Small structures such as rocks, or larger features such as bridges or piers, interfere with a current and sometimes increase its speed, but they also create quiet zones or eddies in which fish can wait for passing food. In some situations, a small rip or turbulent area may form over a sand, rock, or shell bar. Fish often hang around such rips waiting to catch bait confused or tossed about by the turbulent water. While observing currents, watch for signs of feeding or moving fish.

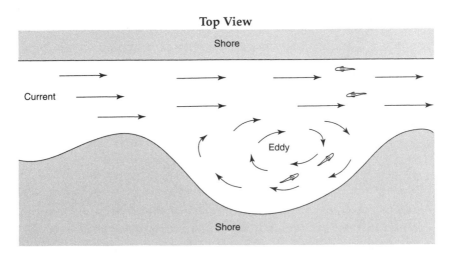

Fig. 9-3 Some of the water moving along in a current may be deflected by a topographic feature, forming a side eddy.

These can include swirls (not to be confused with swirls around the edges of strong currents or submerged objects), tails or fins of fish, or V-shaped patterns or bulges on the water caused by fish moving just below the surface.

The current will usually slow when the water deepens or where it flows into an open stretch of water, such as a pool. Even subtle changes in depth, or the width of an opening, can produce a visible change in the current. Changes in tidal current occur on falling and rising tides. Keep in mind that as the tide falls, fish run out of water in which to hold; thus, with a falling tide many fish move to deeper waters.

One factor that determines the general direction of tidal currents in an estuary is the Coriolis effect, which I discussed in Chapter 3. This is a complicated phenomena, caused by the rotation of the Earth, that forces currents to be deflected to the right in the Northern Hemisphere (and to the left in the Southern Hemisphere).

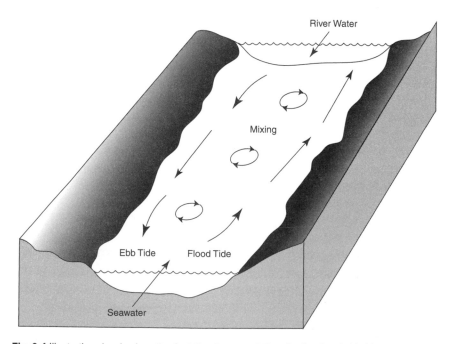

Fig. 9-4 Illustration showing how the Coriolis effect can deflect the flood and ebb tide currents in a large estuary. The deflection of the water, to the right on the incoming tide and to the left on the outgoing, is mainly observable in relatively large estuaries or bays. In smaller bodies of water the deflection is usually obscured by topographic aspects or by wind effects. The deflection can sometimes also be seen in the salinity values in the estuary (see **Fig. 3-5**).

Fishing Tip: Working with the Current

After finding where the fish are feeding in an estuary, you'll have to present your fly or lure in a manner that either simulates natural food or attracts fish and causes them to strike. Fish most often, if not always, expect their food to drift or swim with the current, so it's usually best to cast somewhat upcurrent of a fish and let your lure move naturally down to where the fish is waiting. Retrieving a fly or lure against a strong current will not look natural to most fish, and they will avoid your offering. (When fish are feeding or holding in an area, they will almost always be facing into the current.) A small baitfish would not attack a larger predator, and therefore neither should your fly. As Lefty Kreh has said in several articles " . . . Flies do not attack fish." A good compromise is to move your fly across the current. Putting your lure to the side of a fish (not behind it) and retrieving it so that it appears to be swimming away, trying to escape, is usually the best way to simulate what the fish is expecting. When drifting a fly or lure in a current (a technique called a "dead drift"), you often get a strike

(continued)

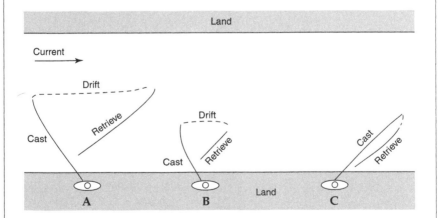

Fig. 9-5 Some ways of working a fly in a current. Your best approach is to let your fly or lure drift with the current down toward the holding fish, as angler (A) and (B) are doing. Angler (C) is mainly working his fly or lure against the current, which is not the normal way that a baitfish would be moving in a current.

FISHING TIP: WORKING WITH THE CURRENT (continued)

when your line comes tight and your fly or lure is pulled up and around through the current. To a waiting fish, this is a normal pattern.

There are several ways to cover an area with your casts. One is a fan pattern in which you cast to different sections of an area, continually increasing your casting distance. If you have no takes, move up- or downcurrent and start the process again. The fan-casting approach assumes that the fish are holding in an area and you have to find them. This is probably a good assumption, and a better technique than just staying in one area and counting on the fish finding you. (Fish in an estuary or along a beach tend to be moving, so it often makes sense to return to a promising area a second time, even if you had no success there on your first visit.)

You should also consider covering the water vertically. By this I mean positioning your fly or lure at various depths in the water as you fish an area. I suspect that many anglers believe that fish usually feed at or near the surface, especially when these anglers see surface swirls or breaking fish. That surface commotion, however, is often made by a fish turning to dive back to some depth, perhaps after grabbing a snack a few feet below the surface.

Another reason for fishing vertically is that the larger fish in a school often stay below the more aggressive younger fish and pick up morsels that fall down from above. Try working your fly near the bottom, in mid-water, and near the surface. By varying the speed of your retrieve, you can get your fly or lure to various depths.

The Coriolis effect deflects tidal currents in moderate to large bodies of water, such as bays and large estuaries. It is less important in small bodies of water, where wind and topographic effects can be more significant. When the Coriolis effect happens, the flooding (or incoming) tide will be deflected or pushed toward the right side of a bay or estuary.

When the tide ebbs, the water will still be deflected to the right, only this will occur on the opposite side of the bay or estuary because the water is now outgoing. The side to which the water is deflected will generally have stronger tidal currents, although the difference may be very subtle. If you want to fish the stronger current, try the right side of an estuary on the incoming tide, and the left side on the ebbing tide.

TIDES

Here, as elsewhere in this book, I'll refrain from suggesting which part of the tide is best for fishing. Fish feed under many conditions in an estuary, and although they prefer to feed when the water is moving, that's not always necessary. In discussions about tides and currents in an estuary, a statement like "Fishing is best two hours after high tide" really makes no sense. The reason is that in some places the tidal current may be at its maximum at that time, whereas in nearby areas the water may be going slack at the same time (see figure 3-8).

One of the best ways to find and catch fish is to think like a fish. Finding food is often their main objective, so to "think" like a fish you should look at the environment and see where bait is or should be, where the water is moving, and where a fish would hold to ambush bait. As a general rule, fish move into an estuary or a flats area with the incoming tide, and work their way out with the falling tide. Following this simple rule can bring fish to the well-placed angler.

Falling tides will carry baitfish, shrimp, crabs, and the like into small channels or creeks. Similarly, a rising tide will allow these creatures to reach recently dry areas that may contain food. Many fishermen like to fish the mouth of an estuary as the tide ebbs, anticipating that fish are waiting there to catch any outgoing food. Another strategy is to continue to move downriver or down an estuary as the tide falls, hoping to stay with or ahead of the seaward-moving fish.

When fishing in shallow water and around structure, many fishermen believe that a falling tide is a good time to start fishing. The ocean side of an inlet or jetty is often an excellent place to fish during an ebbing tide: a predator can wait in the relatively quiet water as bait tumbles out of the estuary.

Spring tides, with their stronger currents, will probably be more productive for fishing than neap tides, the reason being that the stronger currents will do a better job of concentrating bait and attracting game fish. Nevertheless, don't avoid neap tides—there certainly will be areas in

Rising Tide   **Falling Tide**

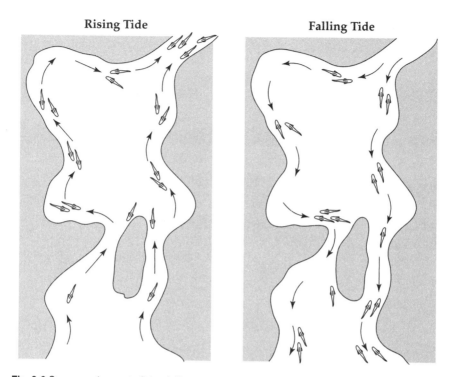

Fig. 9-6 Some good areas to fish a falling or rising tide in a marsh area.

which the currents associated with this tide are adequate for fishing. Let me assure you that fish do not fast between spring tides—indeed, there is no evidence that their feeding rate is any different during spring- or neap-tide conditions. It's usually just easier for anglers to find fish during spring-tide conditions.

Sometimes, a rising tide presents the best fishing opportunities. On a rising tide, fish can enter shallow water with little chance of being trapped. It really isn't clear to me if fish think this way, but I have seen more fishermen trapped by a tidal change than fish. Watching bonefish roar across shallow water, after they are hooked, seems to indicate that they know quite well where to find deeper water. Water entering an estuary from the ocean generally will have a lower temperature, higher oxygen content, and be clearer or less turbid than the water already in the estuary. These aspects may invigorate or stimulate the fish already in the estuary, especially if the water in the estuary is very warm.

Fishing Tip: Lure Selection

The type of bait in an estuary may change over the course of a fishing season. Often the bait is smaller earlier in the year, and gets larger as the season progresses. Estuaries clearly hold a wide variety of food for fish, so most fish do not limit themselves to just one type of food. This may explain why such a wide variety of flies and lures work in estuaries. Factors that can be important to your success include the shape of the lure or fly, the weather, the "color" of the environment, and the contrast of the fly or lure with the ambient or background conditions. Sometimes, you should use colors that contrast with different backgrounds such as the general color of rocky areas or grassy regions. It may not be that simple, of course—a fly with colors that strongly contrast with the environment could appear unnatural to a fish, causing the fish to reject it. In this scenario, the more the fly mimics the realistic colors of the environment, the more effective it will be. There are advocates for both views; if you read fishing magazines, anglers favoring contrast seem to be in the majority.

I cannot offer an unequivocal answer to the question of whether you should use more or less contrast in your lures, but it is evident to me that at certain times, certain colors seem to work better. Chartreuse flies and lures are often successful, and are hard to beat in daytime. The reason seems to be that chartreuse is highly visible—it's probably the most visible of colors in water, and does seem to attract fish. Interestingly, at least to my knowledge, there is nothing in the ocean that is colored chartreuse. In the Northeast, chartreuse-and-white Clouser Minnows are among the most effective, if not the most popular, flies to use for striped bass and bluefish. Another confusing part of the color equation is that there are times when one color seems to work better than others, but later in the day or on the next day another color or pattern seems to be preferred by the fish. Weather variations, such as overcast conditions versus bright sunny conditions, can influence which fly fish will eat. Perhaps the best advice concerning color is to experiment and be patient—if one color works, stay with it.

(continued)

FISHING TIP: LURE SELECTION *(continued)*

Also watch and see what colors other successful, or unsuccessful, anglers are using. There is no catchall lure or fly, but we all have ones that we think come close.

Black, red, or dark flies and lures seem to work better at night, but noise-making lures may also be effective after dark. Flies that "move water," like the Tabory Snake fly, are especially effective by making sound (turbulence, really) that attracts fish at night. On the other hand, popping flies do not seem to do as well at night, perhaps because they make too much noise.

STRUCTURE

When you're fishing an estuary, you cannot go wrong by fishing structure. Structures can be simple topographic highs or lows, either of which can be detected by changes in the flow characteristics of the water over or around the high or low area. Rips will form over high spots, whereas slower-moving surface water and pools will occur over low spots. You might find structure along the edges of flowing water, either on the steep banks or just along the normal slope leading up to a beach or marsh. Often the bottom depth will change at the point where one body of water intersects another. This can be off the mouth of an estuary, where a shallow delta may form, or inside the estuary, where several creeks or drainage areas may converge.

Holes or depressions can attract and hold fish, especially when the tide is low, giving the fish a place to hide. In the summer, the water in a depression is usually cooler than the surface water, and thus may attract fish wanting to avoid warm water. In general, the deeper the depression, the cooler the water in it will be. Some holes (and often shoals, too) are made up of unconsolidated sediment, so their location can shift due to erosion by strong currents or storms.

Structure can also result from an accumulation of oyster or mussel shells on the bottom. When water flows over these natural features, the surface will show a small surface irregularity or rip. Mussel or oyster beds, even if dead, often attract large numbers of crabs and minnows, which are food for big fish. Fishing near active shellfishing areas may also

When to Fish

Anglers sometimes put too much emphasis on trying to determine when the best time to fish is. Remember, fish are present somewhere in the ocean all the time. They may prefer a specific tide that gives them access to a specific area, or a time when the tidal currents are of a specific speed or direction. At times, fish just prefer not to eat. One example might be in shallow water when the sun is bright and the fish feel vulnerable; another is the day following a clear night with a full moon—the opinion here is that the fish will gorge themselves during the bright night and will not or do not need to feed during the following day. Fish often will adjust their feeding patterns to the patterns of their food and mainly eat when their forage is available.

There have been numerous studies on the feeding behavior of fish, but these are typically done in the laboratory using freshwater species, so their applicability to the ocean may be limited. Some research indicates that fish tend to feed at the same times over a 24-hour period. In some instances, a fish's feeding pattern is determined by how long it takes the fish to digest its previous meal. On the other hand, fish that lack a swimbladder and have to expend large amounts of energy constantly swimming may need to eat almost continuously.

Fish frequently show a "crowd mentality." What I mean is that a group of fish may have no interest in food (or a lure) until one fish does. When one fish gets interested, it often triggers a similar response in the other fish and they quickly all start to feed. This might explain how a feeding frenzy begins.

Sometimes, fish stop feeding at the same time. Bluefish often do this—one moment a school is ravaging the bait at the surface and will hit anything thrown at them; and then, almost instantly, everything stops. It would be tempting to blame this behavior on boat noise, but I have seen it happen with no apparent cause. Frequently, the fish will begin to feed again a few minutes later, behavior that maybe is triggered by some unseen but well-communicated message that all the fish receive and respond to.

be a good idea—just remember that clam diggers often leave small holes or depressions that can surprise a careless wader. Clam beds, for example, are continually dug up and overturned, exposing bottom-living creatures and providing a nice collection of food for baitfish and predators.

When you're looking for structure, don't neglect man-made objects, such as piers, docks, jetties, marinas, bridges, and the like (see Figure 9-1). Many inshore species, snook for example, like to hang around such structures, which provide protection and a hiding place from which the fish can wait for a meal.

Man-made coastal structures often have lights that attract baitfish after dark, which means that predators will probably be around, too. The predators will stay in the dark, at the edges of the lighted water, and occasionally charge into the bright water to try for a meal. A lure slowly retrieved through the lighted water may trigger a strike. In a partially lighted area, you should try putting your offering into a dark area and retrieve it so that it passes along the edge of the lighted edge.

Around commercial shellfish or fish-processing facilities, or marinas (especially those that have a charter boat fishing fleet), the carcasses of filleted fish or unwanted parts of shellfish are often discarded into the surrounding water. If so, this "chum" can attract baitfish and thus larger predators. The warm-water discharge areas of coastal power plants may also be good places to fish. This is especially true when the surrounding water is cooling and migrating species are still in the area; the fish often stay around the warm-water discharge pipes.

FISHING SALT MARSHES

There are many places to fish around a salt marsh. These include creeks or depressions, structures formed at the bends of creeks or where two or more creeks intersect, downcurrent of points, around bars or similar shallow areas, and near man-made features such as docks, marinas, and fish- or shellfish-processing facilities. Tide height affects how the fishing will be in these areas. Ebbing or falling tides will drain the marsh and carry food to game fish waiting in adjacent deep water or channels. Flooding tides give bait and predators access to previously dry areas where they can forage.

Many anglers prefer to fish during the later stages of a falling tide, when fish might be concentrated in certain areas of a marsh; during high tides, the fish can be relatively scattered. My preference is to fish by a marsh as the tide is falling, particularly near any distinct body of water flowing off the marsh, which often will be loaded with bait. Sometimes, I try to get a little offshore of the draining tidal creek or channel to intercept those fish waiting in the outflow.

Fishing Tip: Vary Your Retrieve

Whatever lure you use, your goal is to attract the fish and make them strike. To do this best, your offering should bear some resemblance to the bait present, but also should stand out and appear to be an easy catch for a predator. You can often accomplish this by varying your retrieve. The best retrieve often depends on the current speed, light, water clarity, and time of day. A slow retrieve is often better at night or in low-light conditions. When there is good light, a faster retrieve, which gives the fish less time to examine the fly, often works. In a strong current, you may not have to retrieve your lure at all—just let it drift across or down the current. When retrieving a lure against the current, hold it in place and let it flutter a while so that it looks like a struggling baitfish.

Working your fly through a school of bait may make your offering appear to be just one of many similar-looking meals. Putting that fly on the outside or along a school of bait and giving it an irregular or different motion, imitating a wounded or crippled baitfish, often will make it more attractive to a predator. If you are trying to entice fish from a distance, a brightly colored or noisy lure (or both) is best.

If your lure is meant to imitate a shrimp or similar crustacean, use a slower retrieve and keep the lure near the bottom. Some fly fishermen, however, prefer to keep their shrimp flies nearer the surface, as many shrimp are found drifting along with the current. Crab patterns often work best when you let them sink and stay on the bottom for a while before moving them. Poppers and surface flies work by making a disturbance on the surface. If done right, you should be able to see or hear the pop, and see a wake, as a fish strikes a popper at the surface.

Finally, the dark mud of a marsh absorbs heat from the sun when the water level is low. This stored heat will in turn warm the overlying water, which often attracts bait and predators, especially during the cooler months of the year before most of the estuary has had a chance to warm.

Fishing Tip: The Importance of Being Quiet

The estuarine environment, which includes tidal flats, is probably the quietest of the ocean environments we fish. Fish have excellent hearing and can detect sound and vibrations coming from considerable distances. One accidental splash could ruin your fishing for quite a while.

When fishing from a boat, try to drift to where you plan on fishing, rather than using your outboard motor to get you there. Go upcurrent from the fishing area and then pole, paddle, or drift down to your spot; an electric motor can also keep noise to a minimum. If you plan to anchor, have the anchor ready before you get to your fishing area; an anchor makes lots of noise when it's moved around in a boat. When it comes time to drop the anchor, slowly lower it into the water. Even loud talking or yelling may disturb fish.

In quiet water during the day, I frequently move after catching just one or two fish; by catching and landing fish, I may have spooked the other fish in the area. After a period of time I may return to that area to try again.

This approach always seemed reasonable, until I had an experience

FISHING MANGROVE AREAS

Mangrove areas can be home for hundreds of species of fish, including snook, small tarpon, redfish, various species of jacks and snappers, bonefish, and barracudas. Well-known mangrove fishing areas include the Florida Keys and parts of the Gulf of Mexico, the many islands of the Caribbean, and large parts of coastal Central and South America.

A mangrove lagoon often is a superb fishing area, holding schools of small tarpon, bonefish, and other exciting species. In the lagoon you are not limited to fishing the edges of the mangrove swamp; you can also work the lagoon's center. The intertwining network of mangrove roots also provides hiding places for fish. During some high tides the fish may go so far back into the roots that they will be uncatchable. When the tide falls, these fish may leave the security of the mangrove root system and head to deeper, open water. You need to choose the right tide to fish a mangrove swamp: the water must be sufficiently deep for the fish to stay in the area. The tidal range is typically small where mangroves are found, but even small differences in the height of the tide can determine where the fish may be.

that made me question it. I was fishing in shallow water on a fairly bright day at about 10 A.M. and I hooked a striped bass. As I was bringing in the fish, I realized that I was surrounded by several dozen other striped bass; some actually banged my legs. I thought that the struggling fish would spook the other fish, but it didn't; in fact, the other fish just casually moved out of its way as I retrieved it. For the next hour or so, I continued to catch fish out of this close-in school, but the thrashing of the hooked fish did not seem to bother any other fish. All that appeared to bother these fish was my shadow, which they avoided. Another surprise was that sometimes I could see my chartreuse Clouser Minnow disappear for a second in a fish's mouth and, though I had a fairly tight line, I often did not feel the take.

Here are a couple other fly-fishing tips: if you use long leaders, the fish will be less likely to hear the sound of the fly line hitting the water; likewise, it's a good idea to use flies that land gently on the water and slowly sink, keeping the disturbance to a minimum; and using fluorocarbon line as tippet material is always a good idea when you're fishing in shallow water, or when targeting fish that have especially good vision.

Fishing a mangrove area is not always easy. You must place your lure as close to the mangrove roots as possible. The overhanging branches, however, make this difficult. Some anglers will use flies equipped with weedguards and cast them into the overlying branches, then slowly retrieve the line until the fly falls into the water close to the base of the trees. Of course, fish are often hesitant to leave the security of the root system, so how close you place your lure to the roots may make the difference between getting a strike or just a look of indifference from a fish. In fly fishing, a sidearm cast will give you the best chance of putting your fly close to the mangrove roots; an overhead cast is more likely to foul on overhanging branches.

Another challenge when fishing a mangrove area is to keep a hooked fish from getting into the root system and fouling your line. You must keep constant pressure on the fish and, if possible, move your boat away from the shore. If the fish does get tangled in the mangroves, try releasing pressure for a moment; often, the fish will swim clear of the roots.

In some mangrove areas, the water is stained by decaying organic matter, which can make sight-fishing difficult. Clean water around a mangrove area generally indicates that the region is well flushed by tidal action. It's often a good idea to use a fly similar in color to that of the water. The reason is that the baitfish often will be colored like the water; it's a form of camouflage. In other words, a brown or reddish fly or lure might work better when the waters are colored by organic matter, whereas a light-colored or white fly is preferable in well-flushed areas.

If you're fishing a mangrove stand from a drifting boat, try to work the area in front of the boat, where the water has not been disturbed, rather than the water behind the boat, where some disturbance from the boat's wake may have reached the shore. This advice is appropriate for any type of nearshore fishing when you're moving or drifting parallel to the shore.

FISHING TIDAL FLATS

Probably more articles and books have been written about fishing (especially fly fishing) on tidal flats than on any other part of the ocean. In the past, flats fishing has generally meant sight-fishing in Florida, Mexico, the Caribbean, or Central America for species such as bonefish, permit, or tarpon. The resurgence of striped bass along the East Coast of the United States, however, has lead to a type of flats fishing for these fish, which sometimes feed in shallow water. (The West Coast, especially the San Francisco Bay region of California, also has an active striped bass fishery.)

The tide is one of the most important factors when fishing on tidal flats. The flooding or incoming tide usually can be very productive. Prior to the start of the flood tide, fish will often hold in deeper water beyond the edge of the flat. As the tide rises the fish enter the flats area looking for food. One good strategy is to position yourself between the deep water and the flats and try to intercept those fish moving with the rising tide onto the shallow flats. The falling tide also can be good, as the fish may hold in or around drainage channels waiting for bait to be carried to them by the tide. If you can scout the area, preferably at low tide, you may be able to determine where the fish will be or will move to.

Wind can have a strong effect on the tide in the shallow waters of the flats—it can hold water in the shallow areas or prevent or reduce the incoming tide. An offshore wind will reduce the tidal effect, an onshore wind can increase it. Strong winds can stir up the bottom, making sight-fishing difficult, if not impossible. On the other hand, fish tend to be less spooky with a slight wind and a rippled sea surface.

Water temperature on the flats often determines where the fish will be. Species such as snook, bonefish, redfish, and others often move to deeper water and avoid the flats when water temperature gets very warm. They may return to the flats during cooler mornings or evenings, or when the water temperature cools down overall. Warm waters can also lead to some surprising migrations, such as small bonefish or tarpon showing up as far north as New Jersey or jack crevalle off Cape Cod.

The tide or wind can also cause a water-temperature change, as the incoming water will almost always be colder than the water already present on the flats. The incoming tide can also bring in clear water to replace murky water caused previously by wind or rain. Weather, especially the passage of a cold front, can strongly influence the fishing conditions on the flats. A rapid drop in water temperature often will drive many species off a flat. A cold front can also bring clear skies, improving your sight-fishing opportunities.

Barometric pressure changes can influence the height of the tide and affect shallow-water fishing. Storms or fronts usually are accompanied by changes in barometric pressure. (Barometric pressure is a measure of the weight of the overlying air, or atmosphere.) A low-pressure area means that the weight of the air is now less than it was previously. When the pressure is dropping, or is low, it can cause a corresponding rise in sea level because there is now less weight of air pushing down on the surface of the sea. A rise in barometric pressure can cause a drop in the sea level because more weight of air is pushing down on the sea surface. Furthermore, the passage of a front can also cause a quick change in the water temperature, the wind, and the turbidity of the water; the turbidity changes result from increased wave activity caused by the strengthened wind, and may be most evident on the shallower parts of tidal flats. Changes in sea level due to barometric pressure are most obvious in shallow areas, such as on tidal flats, or in enclosed or semi-enclosed bodies of water, such as lagoons or lakes. In shallow water, such as around a mangrove swamp or on the flats, the barometric changes can influence where the fish are able to go.

In *Backwater Fly Fishing in Salt Water,* Swisher and Richards report that normal barometric pressure changes can influence the level of the tide by about 6 inches; under extreme pressure conditions, the tide can change by as much as 12 inches. Because the tidal range on many flats normally may only be a foot or so, it's easy to understand why many flats anglers pay attention to changes in barometric pressure. However, as discussed in Chapter 1, it really isn't the pressure change, per se, that affects the fish, but rather the things that accompany it, such as a change in temperature.

Flats fishing differs from most types of fishing in that you really are hunting for the fish. You do not just stay in one spot on the flats and cast, but rather you move about, often with a well-defined strategy. Most fish that inhabit the flats follow distinct pathways when leaving or returning to deep water and have specific areas where they feed. The challenge is to find these spots and intercept the moving fish.

Although flats fishing is often thought of as sight-fishing, this does not always have to be the case. Blind-casting (casting without seeing fish in the area) can be a productive and fun way to fish in a flats environment. When rough weather or deep or dirty water limits your ability to see fish, blind-casting is the only way to go; however, don't just randomly throw your lure about, but focus on edges, drop-offs, depressions, lees, or any place where there is disturbed or moving water—in other words, any place that looks possibly productive.

Fish in shallow water often give clues of their presence, even though you may not actually see them, via disturbances on the water's surface. This might be the wake of a single moving fish, or what is sometimes called "nervous water." Nervous water appears as ripples or irregularities on the surface, caused by fish moving or swimming just below the surface. Bonefish often make such disturbances, though I have seen similar patterns from striped bass, tarpon, and bluefish.

It's usually best to avoid casting directly into the center of a patch of nervous water. Rather, cast several feet in front of the fish if they appear to be moving, or to the edge of the nervous water if the fish appear to be stationary. If you are casting to a fish's wake, cast at least 10 feet or more in front of it so that your fly doesn't spook the fish and sinks to an appropriate depth by the time the fish reaches it.

A "mud patch" or "mud," which a fish makes as it disturbs the bottom while feeding, is another clue that betrays the presence of fish in shallow water. Often these fish are slowly moving about; if you can determine the direction in which the fish are moving, cast in that direction. Whether you are sight-fishing or blind-casting, be careful not to make unnecessary noise with your fly line or fly. Fish are often extremely nervous in shallow water, certainly more so than in deep water.

Fish on the flats may travel as individuals, in twos or threes, or in large schools. Usually, the fewer the fish, the more spooky they will be; larger groups seem to be more "secure," if that's the right word. This is a general observation—it's still easy to spook a large group of fish. If you are casting to a group of fish, try to pick out one on the edge of the school and cast to it. If the fish are moving cast in front of them and try to intercept them. If at all possible, do not cast to a fish in the middle of the school; you will probably spook the entire school.

Finding or spotting a fish on the flats takes considerable skill. Without polarizing glasses, it is almost impossible. Some fish (bonefish are one of the best examples) are truly hard to detect as they literally merge with the background. Other fish such as stripers or tarpon are easier to see. If the sun is out, the fish will cast a shadow on the bottom, which is often easier to detect than the fish itself. Also, don't stare at one spot when looking for fish, but rather scan a broad area looking for movement, wakes, or bait. Sometimes you can detect these movements with your peripheral vision. The most ideal situation when you're wading on a flat is to have the sun behind you or at your side, and the wind at your back. This will greatly improve your visibility.

Being quiet on a tidal flat is very important. Likewise be careful that the fish are not spooked by your rod or your casting motion. (Remember the Snell's window view that a fish has of the outside world; see Chapter 7, page 150).

When fishing on a flat, you must always be ready to make an accurate cast. You often get only one good chance to cast to a fish. When you're fly fishing, keep your false casts to a minimum and do not let your fly hit the water until the actual presentation cast. Your fly must be where the fish can see it, but not close enough to scare the fish. The fact that the fish is a moving target, combined with the typical winds on the flats, make a perfect cast a formidable chore. If the fish is moving away from you, try to cast to the side of the fish. Try not to cast your line over a fish—the shadow of the line and fly hitting the water usually will spook the fish. Also remember that it's unnatural for your lure to be swimming upcurrent or at a fish.

When you're wading a flat, one approach is to walk into the current. If any fish are present, they should be facing into the current and, if you're lucky, they may not see or sense your approach. You can also follow the current, especially if this keeps the sun and the wind at your back. If there is no or little current, you might want to follow the wind direction.

If you've never fished the flats, it makes sense to take a trip with an experienced guide. There are many subtle aspects and nuances involved with flats fishing that a good guide can demonstrate and explain to you.

FISHING INLETS AND JETTIES

Inlets are where the exchange of water between an estuary and the ocean occurs. Because inlets generally have narrow openings, the flow of the incoming or outgoing water is constricted, which increases the speed of the current and makes the water more turbulent. The strong currents and turbulent areas in most inlets will trap and confuse bait. These currents

Hydraulic Currents

The topic of hydraulic currents is a little complex, but an understanding of these currents can be valuable when you're fishing inlets or any area where one body of water merges with another.

Often the tides, as well as the tidal pattern, between two bodies of water such as an estuary and the open ocean are not in phase and do not have equal ranges in their tide. This is due to a hydraulic current, which is caused by the differences in water height at either end of the inlet that separates the two bodies of water. A hydraulic current can result when the ocean tide offshore is rising but the water level of the estuary is falling, causing an ocean-flowing current in the inlet, which is also called an outflow.

Explained another way, the outgoing or incoming flow of water through the narrow inlet cannot keep pace with the rising or falling tide outside in the ocean. The tidal levels between the two bodies of water, therefore, will be out of phase—for how long depends on the dimensions of the inlet, the size and shape of the bay or estuary, the strength of the tide, and the weather conditions. As a result, the water level inside the inlet, in the estuary, lags behind the water level of the ocean. This will cause the current flow inside the estuary to differ considerably from the flow outside the estuary in the ocean.

Here's an example of hydraulic current. When the ocean has reached its maximum low during an ebbing tide, the water in the estuary has not yet arrived at its maximum low. Thus, as the ocean tide starts to rise, the water in the estuary is still higher than the

(continued)

Fig. 9-7 A graphic description of the process of hydraulic tidal currents occurring between an estuary and the open ocean. It isn't as complicated as it may look. The lines labeled 1, 2, 3, and 4 represent different times. At these different times the tidal currents and water levels will be different in the estuary compared to that of the ocean. In the upper figure the water level of the ocean is rising while the water level in the estuary is still falling. In the middle figure the water level in the ocean is falling while it is rising in the estuary. In the lower figure the same four times, 1, 2, 3, and 4, are indicated on the tidal curves for the estuary and the ocean; in this example, they are out of phase by a little more than two hours.

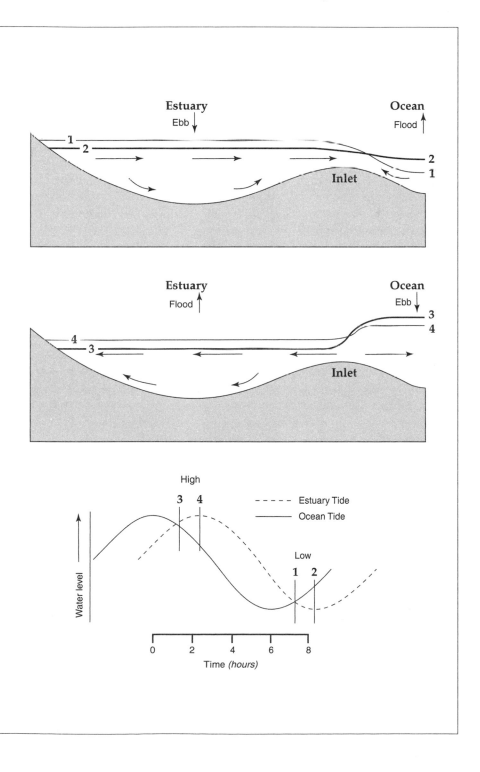

HYDRAULIC CURRENTS (continued)

water of the now-rising ocean. In this situation, which may exist just for a short time or maybe even for an hour or more, the water will be ebbing or flowing out of the estuary through the inlet into the ocean, whereas the tide in the ocean is rising.

Once the tidal levels inside and outside the inlet become equal, there will be a short slack-tide period, but the hydraulic-current process continues and will now start again, only this time in the opposite direction. In this situation, the water in the ocean will rise quicker than the water in the estuary. The inlet often has fairly strong currents, due to the tidal flow as well as to the differences in water level inside and outside the inlet.

When you're fishing the outgoing water near an inlet, you should be aware of the direction of the tidal currents in the adjacent ocean. The direction of the ocean current will indicate how the water, once it clears the inlet, will be deflected. The ocean current will move the outflowing current to one side of the inlet, and in doing so set up some countercurrents and quiet areas; often, the water moves downcurrent of the inlet. This is the best place to fish because it is where the water coming out of the estuary—and the bait in the water—will be carried.

A knowledge of how hydraulic currents work can be very useful to those who fish in and around estuaries. (See Figures 9-8A, 9-8B, 9-8C)

change and shift with the tide, often forming small countercurrents and tidal rips.

Inlets have several key fishing areas, which include along the jetties that flank the inlet, the various depressions and topographic highs found at the inner and outer parts of an inlet, current edges, channels near or in the inlet, and any nearby man-made structure. This is true whether the inlet is a natural feature, is protected by jetties or a breakwater, or is maintained by dredging.

Because fish frequently migrate in or out of an estuary, usually with the changing tide, they often hold along the jetty and channel system that marks and flanks the inlet during various parts of a tide. Generally, these fish seek areas where the currents are relatively slow; thus a cut, creek, or side channel to the main inlet could be a good place in which to cast a fly, especially if there is water flowing toward or away from the main flow.

The area around a jetty or inlet can be fished from the shore, from the jetty itself, or from a boat. If you're fishing from a jetty, be careful—the rocks on even a well-constructed jetty can be difficult to walk on; they also may be covered with algal growth and therefore can be very slippery. Jetty rocks can also be covered with sharp barnacles and mussels, so even a small fall can be dangerous. Falling off a jetty into the swift-flowing current of the inlet can cost you your life. Always wear a tight belt around your waders to prevent them from filling up with water and pulling you down if you should fall in. Check out an inlet jetty in the daytime, before venturing out at night.

An important concern when you're fishing from a jetty is where and how to land a fish. This can be especially troublesome for fly fishermen, who usually wear waders, an awkward casting basket around their waist, and frequently fish at night. Spin and bait fishermen generally do not wear waders and tend to fish more often in daylight. Choose a spot on the jetty from which you can reach down to release or control the fish.

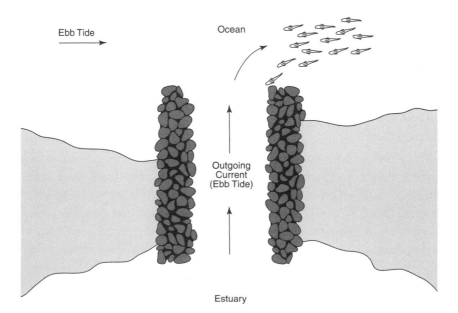

Fig. 9-8A Ebb tide or falling water in the estuary. In this situation the outgoing current is deflected to the right when it leaves the inlet because it is moved by the ebb tide in the ocean. Fishing should be better near the right-hand jetty.

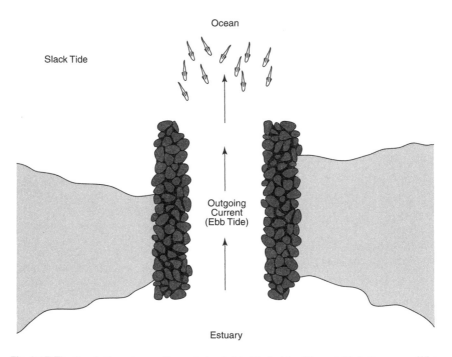

Fig. 9-8B The flow in the estuary will usually lag behind that of the tides outside in the ocean. When the tide is slack outside there will still be water flowing out of the estuary, and fishing will usually be best directly off the mouth of the inlet.

There are advantages to fishing at night in most estuary inlets, foremost of which is that boat traffic at that time is usually fairly light. This allows for more casting opportunities, and the fish will be relatively undisturbed.

Channels or rock piles can also provide good hiding places for predators to find and trap prey. Flies often work well in these areas, if you allow them to drift along with the current looking like confused baitfish.

A break in a jetty, or anything that changes or slows the flow of water in the inlet, can be a place where fish hold. Often the edges or the end of a jetty will have a pocket of relatively quiet water (sometimes called "dead water") where fish may wait for passing bait. Baitfish usually hold near the rocks and tend to hug the side of the jetty as they move in or out of the estuary. Also, there will often be a depression or deep hole near the end of a jetty, farther out from where the jetty ends at the water's surface. This can be a good fishing spot.

My experience is that most areas around the mouth or entrance to an inlet are relatively unproductive when the tide is slack, but the areas

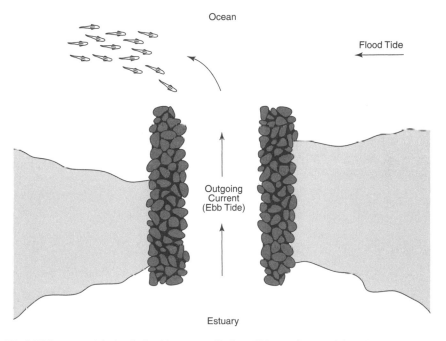

Fig. 9-8C Because of the lag in the tide, water will often still be moving out of the estuary even as the tide starts to flood (or rise) outside. This situation may last an hour or so, and during this time fishing will be better near the left-hand jetty.

inside of an inlet along the jetty may be productive when the water motion is slow or quiet. This pattern will quickly change when the tidal current starts again. With an outgoing current the seaward part of the jetty should be more productive, whereas the inner parts of the jetty walls should be better with an incoming current.

The current speed in the inlet is relatively strong during a spring tide; at these times (and at other occurrences of strong currents) it may be better to work the edges of the current rather than to cast into the main flow.

FISHING INSIDE INLETS

Fishing inside the jetties of an inlet, actually inside the estuary, often is easier than working the ocean side of an inlet but can be just as effective. For wading anglers, the inside of the inlet is usually the place to be. The bottom around the inside of the inlet often has a relatively gentle slope and the waves certainly are smaller here than on the ocean side.

But let me emphasize that many inlets have severe and steep drop-offs along their estuary-side openings. I have been in some areas where the soft-sand, steeply sloping bottom, and breaking waves made entering the water a dangerous proposition. The presence of waves should be taken as a warning sign. Always search out and analyze an area before you fish it, especially if you plan to fish at night.

One of the main problems of fishing from a boat near an inlet is being moved either by the currents or the wind onto the rocks. You can avoid this danger by fishing downcurrent of the jetty, although that will give you only a limited opportunity to cast near the jetty rocks. Anchoring can keep you close to the jetty (within casting range, anyway), but you should anchor up on the downcurrent side of the jetty, just in case your anchor comes loose. Many inlets and their associated jetty systems are areas of high boat traffic, so anchoring around them may be unsafe or illegal.

Some estuary inlets have shallow areas just off their inside and offshore mouths (see Fig. 3-11). These features are actually small deltas resulting from sediment being carried along in the swift flowing water in the inlet, but then dropping out when this water slows as it reaches the more tranquil water either just outside of the inlet or just inside the inlet (in the estuary). These shallow areas usually are not good fishing areas, but they may form surface rips that could lead to better fishing just downcurrent from the shoal area.

It can be dangerous to pass through an inlet in a boat, especially when there are strong tides or breaking waves at the mouth of the inlet. When approaching from offshore, the waves will often appear less dangerous than they really are. Areas where the waves are not breaking are generally where the water is the deepest. You should have some knowledge of an inlet before attempting to enter or exit one by boat.

One good boating technique is to get behind the crest of a wave and follow it into the inlet. This requires considerable seamanship, as you must not overtake the wave and surf down its crest, or you can bury the bow of your vessel; you can't let the following wave overtake you, either.

Chapter 10

Fishing Nearshore Waters

Beaches, the shoreline, and adjacent areas are notorious for changing rapidly due to storms, waves, wind, and the tide. Game fish find the beach, the incoming surf, and nearby rips to be a cafeteria of riches, where bottom structure and currents collect and hold a wide variety of bait. Most game fish are migratory and do not have permanent homes, but, like people, fish like to visit the beach. The beach region is often best fished at night and frequently holds large fish—it is an area where angling legends are made.

The beach and nearshore areas can be intimidating areas to fish. Even expert anglers and old-timers are challenged by the rapid changes and the wave energy that occur along beaches. To successfully fish these nearshore waters, you must pay close attention to the characteristics and structure of the area you're fishing, the bottom topography, the tide, the pattern of the incoming waves, and the weather. The expression "reading the water" is especially appropriate in this part of the ocean environment. Reading the water is relatively easy when it refers to fishing in the quiet backwaters of an estuary, but trying to read the water on a beach while waves are breaking around you is much different. Nothing can replace experience when fishing in the beach and nearshore environment.

BEACHES

Along a typical beach, there are many areas where fish can hold and ambush trapped or confused bait, including longshore bars and troughs, points or cusps, deep holes, areas of steep slopes or drop-offs, and drainage channels. A well-prepared beach angler will explore a potential fishing area at low tide (spring low tide is an especially good time to do a reconnaissance) to locate offshore bars or other structures that are fishable at high tide. Another benefit of such a survey is to determine the location of drop-offs and other potentially dangerous areas. Re-examine the beach

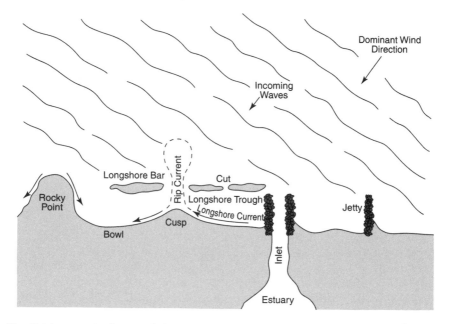

Fig. 10-1 A composite diagram of a beach area showing many of the fishing structures and features mentioned in this chapter and elsewhere. The angle of the waves approaching the beach is exaggerated.

following any strong storms and onshore winds, which can change the depth in the area, as well as the position of many fishing structures.

One of the first things to note about a beach is the general character of the shoreline. Are there any protuberances or points or cusps, any obvious changes in sediment or bottom type, rocky areas or other irregularities, quiet areas, bars and troughs, or other structures such as steep slopes? Fish may hold near any of these features at some time during the tide. Berms, flat areas formed by sediment deposited by waves, are one of the more visible features of a beach. Often there are several berms along a beach. Although beaches may vary in appearance and general characteristics, they often have many features in common.

Tides and Waves

In general, the two factors that most influence how the fishing will be along a beach are the position of the tide and the character of incoming waves. (Details about these subjects were covered in Chapter 2.) These factors combine to produce most of the structure and fish-holding areas along a beach and in the surf zone.

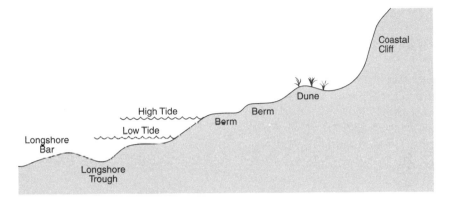

Fig. 10-2 A typical beach profile, with a series of longshore bars and troughs. Most sandy beaches, regardless of their width, will have features similar to this illustration.

You can learn a lot about beach structure by observing how and where the waves are breaking. Breaking waves typically indicate relatively shallow water, such as bars, ridges, or cusps that extend seaward. The pattern of breaking waves often is interrupted when a seaward-moving rip current is present (see Figure 4-6). Changes in the color of the water may indicate changes in water depth; darker colors generally indicate deeper water, and rocks will appear darker than a sand bottom.

Fig. 10-3 Waves will generally break over an elevated feature such as a submerged bar, ridge, or, in this case, a beach cusp that extends seaward.

Summer or Daytime

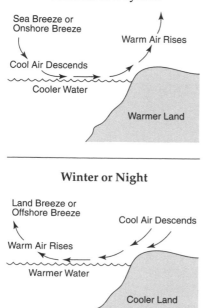

Winter or Night

Fig. 10-4 Sea breeze and land breeze wind patterns resulting from the relative difference in temperature between land and water. In the daytime *(top)*, land is heated more than water. Land also cools more at night *(bottom)*. When the air is heated, it expands, becomes less dense, and rises. Relatively cooler, denser air moves in to replace it, causing a breeze. The breeze is named for the direction from which it comes, not for where it is going. Under less-pronounced conditions, the winds change direction daily, landward during the day and seaward at night.

The time of day also influences the fishing along a beach. Early morning, dusk, and night are favorite fishing times for most beach anglers. The time of day can also determine the general wind pattern. For example, the differences in how land and water respond to heat can affect local wind conditions: when land is cooler than the ocean, an offshore breeze or land breeze may result.

Obviously, the tide stage will dictate what part of the beach you can fish. On some beaches, the best structures or most favorable areas are only reachable at low tide. In this situation, anglers may prefer to fish during a falling tide, so they can move seaward and reach any nearby structures as the tide ebbs. A rising tide increases water depth and often brings in bait and larger fish. The rising tide also creates tranquil areas over depressions, and rough turbulent areas where the tidal current is constricted. The latter effect can also happen during a falling tide. Some anglers believe that the one or two hours before and after the high tide are frequently the best times for fishing along a beach. The time just after slack water may also be productive, as the water motion frequently stimulates bait and predators and could initiate feeding activity. Although tidal currents are important factors in fishing, they usually are not very strong along open exposed beaches; in these areas the swell and wind effects are frequently more powerful than the currents are.

When you track the tide, consider the habits of your target species, as different species have different tidal preferences. For example, if the beach you're fishing is near an estuary outlet, a strong ebbing tidal current carrying bait out of an estuary at dusk or just before morning light should

Global Positioning Systems

You can accurately determine your position literally anywhere on Earth by a system that uses a worldwide net of satellites called the Global Positioning System, or GPS. There are several ways anglers can use a GPS unit. For boating anglers, the most obvious use is to locate and record, then return to, a good offshore fishing location. Even more useful, to me, is returning to a very specific part of that location. I mean not just locating an offshore rip, but locating that small part of the rip where you found fish during a specific tide. You could also use your GPS to track and map the pattern of feeding fish, such as little tunny, and position yourself to intercept the fish as they move along in this feeding pattern. (Catch a few little tunny this way and I'm sure you'll feel your GPS was a great investment.)

GPS units can also be useful for wading anglers, especially for exploring or scouting a new beach, tidal flat, or estuary. With a handheld GPS, you can record the location of significant features and structures and then return to them when they are less visible at high tide or under the cover of darkness. (Most handheld GPS devices are backlit, so you can use them at night.) Also, most GPS units plot an electronic chart of your movement—a nice way of recalling your trip. The compactness of handheld units, which are about the size of a fly box, makes them useful pieces of technology for shore-bound anglers.

Handheld GPS units used to have limitations in accuracy, mainly because of governmental interference with navigational satellite signals due to military concerns. This interference was eliminated in early 2000, and current GPS accuracy is quite adequate for the uses described above.

attract night-feeding fish. Fish such as Atlantic bonito and little tunny tend to avoid heavy surf, probably because the sand suspended in the surf irritates their gills. These fish, however, often come near the beach when surf conditions are modest; you can catch them from the beach, or from jetties that extend into or beyond the surf. Sometimes you can see fish feeding out beyond casting range. If the tide is rising, these same fish may be catchable in an hour or so.

If you're unsure how high the tide will rise along a beach, check the debris that accumulates in lines along the shore. Usually, there are at least two of these lines—the higher line reflects the water level of a recent storm or spring high tide; the lower line probably reflects the last high tide. If there are more than two debris lines, the one with the fresher plant material was probably deposited by the most recent high tide. Unfortunately, at very high tides much of the debris along the beach is usually washed back into the nearshore waters, where it can foul your line, fly, or lure. On rocky shores, the rocks themselves often have a dark band that indicates the general high-tide level.

Keep in mind that the position and strength of rip currents and longshore currents, the undertow, and the location of some bottom structures will change with the tide, sometimes producing hazardous conditions. Rip currents can be especially dangerous during storms and strong spring tides. Getting into a rip current under any conditions can be a serious mistake; fishing the edges of rip currents is the practical, safer, and most-productive approach.

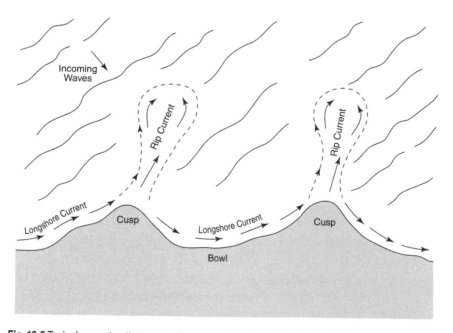

Fig. 10-5 Typical current pattern around a cusp and bowl area. Two basic things are happening, one is that the longshore current builds up and flows seaward as a rip current, often off or near a cusp. The second thing is that the breaking waves will push water up the beach and some will flow in and out along the cusp. Often the topographic high that forms the cusp on land will continue as a high area under the water (see also **Fig. 10-3**).

Cusps

These are among the most important structural features of a beach, and are great areas to fish. Often a cusp or point will continue offshore, forming a small bulge or irregularity on the seafloor, which creates currents. Fishing from this bulge back toward the smoother bowl-shaped parts of the beach can be productive. The longshore and rip currents around a cusp also create many exciting fishing opportunities. If you're fishing a beach and you find cusps and these currents, be sure to fish them thoroughly.

Longshore Bars and Troughs

Out from the beach there may be a sequence of longshore bars and troughs running parallel to the shoreline. At certain tide stages, fish hold along these features and wait for food. In areas where the currents are strong, especially around rip currents, the bar is often cut by a channel, which forms another good fishing area. Such breaks, sluice ways, or cuts in offshore bars or ridges can, on a rising tide, act as funnels and let incoming water flow into the trough between the bars or ridges. The funnel effect can also work in the opposite direction as the tide drops, in this instance draining the trough. Baitfish often get trapped in these troughs.

Fig. 10-6 This low tide photo shows a cut (arrow) in a linear ridge that parallels the beach. The cut allows water to funnel in or out of the deeper trough in front of the ridge. Often such cuts are caused by a local rip current; the presence of the rocky sediment in front of the opening strongly suggests that this is what has happened here.

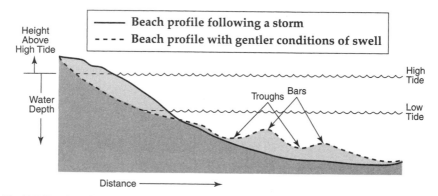

Fig. 10-7 Beach profiles formed under typical summer conditions of swell (dashed line) and conditions following a storm (solid line). Under normal conditions of gentle swell common to summer, the upper part of the beach will be relatively steep and built up, while the lower part of the beach will have a gentle seaward slope. Under storm conditions, the stronger, intense waves and rip currents will erode the upper part of the beach and carry much of the sand seaward, where it can form a single or series of longshore bars and troughs. Following a storm, the normal conditions of gentle swell will move the sand that comprises the longshore bars back up to the upper parts of the beach. This is a continuous cycle of sand being moved back and forth. The bottom structures that are good for fishing, however, are best after storm conditions. The horizontal and vertical dimensions of the beach profiles are dependent on several factors, including the height and period of the incoming waves and the angle and sediment type of the beach.

Along some coasts, there can be a sequence of several bars and troughs that can extend for some distance off the beach. Longshore bars and troughs are temporary features resulting from changing wave patterns that cause erosion and deposition on various parts of the beach. Figure 10-7 shows how a series of bars and troughs can vary with changes in weather and season. Wading and fishing from one of these bars can be dangerous; during a rising tide, the water in the trough between you and the beach can fill pretty quickly, possibly isolating you from the shoreline or maybe just making for a wet return trip.

Some beaches have patches of deep water along their length, which are called holes. They will be darker than shallower areas. Fish can dodge the turbulence of waves by sitting in holes, waiting for a passing meal. A fish might stay in a deep hole throughout a complete tide cycle.

Steep and Exposed Beaches

Breaking waves along steep and exposed beaches cause turbulence and currents that make these areas more challenging to fish than gently sloping beaches. The turbulence often disorients forage species, which attract

Tide Programs

Because tides and their resulting currents are usually the most important factors determining when and where to catch fish, it's important to have accurate information about them. Tide tables published in newspapers or given out in tackle shops or marinas are good places to start, but they usually focus on widely separated areas and lack many of the details that we anglers should have. For example, most tables only show daily high and low tides, and offer no information about currents or what happens between the highs and lows.

Another option is to try tidal computer programs, which often provide useful, detailed information in graphical form. (See Appendix 4.) The data from these programs could complement your own knowledge of specific angling areas.

I live on Cape Cod, where the tides and currents have complex subtleties that, at least for me, are hard to keep track of. For example, the high and low tides in the estuary on which I live, and in others that I fish, do not correspond to the times of maximum current or slack water at their inlets or nearby shoal areas. Similarly, the timing of the tides and currents differ around the Elizabeth Islands, Martha's Vineyard, and Buzzards Bay. I pick representative areas from the computer program and print out either the tide curve or the current curve for each. I then compare the representative areas to the curves for the other areas I fish, and note the differences between the tides. I use this information to develop a tide-adjustment table for the areas I intend to fish. This information makes planning and timing offshore or wading fishing trips very easy. I also record fishing successes and failures right on the tide or current curve, so I can compare these notes with those from past fishing trips.

When I'm in my boat I do not have to trust my memory if I want to know the state of the tide or current in a specific area. And by using my GPS, I can determine how long it will take me to reach a given area. Before I had these tools, I often arrived at a spot too late or too early for good fishing. With them, I can fully fish my local waters, and save considerable fuel and time by knowing exactly where to go, and when. Avoiding just one mistake a year easily justifies the time it takes to prepare these charts.

Identifying Structure

A good place to begin fishing a beach is at any irregularity, such as a point or cusp as shown at the areas marked A on Figure 10-8. These points may continue seaward as a ridge or shoal, sometimes ending in a deep hole or trough. A rip current, or the structure itself, will frequently trap and confuse bait, creating a prime feeding area for game fish.

A second area to explore is along longshore bars, marked B. Fish may be found either outside or inside of a bar. With the right tide and wind conditions, you might be able to cast near the longshore bar and fish parallel to it into the longshore trough (C). Bait can become trapped in this trough, and predators won't be far behind.

The fishing will be even better if there is a passage or sluiceway (D) in the outer bar that fish can use to enter the trough (See also Figure 10-6). The trough and the passageways will be calmer and darker than the surrounding waters, especially when compared to the turbulent, shallow conditions on the top of the bar. Finally, the edges of a rip current (E) also can be productive; this is a good place to cast and let your lure go out with the current on a dead drift.

large game fish. The slope of a steep beach will usually limit your wading. Also, the surf, the undertow, and the rip currents tend to be strong on steep beaches. The strong rip currents are likely to cut a channel through any nearby offshore bar. These channels, if you can reach them, are excellent places to find fish.

The steeper the beach, the harder it will be to see fish. On the other hand, the bottom structures will not be as subtle as they often are along gently sloping beaches. Also, exposed features such as beach cusps and bowls will be more obvious.

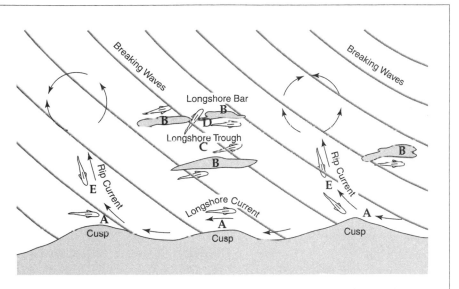

Fig. 10-8 Some of the important fishing features along a beach and in the surf zone include rip currents, cusps, longshore currents, troughs, bars, and cuts. The size of these features is determined by such factors as the character of the incoming waves, the type of beach sediment, and the prevailing winds. Large waves, for example, will form large rips, bars, troughs, and cusps. Along protected beaches, with smaller waves, these features will be harder to detect, but they will still be there, especially after a storm. The letters refer to fishing locations described in the text.

A comment concerning rip currents, which, because of their strong seaward flow, can be dangerous to fly fishers. If caught in a strong rip current, it generally is best to let the current carry you seaward. Do not initially try to swim against the rip current to reach shore. As you get offshore, the rip current will diminish in strength, you can then swim parallel to the beach until completely out of the effect of the rip current, then swim ashore.

Locating Bait

Sometimes you may find bait stranded on the beach, either because they were caught by the falling tide or pushed there by a strong wave; more likely, the bait was pushed up on shore by predators. You may also see bait at the water's edge. Fish all around these areas, including fairly close to shore, as some fish may come very near to the beach, especially when feeding at night.

Finding bait can also clue you in to the types of flies or lures to use. Usually, your lure should closely match the size and appearance of the live bait. In other words, don't use a bulky fly or lure when fish seem to be feeding on small and slim bait such as sand eels. When fishing a beach, some anglers feel that matching the bait's size is more important than matching its appearance.

Spotting a school of bait takes a little experience. Sometimes they can be easily seen, usually as a dark patch in the water, and other times they may be hard to detect. Sometimes a school of bait will make small swirls on the water surface. Another indicator of bait might be birds actively working above and diving into the water.

Fishing near a school of baitfish rarely is a *bad* idea, as predators eventually show up. One way to tell if fish are nearby and feeding on bait is the presence of oily slicks on the sea surface, which are often remnants of recent attacks. (The oil comes from wounded bait, and the slicks usually have a fishy smell.) Such a slick often is elongated or tear-shaped because it's been spread out by a current; the tighter the slick, the more recently it was formed. Your chances of finding fish are better if you fish in front of the slick.

If you are fishing around a school of bait without much success, you might try letting your lure sink, to make it appear like a wounded or dead baitfish. Often this will be attractive to fish feeding below the school— these are frequently big fish. You could also try working the edges of the school of baitfish, sometimes even casting away from feeding fish. You want your lure to stand out among all the natural baitfish, so keeping it a little bit away from the school might accomplish this.

THE SURF ZONE
Surf fishing can be difficult, in large part due to the breaking waves, the shifting bottom, and the rapidly changing conditions resulting from each passing wave. To be successful, you'll need to understand how the water is moving and how this movement can affect where the fish are feeding or holding.

The character of the surf can change from moment to moment. In general, the surf tends to be higher and stronger in the winter than in the summer, as offshore storms are more typical in winter. Winter surf conditions along many areas of the Pacific coast can make fishing dangerous. Wave periods also tend to be longer in the winter, usually causing beach and nearshore erosion; the shorter-period waves of summer move sand toward the beach and thus build it up. Waves caused by a storm or the local winds usually are irregular and unpredictable. In these situations, surf fishing can be dangerous. Never turn your back to the incoming

Fly-Fishing the Surf

There is a wonderful pleasure in having a fish take your fly when you're in the surf. When you're fly-fishing in breaking waves, time your cast so your fly lands behind a breaking wave; if your fly lands in front of a wave, you'll have no control over it. A similar problem can occur if a breaking wave catches your fly line. But if you put your fly in the trough of the wave, you can work it better and maintain contact with it. If you toss a fly into breaking waves, it's usually better to cast at an angle to the approaching waves rather than straight into them. You can't maintain line control when a wave is carrying your fly line and fly straight back at you. Again, you'll have better line control by casting across the wave and retrieving your fly while it's in the trough. If the waves are approaching the beach at an angle, cast your fly so you can retrieve it in the direction that the waves are moving.

You don't have to use a fast retrieve in the surf zone, as your fly is meant to imitate an injured baitfish or a baitfish confused by the rush of water from the waves. Usually a short, well-placed cast is better than a long, uncontrolled one. Also, using a weighted fly is a good idea when you're casting in the surf. Many fly fishers favor shooting heads for surf fishing, simply because these anglers can quickly shoot out line without making numerous false casts—a big advantage in windy conditions.

Landing a fish in the surf zone requires skill and an appreciation for the movement of the water by the waves. Remember that the water in the wave crest is moving toward the beach, whereas the water in the trough is moving back out to sea. When the fish is in the crest portion of the wave, either move back or try to pull it in. Then try to keep the fish from falling into the following trough; if necessary, move seaward and give some line back to the fish. Let the crest of the next wave bring the fish in farther. In other words, let the waves help you land the fish. If the fish darts in the same direction as the water in the wave and you are unprepared, your leader might snap. Keep constant pressure on the fish, except maybe when it is in the wave trough.

waves, especially when you're leaving the water; an unanticipated large wave can easily knock you over. Fishing with a buddy is always a good idea when fishing in the surf, especially at night. Sometimes the safest way to work the surf is by fishing from jetties, inlets, or along points of land.

I've met surf anglers who believe that waves follow a definite numerical pattern as they arrive on the beach, coming in sets of three, five, eight, or whatever. Likewise, I have heard that every 3rd, 7th, 9th, or whatever wave will be larger than other waves. There simply is no scientific evidence to support these ideas. At times, due to the combination of approaching waves of different wavelengths, waves will be especially large. But a few minutes later, the sequence of the arrival of the highest wave will change; later, it will change again.

The main challenge in fishing the surf is to find fish. As in other parts of the marine environment, you can make use of certain clues to do so. Look for gulls, terns, or other bait-eating birds gathering over schools of bait, especially if the bait is being attacked by predators. The baitfish are trapped—they cannot go deeper to avoid the birds because of the predators below. The fishing will probably be best if you see fish splashing below the birds. On some occasions, the birds may just be following the predators, in expectation of their eventual attack on baitfish. This commonly occurs when fast fish such as bonito or little tunny are in the region.

BEYOND THE SURF

You can often fish the surf zone and nearby structures from a boat. It can be a little tricky over a shallow, gently sloping beach, but is frequently easier over steeper-sloping beaches. Obviously, near either type of beach you want to stay seaward of breaking waves, but when the surf is very low, you often can get fairly close to the shoreline. You'll be ahead of the game if you're aware of the beach characteristics and structure before you get close to the shore in your boat.

If you happen to find a school of fish near the beach, you'll almost always do better by putting your lure near the edge of the school rather than in the middle. With a tight school of fish, you have a better chance of hooking up when your offering is moving in the same general direction as the school; a fish may not want to leave the school to chase or attack your lure. You also want to keep your boat away from the school, preferably keeping in front of or to the side of the moving fish. If you get too far ahead of a moving school, just stop and wait for the fish to catch up. Running a boat through a school of fish, even baitfish, will either put down the school or cause the fish to disperse. Staying around the edges of the school is the best way to fish it.

It's also important that your lure does not approach the fish in a threatening manner. It seems almost unreasonable, but even large aggressive predators such as tarpon are often spooked by a small fly moving in an unnatural direction, such as swimming toward the predator. If you're fishing in a current, your lure will appear more natural when it's moving with the current, upcurrent from where you anticipate the fish to be. Many fish deliberately hold in places in which their food will be carried to them by the current. Sometimes these fish will resist moving any distance to feed.

Most fish seem to like lures that are at about the same depth as they are. Some fish, such as tarpon, will rise for a fly, but many are not interested in a fly that is below them or on the bottom. The exceptions are bottom and near-bottom feeders such as bonefish, permit, fluke and flounder, and sometimes striped bass.

Often a fish will follow your fly but not take it. This usually means you're doing something wrong from the fish's point of view. Changing the speed of retrieve, or giving your lure a jerky movement, might induce a strike. Many anglers believes that the worse thing you could do, under these conditions, is to stop the lure; however, I've had some spectacular strikes on flies that I left almost motionless in the water. There are no absolutes in fishing—so experiment.

The behavior of birds, sometimes even a single one, can be an excellent indicator of the presence of fish or bait. Some anglers disagree, how-

Fig. 10-9 Sometimes even a single bird can show the location of fish.

ever, about what birds may be forecasting. For example, some gulls are thought to be relatively lazy and therefore are not reliable fish indicators the way that terns are; terns will dive into the water if bait is available, whereas gulls tend to cruise, looking for a floating meal. Nevertheless, when birds swoop down and flutter near the surface, it's usually a good sign that fish are close and are ready to feed, or are feeding. Of course, the best indication of all is to see fish breaking below the birds. As you move close to the birds, you will eventually start to influence their behavior and they will move away from you unless they are really hungry and a lot of food is available. (If you hook a bird, covering it with a cloth or towel will quiet it down and prevent it from pecking you as you either remove the hook or cut it free.)

Fishing from a Boat

One of the challenges when you're fishing from a boat and you find breaking fish in nearshore waters is to quickly get in position for a good cast. First, consider the forward momentum of the boat once you turn off the engine. If you cast in the direction the boat is moving, you'll probably run over your lure or line before you even get a chance to start your retrieve.

Also consider the wind direction. It's always best to have the wind at your back, blowing toward your noncasting shoulder. Finally, you must factor in how or if the fish are moving. When you're fly-fishing, you might trail some line behind the boat as you approach the fish. That way, you can use the boat's motion to help you load your rod.

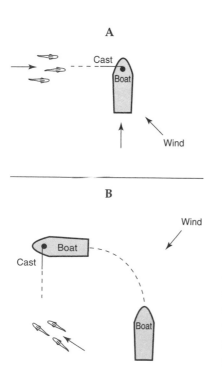

Fig. 10-10 The top drawing (A) shows a good position for a right-handed caster when approaching a school of fish. The cast can be made ahead of the moving fish, and the wind and boat motion should not cause a problem. Sometimes things don't quite work out (B), and a quick turn is needed, to the left in this case. Even so, the wind might still be a problem for our caster, but the boat drift should be okay.

You want to get to the fish quickly, but you also want to avoid spooking them, so the faster you shut off the boat's engine, the better. Try to get ahead of the fish so they're moving toward you. If your boat is drifting, cast toward the stern or amidships and let your lure move with the current—this is the way that a fish would expect to see bait moving.

I like to get ahead of the fish, though sometimes that's not possible. If I have factored in the wind and the boat's momentum correctly, I should be able to cast out at a right angle from the boat to the fish. The boat's momentum will help me keep a tight line. Sometimes, this doesn't work out, and I have to quickly turn the boat to get into a good casting position. If I have to keep my engine running when I chase fish, I try to keep it running at the same rpm. I believe that a quick change in propeller frequency will cause a sound change that can spook fish. I'm not aware of any scientific data supporting this approach—it just makes sense to me.

NEARSHORE RIPS

The term "rip" is used rather loosely by anglers and marine scientists. A rip can be defined as an area that has a faster current and is more turbulent than water in its vicinity. Rips come in a variety of sizes and intensities, ranging from a few feet wide and a hundred or so feet long to those

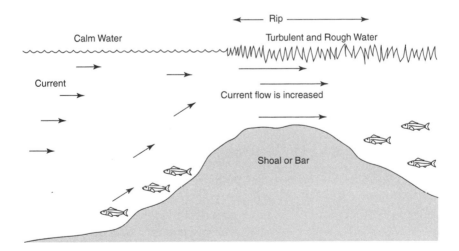

Fig. 10-11 Simple example of how a rip is formed by a current flowing over a shallow area, which constricts its flow and thus increases its speed and creates turbulence. Note how the shallow structure forces some of the water to rise up in front of the rip. Fish often stay away from the strongest part of the current, and often the bigger fish stay in the deeper water.

covering an area of several square miles or more. Every rip tends to have its own distinct character. As most are caused by tidal currents they will flow and ebb or change direction and intensity as the tidal currents change. Likewise, spring tides will produce stronger rips, and neap tides relatively weaker rips.

There are many philosophies about how to fish a rip. The key, I believe, is to both anticipate where the fish are holding and to understand how the water is flowing. In some rips I fish, the water is either flowing directly onto or off the shallow bottom (essentially at a right angle). In these types of rips, the fish tend to stay either in the smooth water, upcurrent of the rip, or within the first wave or so of the turbulent part of the rip. Some fish hold in quiet waters downstream of the current waiting for a meal to be carried to them in the current. Here, drifting a fly into the rip and toward the fish is a good strategy. (Most fish prefer to stay out of the strong flow of a current and will use any type of structure to shield themselves from the faster moving water; in doing so, they conserve energy.)

If you're fishing a rip from a boat, you can anchor upcurrent or use your motor to keep ahead of the current. The latter technique often requires one person to work the boat while another fishes. When you're positioning your boat with the motor, try drifting with the current and then powering forward or to the side of the rip. (You also could just continuously power along off the edge of the rip and troll your lure.) When drifting, your line is at the mercy of the current and you might have to make some fast retrieves. Also, if you're not careful in how you maneuver your boat, the current can suck your boat into the rip.

Fly fishing around a rip often is easier if you anchor the boat, as you'll have better control of your fly line;

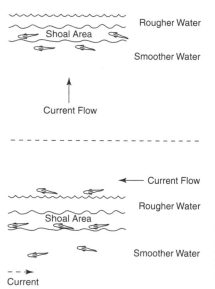

Fig. 10-12 An overhead view of two common types of rips. *Top:* The current flow is at right angles to the shallow bottom. The water in front of the rip is usually relatively calm. *Bottom:* Either two currents flow parallel to each other (example shown) or one flows just parallel to a shallow area. The area of slower or no current will be the calmer side.

however, you'll lose the advantage of drifting along with the current and thereby covering more water.

Some rips are more the result of a current flowing along or essentially parallel, rather than at a right angle, to the shallow bottom. (Usually either a parallel or a right-angle flow prevails.) In parallel-flowing types of rips, the fish seem to hold along the front of the rip, although they sometimes stay deeper than they do in a right-angle flow. Wading fishermen should let their lure drift with the current. Strikes—often hard strikes—usually come as your line tightens and the fly starts moving up toward the surface. If you're in a boat working this type of rip, it can get a little tricky because you have to maintain your position in the moving current as well as stay in front of the rip. Don't sit right on top of the rip or in the first wave or two, you'll probably be on top of the fish, spooking them. Wading fishermen should stay out of a rip completely.

Often, fish will hold in a rip only at a specific part of a specific tide. One approach that works well for me is to determine where the water that forms the rip is coming from. For example, water draining from an estuary will be carrying bait, and will bring good fishing. On the other hand, if the water is coming from a stretch of barren, relatively unproductive coast, I assume it will not hold much bait and will not attract many fish. This simple approach has led me to a lot of good fishing. There will usually be a considerable difference in water depth on one side of a rip; fishing is usually better when the current is flowing from the shallow area toward the deeper end.

Some spots along a rip seem to be more productive than others. This may be due to changes in water depth, or subtle changes in structure or current. I often find that small breaks in the trend of the rip, or where the rip bends or forms a small pocket, are good places to fish. I also like to fish the ends of a rip—this is where I would hang out if I were a hungry fish.

Although most fish avoid the turbulent part of a rip, they sometimes hold at some depth below turbulent areas. (Remember, big fish often stay in deeper parts of the water column.) If you find a good fishing spot along a rip, enter its location into your GPS unit. Such spots will produce fish not only in the near term, but also years later under similar conditions.

PROTECTED OR LOW-ENERGY AREAS

Waves as they approach a shore are usually refracted, and this can cause some areas to have relatively small waves. This often happens where the coast has a concave shape or indentation forming a bay, cove, pocket, bowl, or similar feature. The presence of offshore bars can also absorb some of the energy of the incoming waves, making that coastline fairly quiet. Fish often feed or stay in these low-energy environments. Even though the wave action may be minimal in these protected areas, the modest waves and the tidal currents can provide enough water motion to attract large fish.

Coves or bays may have similar bottom features as other parts of a beach, with bars, troughs, channels, and the like. Bowls are often found between cusps, a pattern that might continue along the entire length of a beach. Some coves can be almost completely sheltered from waves and have a small or restricted connection with the ocean. Aside from not having freshwater input, such a cove or bay is essentially like an estuary. Fishing conditions on a quiet beach, a cove, or a bay are usually best with a rising tide, which often brings in bait.

FISHING ROCKY COASTLINES

A substantial portion of the world's coastlines are rocky. This is usually a harsh environment with breaking waves and strong currents, and can be a dangerous place in which to fish—the rocks may be treacherous, especially if covered with slippery algae. Nevertheless, many fish hang around rocky structure.

When you fish by rocks, it's important that you get your lure within inches of the structure. Some anglers even cast onto the rock, if it is exposed, and slowly pull the lure into the water. Another technique is to put your lure in front of a rock just as a wave is approaching, so that the wave will carry the lure up on the rock. After the wave passes, your fly or lure will flow back with the withdrawing water and tumble about like a confused baitfish. Fishing between rocks, in their crevices, or near bottom can also be effective tactics. Crevices or gaps between rocks are pathways for fast-flowing water and thus trap and confuse bait. Big fish hide and wait behind these rocks and other structure.

Cliffs or Ledges

Fishing from a cliff or ledge is a popular sport for adventurous anglers, particularly along the rocky coasts of Maine or Oregon. You have to be careful not to get too close to the breaking waves and always have some way of escaping if bigger waves start to come in. Likewise, look out for slippery rocks. Cliff fishing is something you should do with a buddy, and preferably not at night.

From a cliff, you'll be looking almost straight down into the water;

often you can see the fish. The water may be turbulent, but some fish seem content feeding there. One benefit of fishing from a cliff is that it's pretty hard to spook a fish living in such turbulent waters.

You don't need the prefect lure when fishing in the turbulent waters off a cliff or ledge, as the fish will not get much of a chance to examine it. Whatever you use, however, should exhibit some motion. Your lure will be tossed about by the surging water, although it's best to get it in the outflowing or seaward surge of waves. If you cast into a channel just as the water is moving out, the backwash will often carry your lure into relatively quiet water where fish may be holding. If you catch a fish from a cliff, you might have a problem landing it. For safety's sake, try to get the fish to a relatively protected area away from the direct approach of the waves.

You can fish rocky areas or cliffs from their seaward side if you have a moderate-size boat. This type of fishing, also called white-water fishing, can be a little hairy and dangerous, but can also produce some very nice fish. Don't do this alone, unless you're a competent boatsman. You'll need to get within casting distance of the rocks or cliffs, which can be dangerous if there are strong incoming waves and/or wind. Closely watch the incoming swell, in case an unexpected large wave comes up behind you. Once you hook a fish, get away from the rocks as quickly as possible.

Put your fly—flies usually work better than lures in white-water fishing—on the face of the rocks or the cliff and then let the surge of a falling wave carry it back to the ocean. Ideally, you want your fly to reach its location just as the water is starting to withdraw off the rocks. It's important to retrieve fast enough to keep control of your line, as a fish's strike may be subtle compared to the other forces acting on your offering. Fish both the upcurrent and downcurrent parts of a rocky area.

Fish any open areas or pockets between rocks, which act as channels in which water and bait are carried to deeper holes. Submerged rocks and ledges can also be holding places for big fish. One of the interesting things about fishing among the rocks is that you never know what species you might catch.

Jetties

Because they interfere with the incoming waves, jetties often cause the waves to break, so you will often find turbulent water on a jetty's seaward-facing side. Strong waves and longshore currents can sometimes cause small rips to form at the end of the jetty. The water moves along the beach and is interrupted by the jetty and starts to flow along its windward side

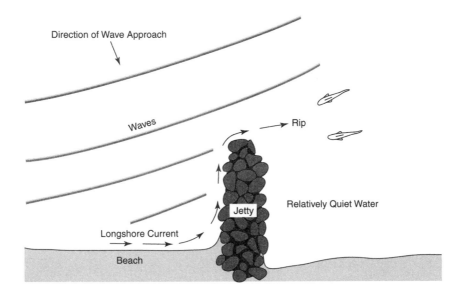

Fig. 10-13 The presence of a jetty and strong waves coming in at an angle can, along with the longshore current, form a small rip off the end of the jetty. Fish may well be at the end of the rip, along its edges, in the quiet water on the leeward side of the jetty, as well as any place along the jetty.

to the end of the jetty. Fish may wait for the bait being carried by this current near the end of the jetty, in the rip, or even on the leeward side of the jetty.

If there are two jetties (say, at an inlet), usually the downcurrent side will be the best one from which to fish because the current should push the bait and the predators toward that jetty. If there is only one jetty, the side facing the current often is best for fishing.

NIGHT FISHING

Nighttime is often when beach and surf-zone fishing is most productive, most challenging, most dangerous—and most enjoyable. Big fish come closer to shore to feed at night. These fish won't be able to examine your fly too clearly, which can improve your chances of hooking up. Another advantage of nighttime fishing is that a beach that may be crowded during the day will usually be deserted at night. If you cannot fish at night, the early morning or around dusk are good, too.

From the fish's point of view, it may be easier to feed at night. Many of the tricks and camouflage techniques that baitfish use to elude predators do not work at night. Furthermore, food such as crabs and worms

Bioluminescence

You may encounter a strange phenomenon when you're fishing at night along a beach or even offshore—bioluminescence, or what some anglers call "fire in the water." Bioluminescence is caused by floating phytoplankton, or other small creatures that emit an eerie patch or flash of light when disturbed. The effect is especially noticeable on very dark nights, but whether it limits fishing or not is debatable. It certainly will make the fishing different—your line and fly will appear to be illuminated, which is not exactly something a fish might expect. Many anglers I know call it quits when there is intense bioluminescence in the water, although good fishing may still occur—especially when the moon is bright, which may reduce the bioluminescence impact. Little is known about how bioluminescence affects fishing. The bioluminescence around your lure might make it more attractive (certainly more visible) to fish; for instance, live bait often cause bioluminescence flashes. You might try reducing the speed of your retrieve during periods of bioluminescence—in doing so, you'll probably disturb the bioluminescence-producing creatures less.

will come out of hiding and move about at night. Another advantage for a predator is that the water temperature is usually lower at night, a condition that many fish find favorable because they will expend less energy while feeding in cooler water. Finally, many nocturnal predators have good night vision and can capitalize on the reduced level of protection that the baitfish have.

Always carry a flashlight (and spare batteries) when you're fishing at night. I use a small Mini Maglite flashlight and keep it on a string around my neck. You'll find yourself using your flashlight to find bait; change flies; tie knots; release hooks from fish, fingers, or other places; fix line foul-ups; signal your partners; and to light your way back to your car. Fish can be spooked by flashes of light, so don't shine your light in the water in the area you're fishing.

Scout out an area during the day before you fish it at night. Never forget how a changing tide alters the appearance of the coastline and hides or exposes structure and key locations around a beach. Many anglers use darker flies and lures at night because they make a better silhouette against the sky than bright flies do. Vibrating lures often are effective at night, although poppers generally do not work well.

One limitation of night-fishing is that you probably won't see the fish strike. Fish also strike more gently at night than they do in the daytime, which means you should be especially attentive when retrieving your fly or lure.

At night, you have to manage your gear with considerable care to make good casts and prevent your line and flies or lures from fouling. You'll have to use more of your senses at night: sounds will seem different and distances can confuse; your hearing and even your sense of smell will compensate for your reduced vision. Ocean fishing is always a challenge—doing it at night just makes it more interesting.

Chapter 11

Fishing Offshore Waters

When you're buying real estate, the rule is "location, location, location"; for offshore fishing, the appropriate phrase is "structure, structure, structure." This can be a depression, a slope, or a topographic high in the ocean bottom, or a feature such as the thermocline, a tidal rip, a front, or other irregularities in the water. Structure can also be formed by man-made objects such as drilling platforms, wrecks, or reefs formed by materials dumped on the seafloor. You can often find bottom structure by locating surface rips or by following nautical charts that show bottom irregularities; or you can learn the location of warm- or cold-water spots, eddies, or temperature breaks via satellite temperature services. It's hard to quantify fish distribution in the ocean, but many offshore fishermen believe that areas where the bottom is flat (with no structure) and no over- lying water irregularities are essentially deserts for fish, whereas areas of structure are oases. Basically, you should look for an area of change—a change in the bottom character or slope, a change in water characteristics, a change in the color of the water, a change in temperature, any change.

Offshore fishing is always chancy, so it's helpful to seek out any infor- mation that might tip the odds in your favor. Many offshore anglers keep in close contact with other fishermen to share information about water temperature, birds working over the surface, recent catches, or fish sight- ings. Anglers who keep fishing records often note that fish appear in cer- tain areas at relatively similar times over the course of many years. This does not necessarily mean the same fish are returning year after year, although some tagged fish have been recovered in areas in which they were tagged a year or two earlier. Why these fish reappear is unclear, but obviously something about the area, perhaps a source of food or shelter, is bringing them back. Sometimes the fish return not just to a general area, but to a specific part of the area or structure. Such behavior is especially noticeable over large features such as submarine canyons or major shoals or rips; it also can occur in the nearshore region along certain parts of a beach or estuary. Whatever the reason for the behavior of these fish, it's a persuasive argument for keeping good records about fish sightings and catches. Your records should also include weather, water temperature, the presence of birds and bait, and any other relevant data that might help you recognize a fishing pattern.

Of course, there are certain locations, times, and conditions when offshore fish are nowhere to be found, even though the conditions might look good to you. Note these experiences in your records, too. Experienced offshore anglers, for example, often believe that the days around the full moon are not a good time to fish. They reason that offshore fish such as marlin and bluefin tuna feed mainly during the day and therefore may also feed under the bright light of the full moon. As a result, the theory goes, these fish will not feed the day following a full moon. I get a similar impression when fishing for striped bass in the early morning after a full moon.

OFFSHORE NAVIGATION
Often, you'll have to travel considerable distances to reach good offshore fishing areas, which is most safely accomplished in seaworthy boats of 24 feet or more. (Offshore fish do come close to shore and sometimes can be caught from smaller boats in nearshore waters.) Off the coast of New England, you may have to travel 40 miles or so to find big offshore fish, whereas off the eastern coast of Florida a trip of 10 miles or so can get you to offshore fish feeding at the edge of the Gulf Stream.

When you're headed offshore, you need appropriate nautical charts, a working echo sounder/fish finder, radar, and navigational aids such as Loran or GPS, or both. A radio is essential in case of emergencies; you'll also use it to communicate with other boats about the location of fish, and to keep track of the weather. Other valuable devices are a cellular phone and an EPIRB (emergency positioning indication radio beacon), which transmits a satellite signal that gives your position to rescuers should you have an emergency. It's also a good idea to file a float plan before you go, and to share it with others.

A relatively new gadget that can be useful to offshore anglers is underwater video. With this device you can watch and record the action of the lures you are trolling, see the strike and possibly some of the fight once you hook up, observe the fish as it is brought to the boat, and finally watch it being released. Some models of these underwater televisions, which start at a little less than $1,000, work in low-light levels and therefore give you a view into dirty or murky water; more expensive models have lights so you can record at night. These devices are portable and can be used in shallow water to explore around bridges, docks, and jetties.

Vision of Offshore Fish

Offshore fish are usually color-limited or even color-blind. Most have what is called monochromatic vision, which means that they only see one color, which usually is blue. (Monochromatic light is similar to the image shown on a black-and-white television screen.) A few offshore fish, such as albacore and mahi-mahi, can also detect green. Recent research by Australian scientists indicate that marlin may be able to detect some colors when they look up toward the surface. The lack of color vision among offshore fish is not really a serious handicap, as blue is clearly the most common color in the open ocean, followed to a lesser degree by green. Even if an open-ocean fish could detect more or all colors it would have little opportunity to use such an ability.

The fact that tuna and billfish are not able to distinguish the colors red or yellow is somewhat surprising since one of their main foods is squid, which often turn red when agitated. Likewise, many supposedly successful tuna lures are red. A fish with monochromatic vision, however, can still see a red squid. The squid's contrast with the color of the surrounding water would give it away. Likewise squid's size, shape, and type of motion would be clues to a fish with monochromatic vision. On the other hand, if the squid were at a depth of 30 to 40 feet or more and the fish was looking down at it, the squid would appear black against the dark blue background and would be difficult to see. So red lures or flies still can work, though at a few fathoms depth there will be very little color difference between a red, orange, yellow, or pink lure or fly and the dark background. If the fish is looking up, the lure or fly will contrast against the bright surface of the ocean; the fish will see the lure or fly as a dark object against a bright background. In fact, monochromatic vision may make the lure or fly stand out even more—at least that is what the scientific research indicates.

Most game fish have very good eyesight and usually use their vision for the actual attack on a prey, bait, fly, or a lure regardless of how they were originally attracted to it. Although vision is important in feeding for many species, other senses may be initially more critical in various parts of the feeding process. For

(continued)

VISION OF OFFSHORE FISH (continued)

example, the senses of hearing or smell may indicate prey before the fish actually sees it. Regardless of how a fish finds its meal, some movement of the prey is usually necessary to trigger or provoke the final attack. Therefore, motion may even be more important than color in some instances, since most predatory fish are very curious and will examine anything that crosses through their fields of vision. Indeed, scientific studies in aquariums have often shown that predatory fish get agitated and excited by movement. Fish in offshore waters seem to prefer fast-moving lures or flies, such as those trolled at speeds of 6 knots or more.

OFFSHORE FLY FISHING

Fly fishing for sailfish, marlin, or tuna has in recent years become fairly common. One way to fish is by trolling a hookless teaser of some sort, either bait or a lure, behind the boat. Once a fish finds the teaser, it is "teased" to within casting range of the boat. As the fish gets closer to the boat, the boat captain takes the engine out of gear, the teaser is pulled completely out of the water, and the fly fisher makes a short cast to the excited fish. If everything goes right, the fish will take the fly and the reel will start to sing. Hooking one of these big-game fish is not as hard as it may sound. The really difficult part is done by the teaser and the person running the boat. Landing the fish is another matter. Trey Combs, in his excellent book *Bluewater Fly Fishing,* devotes an entire chapter to teasing procedures. In the time since this technique was developed in the early 1960s, almost all varieties of billfish, marlin, and tuna have been caught on flies in the Atlantic and Pacific Oceans. Teasing is probably the only practical way to catch these fish, except for the very rare opportunity when you find them feeding on the surface and can get close enough to reach them with a fly.

Many of the fish that you might catch in offshore waters are superb fighters. Tuna, for example, can swim faster than 40 mph; a run at that speed will strip about 300 yards of backing off your fly reel in 15 seconds. These fish usually will not jump, but they are amazingly strong. In deep water, tuna will often dive straight down, so getting them up to the boat requires muscle and strong equipment.

The sport of bluewater or offshore fly fishing may have entered a new phase in the early 1990s when a group of experienced fly fishers went on a week-long charter from San Diego. The trip, organized by Steve Abel, was aboard the *Royal Polaris,* a luxurious 113-foot sport-fishing boat fitted out with the latest electronic equipment and carrying three skiffs. Launching the skiffs, anglers could fish away from the big boat and have better maneuverability when fighting fish. The charter probably was the first long-range fly-fishing trip; the group traveled about 1,500 miles. One of the chief reasons for the trip was to test new tackle against some hard-running fish such as tuna. Judging from several magazine articles, the trip was very successful: Close to 400 tuna and numerous wahoo, dorado, and other fish were caught, three of which were pending world records. Chumming, working around structure and temperature zones, and using fish-finding electronics were the principal methods used to find fish. Much of the fishing was done over a series of banks about 400 miles south of San Diego. Interestingly, most fish preferred relatively small and sometimes sparsely tied flies. Subsequent fly-fishing trips from San Diego were even more successful. One trip yielded 11 pending International Game Fish Association (IGFA) world records for wahoo and skipjack tuna.

As exciting as these trips may have been, most offshore fly fishing is done in combination with conventional rod-and-reel techniques. As the interest in offshore fly fishing grows, however, I expect that exclusive fly-fishing charters and expeditions will become more popular.

Tackle
Offshore fly fishing requires sturdy rods, reels with dependable drags and considerable line capacity (300 yards of fly line and backing, at a minimum), and well-tied and shock-absorbing leaders. Flies are important, of course, but without a solid rod, reel, and leader system, you will not land big offshore fish. You'll want a 12- or 14-weight rod handy, rigged with the appropriate line and leader, should billfish or tuna appear. Keeping several fly rods rigged as you're fishing is a good idea, as you may encounter several different offshore species in the course of a trip and there will be little time to change gear—in the heat of the moment, you won't be able to instantly attach a wire leader for sharks, wahoo, or barracuda, or a fluorocarbon leader for tuna, bonito, or false albacore.

Leaders are especially important in fly fishing: they must absorb the shock of the strike, which can be awesome with some species, and the pulls as the fish jumps, twists, or runs. The leader must also resist abrasion from the fish's teeth, scales, or its bill (in the case of billfish). If you're interested in catching record fish, your leader system must conform to IGFA require-

Offshore Tides and Currents

Tides in the open ocean (where they are not restricted by land) are often less of a factor for fishing than tides in nearshore or estuary waters. In general, offshore tides follow a circular or rotary pattern, completing one loop within one tidal period, with the direction of the current moving in a clockwise manner in the Northern Hemisphere. The tidal currents that flow in this rotary pattern do not have a period of slack tide.

Since the offshore tidal currents are not restricted by surrounding land or by a shoaling bottom they generally have less strength than the tidal currents closer to land. The offshore tidal current will vary, usually having two minimums and two maximums over a tidal period. These currents also have a periodic variation similar to that of nearshore tides, being stronger during full and new moons and less during quarter moons.

Offshore tidal currents can be important for fishing in several ways. One is by forming rips. This happens when the tidal current flows over a shoal area, and the reduction in the flow area by the shoal causes an increase in the speed of the current and often a tidal rip. Tidal currents can also cause upwelling. This process often depends on some struc-

ments. If you're fishing for fun, you can use a shock tippet of as much as 100-pound test (or wire, for toothy fish) when you're fishing for strong and large bluewater fish; use fluorocarbon leaders for tuna and similar species that have good eyesight. You may get only one or two casts to a fish, so proper preparation is crucial. Serious offshore fly fishers often rehearse the procedures of teasing, hooking, playing, and releasing a fish with the captain and crew of the offshore fishing vessel before they set out to fish.

Often, it's crucial when fly-fishing in offshore waters to get your fly deep. Rapid-sinking fly lines and heavy flies will certainly help in this regard. Some fly fishers use LLC-13, a lead-core vinyl-coated line made by The Cortland Line Company, cut to appropriate lengths. This line weighs 13 grains per foot, so specific lengths can be used for various weight rods or to get deep in various current speeds. The combination of

ture or bump on the seafloor that interferes with the flowing current and deflects deeper colder water toward the surface (see Figure 5-5).

Currents, almost always, are an important factor in determining where fish will feed. Most fish often stay on the edge of the current, or near the bottom or behind some obstructions where the current velocity is less and thus less energy is needed to maintain their position. From these spots a predator can quickly dart out and grab a meal as it drifts or swims by.

Since many offshore currents are driven by the tides, they will have peaks in their velocity, both within the daily tidal cycle as well as over a 28-day period. Usually there are certain times during the tidal period or certain directions of flow that produce better than other times. Keeping good records of fish catch and failures related to currents and other factors such as weather, tide strength, and so forth, can help you to determine the best times to fish.

Currents in offshore waters can also form boundaries between waters of varying physical characteristics, especially temperature differences. Fish may be restricted by these boundaries as well as be attracted to their edges. Most boundaries caused by currents are usually visible, but sometimes they can only be detected by changes in water temperature or salinity.

a lead-core shooting head and monofilament running line is an especially effective setup for getting deep. With this line rigging, you can work a fly at depths of 50 to 100 feet. Sinking fly lines are also available, including some that are much easier to cast than lead core. Even with heavy lines and weighted flies, it still might be difficult to get deep when you're fishing in a strong current, such as in an inlet or over a rip. If you're drifting in a current, you can get your fly deep by casting downcurrent and then letting out line as the boat drifts with the current. When the fly line tightens, you can start your retrieve.

There's considerable potential in offshore fly fishing for innovation and experimentation. Up till now, most offshore fly-fishing techniques have been derived from conventional-fishing techniques. This may change as anglers test new methods to find and attract the exciting fish that inhabit offshore waters.

TROLLING

Trolling is a common and effective way to find and catch a variety of fish in offshore waters. In most cases, anglers put out numerous lines, usually in a specific pattern at defined depths and distances behind the boat. The trolling setup often includes a combination of plastic or wooden lures, several on one line, as well as live or dead bait rigged on hooks. Often the last lure in the group, the only lure with a hook in a string of lures, will be different in color or size than the others. This is to make it stand out and to create the impression that it is chasing the other baits, either of which might provoke an attack by a predator. Many captains feel that even if just one lure is catching fish, that nothing should be changed, since it is the total pattern that is attracting the fish, who then for whatever reason find a favorite to bite on.

The position, type, and pattern of the lures relative to the boat's wake serve to attract fish and prompt them to bite. Fish in the open ocean could avoid a boat if they wanted to—indeed, fish probably hear the noise from a large boat many miles away—but it seems clear that the boat and its engine may actually attract fish. In the sport of billfishing, some boats seem to always do better than others. Rather than this being a matter of luck, maybe the sound of that boat's engine, or its propellers, attract the fish. Likewise, maybe the noise emitted by the unproductive boats keeps fish at a distance. It's possible that when offshore fish hear a sportfishing boat's engine, they may associate the noise with that of a dragger or net-

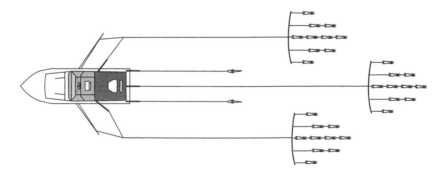

Fig. 11-1 A typical trolling pattern for tuna. Many variations are possible. This pattern comes from Capt. Al Anderson's 1990 book, *To Catch a Tuna*. Multiple lures, such as a squid daisy chain or rigger baitfish, can be trolled. Throwing a fly into this pattern could be a disaster, but the goal of such a pattern is to first find and attract fish. Generally, when a fish is hooked on one line, the other lines are quickly retrieved. After the other lines are out of the water, or better still, when the fish is released, it may be possible to cast a fly at any remaining fish.

fishing boat and anticipate an easy meal from material dredged up off the bottom or from the catch.

Many trollers work their lures in a zigzag pattern rather than in a straight line. By moving at an angle, especially along the coastline, you can fish over changing depths. Trolling in different directions is also a good idea. In other words, you troll against the waves, with the waves, and at angles to the sea. You also should change the trolling speed, which usually ranges from 4 to 8 knots or so, every now and then. This will vary the depths at which the lures run, and will place the lures at different angles to the current or to light from the sun. (Some offshore anglers, especially those going after marlin, troll at speeds of 10 knots or more.) The length of the trolled line will influence the depth at which the lure runs, too.

Many offshore fly-fishing techniques depend, in large part, on conventional trolling procedures. Once fish are found or hooked then you can throw a fly at them. This approach often works since many times more than one fish is either attracted to the trolled lure or will follow a hooked-up fish trying to get some of its meal. Lou Tabory in his 1992 book, *Inshore Fly Fishing*, suggests trolling a fly between two trolled lures; the fly should be closer to the boat than the lures. Once fish are found quickly get the fly farther out to the following fish and away from any hooked fish, if possible. The technique requires close cooperation and teamwork between the person running the boat and the angler. If you hook one on a fly, you may have to break off the fish hooked on the conventional trolling line. This is done not just to prevent a foul-up, but because you may have to chase after the fish on the fly rod.

Trolling Equipment
Offshore trollers sometimes use special equipment such as outriders or outriggers, which are long poles that extend out and away from both sides of the boat, to spread out the trolling pattern. Downriggers, heavy weights attached to strong line or cable, are used to get lures down to depths of 100 feet or more. Another way of getting a lure deep is by using a planer, a device attached to your fishing line that pushes the line downward in the water.

To troll successfully, you need a fish finder or depth sounder, preferably one that displays the water temperature. You can use these electronic devices to find structure and wrecks, as well as to detect fish or bait in the water column or near the bottom. This information will indicate the depth at which to place your lures.

Fly fishers who troll generally use sinking lines and heavy flies. Some anglers say that this is not really fly fishing, and IGFA rules state that any

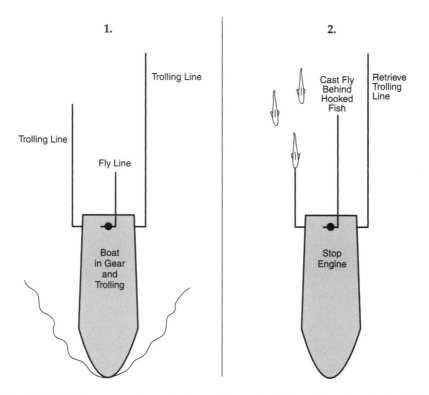

1.

Trolling Line

Trolling Line

Fly Line

Boat
in Gear
and
Trolling

2.

Cast Fly
Behind
Hooked
Fish

Retrieve
Trolling
Line

Stop
Engine

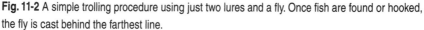

Fig. 11-2 A simple trolling procedure using just two lures and a fly. Once fish are found or hooked, the fly is cast behind the farthest line.

fish caught in this manner do not qualify for world-record consideration, if the boat's engine is engaged when the hookup occurs. On the other hand, catching a fish by trolling a fly can be fun and allows you to test your gear and knots and to develop your fish-fighting skills against big and powerful fish. There is enough room in the ocean for both viewpoints.

CHUMMING

Chumming is a common technique used by offshore fishermen to attract a wide variety of fish. It works because most fish have a superb sense of smell and often enthusiastically respond to what promises to be a free meal.

A few rules apply to chumming. First, always keep the chum flowing, even when you're hooked up to a fish. Second, whether you're anchored or drifting, pick your position very carefully so that the chum reaches the fish in that area. Obviously, you need moving water to be able to chum; you should position your boat in the upstream portion of the current. The strength of the current, as well as the weight of the pieces of chum, will determine the angle at which the chum sinks. For example, in a strong current the chum will drift farther before reaching a specific depth. The geometry of chumming gets more complex when you're drifting and/or when the wind is strong.

Chum can range from live bait, ground-up material, frozen blocks of fish parts (suspended overboard in a mesh or chain bag), to chunks of fish, clams, or other fish-attracting material. Chum can also be mixtures of macaroni, corn kernels, oatmeal, bread, or other food scraps. Pet food, especially canned cat food (which often has fish by-products) can work well, too. Just punch a few holes in the can and hang it over the side of your boat. Another trick is to mix menhaden oil (or other types of fish oil) with your chum material. This is a good way to prepare dried dog food that you're using as chum. Fresh chum will usually be most productive. Because fish have an acute sense of smell, many species will not find the scent of rotten or spoiled material attractive and generally avoid such dreck.

When fishing for bottom-living species, some chum fishermen use weighted containers or pumps to get the chum closer to the bottom. One trick is to mix the chum with sand to make it sink.

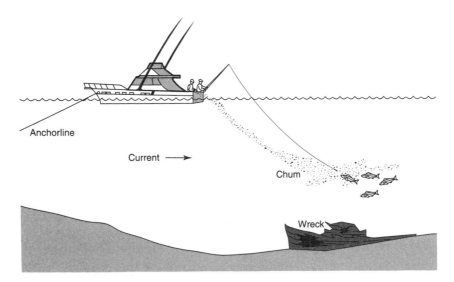

Fig. 11-3 Chum fishing over a wreck (or bottom structure or current). In this instance the boat is anchored upcurrent of the wreck and a continuous line of chum is being used to attract the fish. A fly similar in appearance to pieces of chum is drifted along with the chum.

The rate at which you chum is important: too little or too slow and the fish may lose interest and move away; too fast or too much and you may quickly fill up the available fish. Experienced chummers say that it takes about ten to fifteen minutes after the release of chum before the fish start showing. (The sound of fish feeding can also attract other fish.)

You can easily fly fish in a chum trail. Most fly fishers use a fly that resembles the chum material and sinks at the same rate. (Some tinsel is probably a good idea, it simulates the skin of a fish. To get the fly to the appropriate depth it often must be weighted, lead wire can be used and added as appropriate.) For the best results, you should let the fly drift out with the chum without any tension in the line; if you put tension on the line, the current will cause the fly to rise out of the chum trail. Alternately, you can cast into and around the chum line hoping to hook up any fish that might be hanging around.

Sometimes you can let someone else do the chumming for you. For example, you can follow a lobster or fish-trap boat as the crew pulls and rebaits their traps. Their work often stirs up the bottom, attracting baitfish and thus predators. Another approach is to hang around dragger boats, which stir up the bottom with their nets and then toss the by-catch from the nets overboard. In the Gulf of Mexico, many fly fishers hang around shrimp trawlers, casting to the jack crevalle and other species feeding on material discarded by the trawler crew.

Fly fishers often use chum to attract sharks. Blue sharks, which can range from 10- to 12-feet and weigh several hundred pounds, are a species commonly targeted by fly fishers. Blues and other species of sharks make fast, strong, and long runs. Things can get exciting and dangerous when several sharks come up to a chum slick. Often, a feeding frenzy may begin and one shark may take a bite out of another. Freeing a hook from a shark or bringing it into the boat is for experienced shark anglers only. I've seen pictures in which an angler was holding a shark by the tail when it bent around and bit him on the foot. Most anglers just cut the leader once they get the shark up to the boat.

FISHING OFFSHORE RIPS

A rip is the result of water either flowing into an area where the bottom shoals or where two different bodies of water come into contact with each other. In either case they are usually visible surface features and often attract many boats, as well as fish. The rips may form a line or several lines of choppy water that, in some instances, can extend for miles. The intensity of the chop is determined by the tidal flow and often either reinforced or decreased by the wind. Offshore rips tend to have more of a steady but less intense flow than nearshore rips. This in large part is

Top View

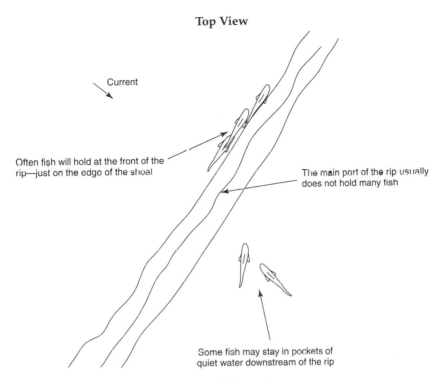

Current

Often fish will hold at the front of the rip—just on the edge of the shoal

The main part of the rip usually does not hold many fish

Some fish may stay in pockets of quiet water downstream of the rip

Fig. 11-4 Some of the places where fish may hold along a rip.

due to the stronger but changing tidal flow common in nearshore waters, offshore waters generally have a continuous but less intense tidal flow.

Rips attract predators because the turbulent water traps bait, often keeping them confused and vulnerable. Often there are pockets or patches of relatively calm water just behind the shoal, where predators may hold, waiting to catch bait. If something appealing is carried by the current a fish may dash out to grab it and then return to its holding place. The fish feeding around fast-moving water have to move quickly and make fast decisions so often they will not be bothered or even have the time to notice heavy leaders. For a fly to work in a rip it must be placed in the right spot; the sinking ability of your line and the positioning of your boat are the keys.

A common trolling technique used by recreational and charter fishermen for fishing rips and deep water is using wire line. The technique can work to catch large stripers, bluefish, salmon, and other species. The concept is simple: the wire line, or extra-fast sinking line, gets your lure or fly down deep to where the big fish are holding and feeding. Some big fish literally have their stomachs on the bottom. In areas where the currents are especially strong, the wire or sinking line will at least get your lure below the rough surface water.

Probably the most common wire-line lure used in New England waters is the parachute jig, a heavy jig (4 ounces or more) with a fiber skirt that extends both fore and aft of the hook. The forward part flows back when trolled in a pulsating motion that mimics a swimming squid. The hook of the jig is usually tipped with a strip of colored pork rind. Jigs are often white, red, or chartreuse; similar colors are used for the pork rind. The tail of the pork rind can be split to make it flutter.

Capt. Ron Murphy, a charter captain who fishes out of Hyannis, Massachusetts, has developed a fly that resembles and behaves like a parachute lure. It is composed of layers of different-colored fibers (usually reds, pinks, and whites) tied around the middle of a long hook. He positions his fly-fishing clients near the edge of a rip, holds his boat's position using his engine, and has his clients drift their flies out into the rip. The method can be very successful.

Anglers work the jig-and-pork-rind combination or the parachute fly by rapidly moving the rod forward every few seconds and then letting the line and jig drop back; with a fly rod, you're better off working the line by hand, rather than moving your rod. However you do it, the parachute jig or fly will puff out when it drops back, looking like a swimming squid.

Trolling Along Rips
Regardless of what kind of trolling line you are using, trolling speed when fishing a rip can be very important to your success. Fish such as bonito and Spanish and king mackerel often prefer lures trolled at speeds up to 7 knots, whereas bluefish and striped bass are more responsive to lures trolled considerably slower. Sometimes a change in speed of just 25 to 50 rpms on your engine can make a major difference in hookup rates. Likewise, you might want to adjust your speed depending on whether you are trolling with or against the current.

Often fish will only strike lures or flies trolled in a certain direction, which makes sense if they are holding on a structure or facing into a current. (Remember, fish almost always will face into a current.) If so, save time and speed up when going in the other direction, rather than troll. I often find fish where there is a bend or curve in the rip, or where there is a break in the rip pattern. Such a break presents an edge or boundary, which often attracts fish.

It usually is best to keep your boat positioned at some angle to the rip. Often, you'll have to experiment to find the best trolling speed. (In my experience, it's easier to go too fast than to go too slow.) When you get

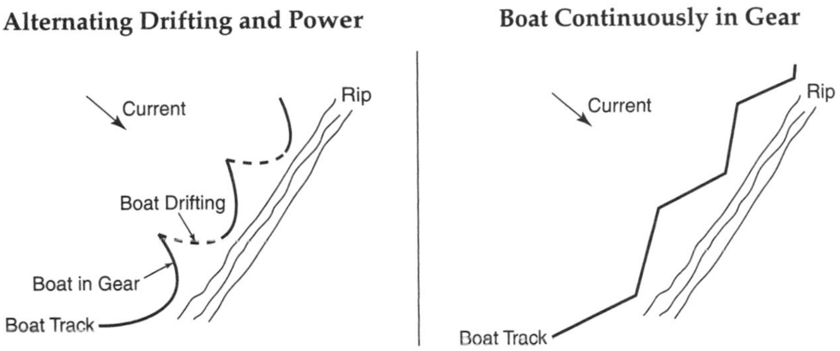

Alternating Drifting and Power

Current

Rip

Boat Drifting

Boat in Gear

Boat Track

Boat Continuously in Gear

Current

Rip

Boat Track

Fig. 11-5 Various ways to position and move your boat in a rip area.

your line sufficiently close to the rip, turn toward the rip, which will make your lure or fly look like bait caught in the main part of the current. Strikes will usually come as your lure or fly gets carried over the top of the rip and underlying shoal. Once in this position, at an angle to the rip about 50 or 100 feet out, try to hold the boat in place by moving forward or dropping back, either keeping the lure or fly in front of the rip or in a quiet area behind the rip. Basically, you want to move your boat along but outside of the rip, keeping your lure on the edge of the rough water over the shoal. (These maneuvers are easier to do when there are few boats in the area.) Keep your boat out of the rip—it can be dangerous and certainly will spook the fish

When a hookup occurs, the best approach is to move away from the rip. If this is difficult to do, just turn off your engine and drift through

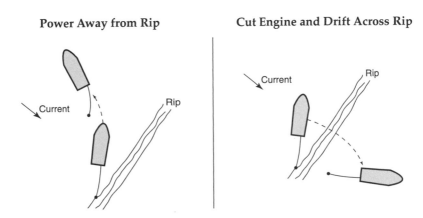

Power Away from Rip

Current

Rip

Cut Engine and Drift Across Rip

Current

Rip

Fig. 11-6 Some ways to position your boat following a hook-up while trolling near a rip.

the rip and fight the fish farther downcurrent. Some charter-boat opera-
tors will stay in gear and maintain their position in front of the rip while
their clients fight the fish. This means pulling the fish in against the current, which may unnecessarily exhaust the angler and the fish.

During periods of strong tidal currents it can be difficult to fish
rips with any technique. This is especially true around spring tides, when
the strong currents will make it very hard to get your fly significantly
down into the water. On such days, you might do better fishing nearer to
the period of slack current, when the current flow is lessened. Another
problem that occurs after high tides or storms is that gunk and seaweed
are washed off the beaches and may accumulate in the rip. When this
happens, trolling is essentially impossible, as your lure will constantly
foul.

There is an etiquette for fishing a rip. Often, boats line up to move
down along a rip line. Part of the etiquette is to maintain sufficient spacing so that your boat and its noisy engine is not sitting over the lines from
another boat. Also, don't troll through the rip. Besides spooking the fish, it
shows others that you just don't know what you are doing. Similarly, it's
poor boatsmanship to go between another boat and the rip, as you may
run over trolling lines from the other boat.

Anchoring Techniques

If you are the only boat in an area, and the water is not too deep, you
might consider anchoring up ahead or upcurrent of the rip and then drift
your fly (on a sinking line) into the rip. Fishing from an anchored or drifting boat sometimes will be more successful than trolling. This is often
so when fishing for fish such as bonito and little tunny; species that are
also found in nearshore waters. These rapidly swimming fish will appear
in one area for a few seconds and then disappear only to show again a
quarter of a mile away, again for a few seconds. Some fishermen, often
to the dismay and annoyance of others, race after these fish hoping to
get one cast into the school before it takes off. A few of these high-speed
maneuvers often result in the entire school taking off and fishing being
ruined for all.

Most success with these elusive fish often will come by staying in the
general area where the fish are feeding. Bonito and little tunny generally
have a pattern to their feeding, moving along the shore or around a rip. If
you position yourself in this pattern you should get numerous chances to
put a fly where they can see it. It is possible that your anchored or drifting boat may even attract these fish. Actually, what may be really happening is that your boat is attracting small baitfish, which in turn are
attracting larger fish.

FISHING WRECKS AND ARTIFICIAL STRUCTURE

Offshore waters can have sparse pickings for fish except around unique areas such as rips and canyons, and over bottom structure. The wrecks of boats, barges, or other similar objects on the seafloor are types of structure that almost always hold fish. The locations of some wrecks are published or listed in fishing magazines, but the whereabouts of the really good ones are closely guarded secrets among fishing guides.

A wreck often provides a solid surface on which organisms attach and grow, becoming the setting for a large marine food chain, starting with microscopic creatures, plankton, barnacles, crabs, baitfish, and many other good things for fish to eat. The wreck structure also provides shelter and an attractive habitat for many species of fish, such as cod, tautog, sea bass, and pollack in cooler waters; and bonito, cobia, permit, amberjacks, jack crevalle, barracudas, sharks, tuna, billfish, and various species of mackerel in warmer waters.

There are many ways to fish a wreck, but first you must find it. For that reason, a Loran or a GPS navigation system and a good echo sounder are a must. Once the wreck is located you can either anchor near it, troll over it, or just drift over the area. Anchoring takes some skill, especially if the water is deep. When trolling, you risk getting your line hung up on the wreck, unless you keep your line well clear of the structure.

If the wreck is not marked by surface buoys, you can make your fishing easier by laying out your own floats or markers, which can range from plastic jugs to more elaborate setups; however, remove whatever you use for a marker when you are finished fishing. Often the downcurrent or downtide part of the wreck will be the area to fish. Sheltered from the current by the wreck, fish expend less energy as they search for food.

You can also use chum to attract fish to the boat. Generally, the best approach is to anchor upcurrent of the wreck and let your chum drift out over the wreck; usually less chum is better than more. Or you can tease the fish to within casting range.

Artificial Reefs

In Chapter 5, I briefly discussed the general character of the seafloor and noted the relatively high amount of boulders and irregularities on the seafloor of the recently glaciated parts of the continental shelf. In the unglaciated areas south of New York City along the Atlantic coast, however, the ocean bottom is fairly smooth. For this reason, many coastal states have developed offshore habitats for fish called artificial reefs. Florida probably has the most—more than 300 have been sunk in the state's waters. New Jersey has spent more than $20 million in recent years to develop artificial reefs at fourteen offshore sites.

Developing artificial reefs is not as straightforward as it may seem. Federal and state rules limiting the disposal of material in offshore waters can impede the creation of an artificial reef. The materials used for artificial reefs range from defunct airplanes, tanks, ships, old drilling platforms, and subway cars, to rocks, tires, logs, branches, and building material (especially concrete). Some people just drop concrete blocks near their dock to attract fish. Whatever is used must be cleansed of any hazardous materials, such as asbestos, PCB, oil, or gasoline. More recently, specially built structures have been developed to provide habitat for offshore fish, sometimes even for specific species. For example, certain prefabricated structures form small habitats for individual octopuses. Controversies have arisen over artificial reefs, due to the extensive fishing that occurs around some of them. The concern is that heavy fishing over the reef could result in an overexploitation of the local fish population.

Why are fish attracted to the reefs? Simply because there is something about the artificial habitat that influences their behavior or creates some favorable environmental aspect, including providing food. Artificial habitats, the same as natural structure, sometimes interfere with currents and produce a small area of upwelling. This upwelling can increase biological productivity, making more food available and thus attracting predators. Artificial habitats can also be suspended in the water column or even placed on the ocean surface. Tuna and various species of jacks, for example, hang around such habitats for periods of time.

Drilling Platforms and Navigation Towers

A surprising number of man-made structures are placed on the continental shelf, and even the upper parts of the continental slope. In the Gulf of Mexico, there are literally thousands of drilling and production platforms. Similar features or navigational platforms or towers can be found offshore of most coastal states. These structures attract fish such as dolphin, wahoo, yellowfin and blackfin tuna, sharks, barracuda, cobia, and various species of mackerel.

One fishing strategy is to first troll in the vicinity of the platform, which may bring dolphin, wahoo, and other big-game species (including marlin) to the surface. Anglers then use chum to keep the fish nearby, so fly fishers and light-tackle anglers can cast to them. Below the surface, these artificial structures are covered with marine life, which attracts a steady supply of baitfish. Because these structures extend to the seafloor, they can supply a considerable source of food—the structure is literally a living reef that spans the entire water column, from the surface to the ocean bottom. Some of these man-made structures are built close to natural seafloor structures such as topographic highs or rock outcrops, around which fish may also hold.

It's been suggested that fish such as tuna and marlin may be attracted to the magnetic fields produced by these metal structures. Such a structure, and its magnetic characteristics, could be used by these fish to navigate when they migrate. True or not, these structures clearly attract fish like magnets. It seems that fish may also be drawn to active drilling platforms, some of which are floating rather than attached to the seafloor. The noise made by the drilling does not seem to spook the fish, but rather may attract them.

OBJECTS IN THE WATER

When you're fishing offshore, never overlook floating objects such as logs, cans, or pieces of plastic. Many species of fish, such as dolphin, yellowtail, and cobia, tend to hang around such objects, apparently using them as some sort of landmark. Fish have little by which they can orient themselves in the relatively featureless open ocean, and a boat or even a buoy will often attract some species. Also, because most fish do not have eyelids, when the sun is strong they may be attracted to shady areas formed by floating debris. Often, a single piece of flotsam will have an accompanying population of fish. Sometimes a long weed or flotsam line may form along the edge of a current—always fish these locations, as bait and larger game fish will hold nearby.

One way that commercial fishermen exploit the behavioral trait of fish to gather around structure is the use of contraptions called fish aggregation devices, or FADs. This works because fish are very social animals, and many species gather in groups. FADs can be as simple as sheets of plastic or tree branches put under a raft, the commercial fishermen then use nets to catch the fish after they aggregate. The concept is similar to what occurs around natural or artificial reefs.

Recent research by scientists from the Universities of California and Hawaii on small yellowfin tuna has shown that the fish tend to hang around FADs in a continuous manner. In some instances, these fish would stay near a specific FAD for up to two months. Their visits could last as long as ten hours, but more often they stayed for an hour or less. Perhaps more interesting is that their departures and arrivals tended to occur at about the same time each day. These observations suggest that yellowfin tuna have a good sense of time, as well as feel for where they are in the open ocean.

Another way to attract fish in the offshore ocean is to put hooked live bait in the water near your boat. The baitfish's struggle often will attract

Fly Fishing Coral Reefs

Coral reefs are an exciting environment for fly fishing. Fishing a coral reef or rocky reef is not much different from working a wreck or other deep structure. There basically are two challenges: getting your fly down to the fish and, when hooked up, preventing the fish from cutting the line on rock or coral.

A sinking line is a must for getting your fly down deep. Because most fish will hug the reef, you'll want to get as close to the rocks or coral as possible. Snagless and weighted flies are needed; Clouser Minnows, with their upward-pointing hooks, are good patterns to use.

Once hooked up, you must prevent the fish from running for the shelter of the reef. With spinning tackle, this means using strong line and a tight drag. When fly-fishing, however, it's a little more difficult to control the fish's run. Your leaders, reel, and rod should be strong enough that you can turn the fish as soon as it is hooked. Use a 50-pound-test abrasion leader, or even some wire.

Positioning your boat is critical to getting your fly in the best position. Never anchor on a coral reef, as the anchor can cause serious damage to the coral; it's usually illegal to do so anyway. One of the great things about fishing on a reef is that you rarely know what you've hooked until you see it.

---

other fish (generally because of the irregular sounds made by the baitfish as it tries to get free). Some species are attracted to the struggles of hooked members of their own species, perhaps interpreting these movements as having something to do with feeding. Many times one fish will follow another hooked fish literally up to your boat, often trying to pull your lure or fly out of the other fish's mouth. The hooked fish knows that it has a problem, but the other fish may be interpreting its movements as an enthusiastic feeding behavior.

Anglers fishing for dolphin (or mahi-mahi) often will let the first hooked fish stay in the water; this frequently will keep the other members of the school nearby. I have heard that this technique can also work on bonito, bluefish, and even striped bass. I personally have never tried it, but it seems reasonable.

TEMPERATURE CHANGES

A temperature change will often determine where offshore fish are located. Sometimes an intrusion of warmer or colder water called a finger will create an edge or boundary where bait may hold. Fingers can result from upwelled water or by the convergence of one current with another, or with a relatively quiet piece of water. Sometimes, part of the Gulf Stream will branch off and form a finger of warmer water that flows close to shore. When you find such a change, fish the edges—fish will often feed there.

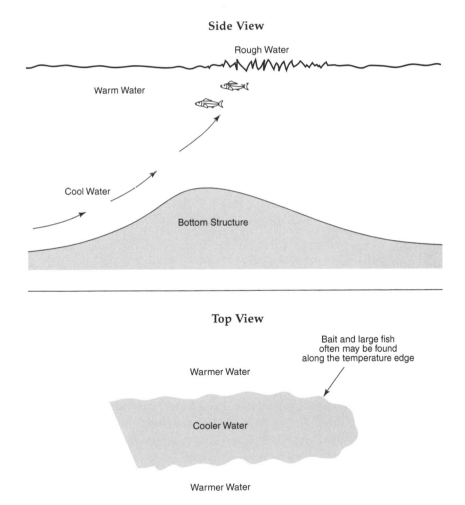

Fig. 11-7 Bottom irregularities can often interfere with water flow, causing upwelling and temperature irregularities, or fingers. These are areas where bait and larger fish may accumulate. Sometimes flotsam will accumulate around the edges of the temperature irregularities.

Having up-to-date temperature data, such as from a satellite service, is a good way to find and track these productive offshore features. You can also detect temperature changes by carefully monitoring the temperature gauge on your fish finder.

Large underwater structures such as wrecks may interfere with current or tidal flow. This interference can be seen on the surface in the form of a rip or similar irregularity, or some temperature variation. In some instances, however, the interference with the water movement causes an irregularity to the flow only below the surface. Both types of areas will attract bait and larger fish. One example of the subsurface variety is "The Hump" off Islamorada, Florida.

WEATHER

Weather can greatly influence offshore fishing. Obviously, bad weather can keep you at home, but there can be more subtle weather effects that can spoil your fishing. For instance, cold weather, winds, or the passage of a front can cause fish to move away from your fishing area. These conditions frequently push nearshore-living fish to offshore areas. Then, after the weather quiets down, the fish may return to nearshore waters. Tarpon seem to follow this pattern along the west coast of Florida. Cold and windy conditions may cause the fish to leave areas such as Charlotte Harbor and temporarily move offshore to the Boca Grande Pass area.

Winds blowing directly against a current or tide will frequently produce high waves and uncomfortable offshore conditions. Don't be confused by descriptions of the direction of the wind and the direction of the current. The wind direction is given according to the direction from which it comes—a southwest wind, for example, comes from the southwest and blows to the northeast. An ocean current, however, is described by the direction in which it flows. In other words, a southwest current flows to the southwest. Using these examples, a southwest wind and a southwest current would be opposing each other.

Basic information about anticipated winds can be obtained from marine radio, local NOAA offices, weather forecasts, or newspapers. If you watch the direction of change in the wind pattern, you can predict the near-term weather. Making such predictions comes from understanding how the wind flows around high- and low-pressure areas. For example, the wind circulation around high-pressure areas generally brings fair weather, whereas the wind circulation around low-pressure areas generally brings bad weather. Winds move clockwise around a high-pressure area and counterclockwise around a low-pressure area. If you note that the wind direction is changing in a counterclockwise direction (for example,

Fishing the Gulf Stream

The Gulf Stream is a favorite area for many Atlantic big-game anglers. This current is the largest in the ocean and moves 100 times more water than all the rivers of the world combined. The Gulf Stream travels at a speed of about 3 to 4 knots, sometimes more, sometimes less. The water in the Gulf Stream, which can be 10 degrees or more warmer than the adjacent water, moves along the east coast of the United States and Canada, then crosses the north Atlantic, and eventually reaches and warms parts of Europe. The Gulf Stream current comes within a few miles of south Florida and within 20 miles of Cape Hatteras, North Carolina. Elsewhere, it's farther offshore; it's as far as 50 to 100 miles away from land where it passes New England.

The water in the Gulf Stream is deep blue in color and is not biologically productive. The blue color is due to the absence of plankton and other floating material in the water. The principal areas to fish are the temperature boundaries or edges between the Gulf Stream and the adjacent water. Here, strong mixing occurs and the waters are biologically productive.

Rings or eddies of warm or cold water often spin off the Gulf Stream and travel as separate entities in the adjacent waters. These eddies sometimes contain significant numbers of fish. Sometimes, small parts of the Gulf Stream branch off, moving fingers of warm water close to shore. This happens off the Florida Keys—in fact, the edge of the Gulf Stream off Florida is well known for its many sailfish.

Anglers who fish the Gulf Stream point to several key factors to determine where to fish. Among the most important are temperature changes, bottom structure, currents, and water color. Some anglers prefer to fish in clear blue water; others like green water near the edge of the Gulf Stream.

from south to east), bad weather with high winds and rain may soon follow. If the winds shift in a clockwise sense (for example, from north to east) fair weather is probable, but the winds may increase as the high pressure crosses your area. These general rules also apply to conditions on land.

Appendix 1

Classification of Ocean Life

L iving things can be classified in many ways, such as by considering various aspects of their body structure (for example, whether or not they have a backbone), where they live, or if they produce their own food. Among scientists, a common way of classifying marine organisms is based on how the organisms move. In this way, marine creatures are divided into three main groups: plankton (organisms that float), nekton (organisms that swim), and benthos (organisms that live on or in the seafloor).

PLANKTON

The word plankton is derived from the Greek word for wandering and applies to a broad and general category of organisms with very weak or limited abilities of movement—if these creatures do move it is generally because they are being carried in a current. Plankton can be animals (zooplankton), plants (phytoplankton), or bacteria (bacterioplankton). Most of the plankton in the ocean are microscopic, although some large floating forms include jellyfish and sargassum weed. In terms of numbers or biomass, plankton are the largest group in the ocean. The density or amount of life in the ocean is called the "biomass," which is defined as the weight of living organisms expressed in grams in a square meter of the ocean bottom or in a cubic meter of sea water (a meter is equal to 3.28 feet, or a little more than a yard). The biomass value typically is higher in nearshore waters and lower in offshore and deep water. Some plankton spend their entire lives as planktonic organisms, others, such as most young fish, may spend only a portion of their lives (usually their early larval stage) as plankton. Those that only spend a portion of their lives as plankton grow to become nektonic (swimming) or benthic (bottom-dwelling) organisms.

Phytoplankton, or floating plants, are the most important individual group of marine life. Through the process of photosynthesis, these plants convert water and carbon dioxide into organic matter, which is the basic food and foundation of the marine food chain. Because phytoplankton are plants and require light for photosynthesis, to survive they must live in the upper, lighted parts of the ocean.

The vertical distribution of phytoplankton is mainly determined by the depth to which sufficient sunlight for photosynthesis can penetrate. This can be just a few feet in nearshore sediment-laden waters to possibly as much as 600 feet in the clear open ocean. Seasonal variations in phytoplankton distribution can be due to the supply of their needed nutrients, to the water temperature, and to the presence of herbivores (organisms that eat plants). Phytoplankton growth can be very rapid—some may have as many as six cell divisions per day—and each cell division doubles the number of organisms, so that 500 organisms could become 32,000 in just one day with six cell divisions.

Zooplankton, or floating animals, are also important in the overall biological cycle of the ocean because they generally feed on the phytoplankton. Many marine animals, including fish, begin their life in a zooplankton stage, during which they float freely in the ocean, relocating and feeding (and also being eaten) as they drift. When zooplankton eat phytoplankton, they make the phytoplankton-derived energy, in the form of organic matter produced by photosynthesis, that's available for higher forms of life. In other words, the zooplankton concentrate the phytoplankton into "bite-size" pieces upon which larger animals can feed. Those organisms feeding only on phytoplankton frequently are called grazers or herbivores.

NEKTON

The word nekton comes from the Greek word for swimming. This category includes animals that are able to swim and move independent of ocean currents. Nekton, as a group, excludes plants, but does include most advanced forms of marine animal life, such as fish and whales. Because nekton are able to swim, they can search actively for food and move about to avoid predators or unsatisfactory environmental conditions. Nekton, especially many species of fish, have voracious feeding habits and thus can impact or limit the survival of other species. Many nekton feed on plankton, including young fish (sometimes even the young of their own species), and in this manner can control their own numbers.

Nekton, because they can swim, are the least restricted form of life in the sea. They can inhabit all parts of the ocean, but the distribution of many species is limited or controlled by water temperature, or other factors; however, the influence of environmental factors on nekton is often not as well understood by scientists as it is for benthic and planktonic life forms.

BENTHOS

The term benthos is derived from the Greek word for deep or deep sea. It is applied to organisms—plants or animals—living on or in the seafloor. Many benthic organisms, such as barnacles and oysters, begin life as plankton and then, after a period of time, attach themselves to the bottom, thus becoming benthos for the remainder of their lives. In water shallow enough for photosynthesis, plants attached to the bottom are part of the benthic life. In the deeper parts of the ocean, the benthic organisms live in perpetual darkness, where the availability of food is limited.

Appendix 2

Some Aspects of Water

Our planet is unique because of the vast quantities of water on its surface. Without water, life as we know it would be impossible and, of course, there would be no ocean, no rivers, and no fish.

For centuries, water was thought to be a separate and indivisible element, rather than a chemical compound consisting of two different elements. It was not until 1783 that water was discovered to be composed of the elements hydrogen and oxygen. The actual chemical composition of water is deceptively simple: two parts hydrogen to one part oxygen or H_2O. Although water is an extremely simple compound, its chemical and physical properties and the way it behaves under certain conditions are remarkably complex.

Water has an ability to literally bond with and dissolve anything that crosses its path. Because of this ability there is a wide variety of chemical compounds dissolved in the ocean. The process starts with rainfall on land that erodes and dissolves minerals and rocks. This material is eventually carried to the oceans by river runoff and rainfall, and ultimately causes most of the ocean's salt content (called its salinity). Volcanic eruptions also add to the ocean's salt content. When sea water evaporates into water vapor, these salts are left behind; the water vapor subsequently condenses and falls as rain. This movement of water between the ocean, atmosphere, and land is called the hydrologic cycle. Some water is always moving from one environment to another.

WATER—SOLID, LIQUID, OR GAS
Water is one of only a few compounds that can occur naturally in three different phases or states: solid (ice), liquid (water), or gas (water vapor). The liquid phase of water dominates on Earth for a single reason: water's high boiling point. Without this high boiling point, life as we know it would be very difficult, if not impossible. The change from one phase to another requires either an addition or a loss of heat. Water is a liquid at

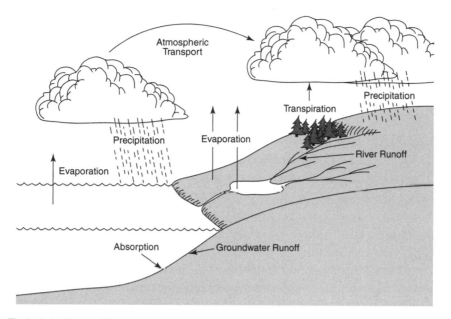

The hydrologic cycle. Transpiration is the evaporation of water through the leaves of plants. Many of the biological uses by plants and animals are not shown.

temperatures where many similar chemical substances have already vaporized into a gas.

When water is in its ice phase, the individual water molecules are tightly bound to each other. However, the structure of the ice keeps the molecules separated by a relatively large distance. In the liquid phase, individual water molecules are not as tightly bound to each other as they are in the ice phase, but this lack of structure in the liquid phase actually allows the individual molecules to be packed closer together. The result of this is that ice is less dense than water, and therefore ice floats on water.

When sea water freezes, the salts it contains are excluded from the ice, which then is composed of relatively pure water; pure water is less dense (or weighs less) than sea water. This fact, combined with the wider spacing of the water molecules in ice, also contributes to the fact that ice floats on sea water. This is very important, because if ice sank (in other words, if ice was more dense than sea water), the ocean would freeze from the bottom up, rather than from the top down. If this happened, it would be catastrophic for those organisms living on the ocean bottom.

Since water constitutes a large portion of the tissues of animals and plants, these organisms must avoid freezing, because the growth of ice crystals will damage or rupture their cell strictures. Some marine fish that live in cold polar or deep-water regions have evolved an antifreeze-like compound to counter this potential problem.

Several properties of sea water can affect the organisms that dwell in the ocean. Some properties offer certain advantages to the creatures that inhabit the ocean; others are not very helpful. The following is a brief list of, and commentary on, some biologically important properties of sea water.

Density

The definition of density is mass per unit volume, usually shown as grams/cubic centimeter (g/cm³). Sea water density has a narrow range, from about 1.022 to 1.030 g/cm³. It is slightly denser than pure water, which is the standard density reference at 1.000 g/cm³.

The density of sea water is sensitive to temperature, salinity, and pressure changes (or depth changes, as pressure increases with depth). Density is an important property of ocean water because it can determine both the motion of sea water (denser water sinks) and the relative position or layering of water with different temperatures or salinities. Looking at density in a vertical sense, the upper 200 to 300 feet of the ocean is usually sufficiently mixed by waves and the wind so that it has a relatively uniform density. Around or below this depth there will be rapid changes in temperature and salinity that will produce a corresponding rapid change in the density. The density usually then slowly increases from there to the bottom.

Buoyancy

Because the density of sea water is generally similar to the density of most marine organisms, sea water provides some support or buoyancy for many ocean creatures. One benefit of this buoyancy is that it eliminates or reduces the need for organisms to have a supporting skeletal structure. Examples of animals without a complex supporting structure are jellyfish and other small floating animals, including some fish. This buoyancy allows extremely large animals, such as whales, to grow and live in the ocean; similar-size animals on land would be too heavy to move about or to survive. The buoyancy provided by sea water also makes it easier for the various forms of plankton to float.

Pressure

Pressure in the ocean results from the weight of the overlying water and air. It ranges from 1 atmosphere (or 14.7 pounds per square inch) at the ocean surface to about 1,100 atmospheres (more than 8 tons per square inch) in the deepest parts of the ocean (slightly more than 36,000 feet). Although pressure does affect some biological aspects of marine life, many organisms have adapted to it. If an animal has a swimbladder, as many fish do, changing its depth will cause a pressure change on its swimbladder that can cause internal difficulties. In particular, the animal will have to expel gas if it goes deeper, because of the pressure increase. For those marine organisms without a gas bladder or internal air spaces, the pressure inside and outside the body will be the same, so little or no special protection or behavior against pressure is needed.

Viscosity

Viscosity, a measure of the internal resistance of a fluid to flow or motion, can be a handicap for swimming organisms such as fish, who must move the water in front of them as they swim forward. The more streamlined an organism, the better it can overcome the slowing effect of the viscosity of water. In nature, many marine organisms are streamlined, especially fish such as tuna and mammals such as porpoises. The streamlining of fish has been applied by engineers in ship design to help hulls move faster and more efficiently through the water.

Heat Capacity

The high heat capacity of water has implications for the ocean and for the creatures that live in it. Water temperatures in the ocean range from about 28.4 to 86 degrees Fahrenheit, a range of about 58 degrees. The surface of the land has a much wider range of temperature, about 180 degrees, and the atmosphere's range is even greater. The high heat capacity of the ocean, combined with its ability to store heat below the surface, helps moderate the temperature on Earth, and prevents wide variations in temperature, making the planet more inhabitable. That water stores large amounts of heat also has an important influence on various weather phenomena. For example, evaporation removes considerable heat energy from the ocean and transfers this energy into the atmosphere when the evaporated water (warm-water vapor) rises. The heat is stored in the atmosphere until the water vapor cools and condenses. Condensation releases this stored energy harmlessly as rain, or destructively as violent storms or hurricanes.

Stability

In general, the physical and chemical characteristics of sea water are stable, and do not change quickly. Therefore, most marine organisms are not exposed or subjected to any sudden environmental changes in temperature or salinity. Shallow coastal areas, especially near rivers, can be an exception.

Carbon Dioxide

In the ocean, CO_2 occurs both as a gas and in various compounds. It is involved in complicated, interrelated, and important biological and chemical interactions, including serving as one of the components in the calcareous shells of organisms, and as part of a chemical buffer system that stabilizes the pH of sea water. Although not directly related to the well-being of marine fish, the ability of the ocean to hold large amounts of CO_2, a major greenhouse gas, is of considerable importance in the understanding and prediction of the future implications of global warming due to the increasing amounts of greenhouse gases in the atmosphere.

Buffering

Sea water is what is called a buffered solution, which means it behaves like a chemical shock absorber, limiting changes in its acidity/alkalinity, or its pH. Sea water usually is slightly alkaline and has a pH between 7.5 and 8.4. (A value of less than 7.0 is acidic, and above 7.0 is alkaline.) That sea water is alkaline is critical for organisms that form calcium carbonate shells, such as clams or oysters—if sea water was acidic, the calcium carbonate could be dissolved.

Appendix 3

Photosynthesis and Respiration

The photosynthetic and respiration processes together make up the organic cycle in the ocean. Photosynthesis is what is called an endothermic reaction, which means that it is driven by energy. The energy in the process comes from sunlight. Certain nutrients and various trace elements are also necessary for photosynthesis to occur. The principal nutrients are nitrogen and phosphorus compounds. Chlorophyll, a green-colored pigment in plants that lets them use the energy from sunlight in the photosynthetic process, also plays a role. The basic photosynthetic equation is:

$$CO_2 + H_2O + \text{solar (light) energy} \rightarrow \text{organic matter} + O_2$$

Solar energy, combined with carbon dioxide gas and liquid water, yields organic matter (generally expressed as some variation of CH_2O, commonly the carbohydrate called glucose, $C_6H_{12}O_6$) and oxygen gas. This process releases oxygen into the water.

The reverse of the photosynthesis reaction is called respiration or oxidation, during which organic matter is consumed either by the plant itself or by whatever eats the plant. This process uses oxygen and ultimately returns nutrients back to the water. Respiration, unlike photosynthesis, does not require light energy and can therefore occur at any depth and at any time. The respiration equation is simply the reverse of the photosynthetic equation (without solar energy):

$$\text{organic matter} + O_2 \rightarrow CO_2 + H_2O$$

Because sunlight is necessary for photosynthesis, how far light penetrates into the ocean determines the depth at which plants can live. In the clear open ocean, under the best conditions, light can reach a depth of 600 feet, but in most areas of the ocean light doesn't reach that deep. This explains why plants attached to the seafloor are restricted only to the shallow and well-lit portions of the ocean. The need for sufficient sun-

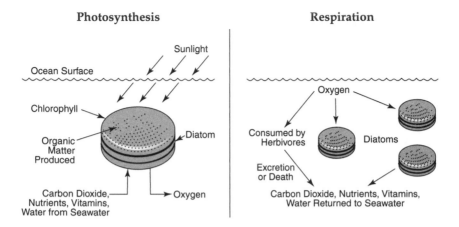

The organic cycle in the ocean, using a diatom (a floating plant or phytoplankton) as an example.

light also explains why essentially all marine plants are planktonic—they must float in the nearsurface waters to receive the light they need for photosynthesis; thus most marine plants are small, and many are microscopic, so that they can easily float.

The key nutrients for plant growth, nitrogen and phosphorus, are initially supplied to the ocean by rivers, but they quickly can be removed from sea water by plants. Once the nutrients are incorporated into plants, they return to sea water only when the plants die, or when the animals that eat the plants die and decompose or excrete the nutrients. If the nutrients are returned to the sea water below the zone where photosynthesis can occur, then some mechanism, such as upwelling is required to move the nutrients back to the surface waters for their use by the plants. Areas of upwelling, or where the waters are well mixed, such as coastal areas, usually are areas of high biological productivity and frequently have large numbers of fish.

Appendix 4

Computer Tide Programs

A detailed review of all tide computer programs is beyond the scope of this appendix. I suspect that there are many other programs than the ones mentioned here, including those for foreign countries as well as some that provide very localized information. Advanced navigational or charting computer programs also may come with tidal packages.

The programs here all use the same basic tidal data, mainly from National Ocean Survey of the National Oceanic and Atmospheric Admin istration, and similar organizations such as the Department of Fisheries and Oceans in Canada and other countries. Let me emphasize here, as I did in Chapter 2, that these programs make tidal *predictions*—the actual tidal stage may vary due to factors such as the weather.

HARBOR MASTER

As best I know, there is only one tide-and-current-prediction program that runs on Macintosh computers, and that's Harbor Master, produced by Zihua Software (P.O. Box 336, Marlborough, CT 06447, 1-800-659-0155 or zihua@tiac.net). The same as most Macintosh programs, it is very easy to use. Harbor Master can also run on any IBM-compatible PC using Windows 95 or later, or Windows NT. The program provides ten years of tide-and-current data for the East and West Coast of the United States, as well as for Mexico, Bermuda, Belize, Guatemala, Honduras, and the West Indies. The cost is $100.

The program shows tidal-and-current data in various formats, from a single day to a month in duration, and can include the stages of the moon, sunrise, twilight, sunset, and lunar perigee and apogee. The resulting tidal-or-current curves can be stacked one above the other, shown in sequence, or in a calendar mode; the data can also be displayed in a text format. You can also add notes for favorite locations, search for tides of a specific height, and be warned about unusually high or low tides. Check www.zihuasoftware.com for more information.

TIDES AND CURRENTS

Perhaps the best-known, most-versatile, and best-selling tidal computer program is Tides and Currents, produced by Nautical Software in Beaverton, Oregon (call 1-800-946-2877; send e-mail to info@tides.com; or check out the Web site at www.tides.com). The program runs on Windows 3.1 or MS-DOS 5.0 or later versions. The DOS version can be configured to work on computers with limited memory, such as laptops. With Tides and Currents, you can get data packages for essentially any part of the world, and the predictions will work out to the year 2100. The Windows version for either the East or West Coast of the United States sells for $129; the DOS version is $79.

Tides and Currents is a sophisticated and impressive program, with many bells and whistles that can produce a wide variety of reports and data. You can easily change from a screen showing currents to one showing the tide and you can display several screens at once. You can also use the program to look at past tides, such as the tide on that great day you had several years ago. Tides and Currents can also link up with various navigation programs that Nautical Software produces.

ELDRIDGE TIDEWARE

This tidal program is based on the famous *Eldridge Tide and Pilot Book*. The program contains six years of tidal data, from 1999 to 2004; more data is available from the company's Web site, www.tideware.com, or call (877) 843-3927. The program works on PC-compatible computers using Windows 95, 98, or NT 4.0 with a 486DX or better processor. The program sells for $119. I have not tried TideWare, but it seems to be sophisticated and useful. Among other things, it will provide a real-time graph of the level of the tide over a period of time for a particular area; therefore, you can watch the ocean come into and move through the areas you might want to fish.

Appendix 5

Classifying Ocean Fish

CLASSES OF FISH

Jawless Fish—Lampreys and Hagfish

These fish are generally eel-like in appearance and distinguished by their lack of a jaw, scales, and paired fins. About forty known species of lampreys are found in fresh and salt water; hagfish only occur in the ocean. Some lampreys are parasites and attach themselves to other fish and kill or weaken them by sucking out their internal fluids. Hagfish, of which there are about fifty known species, are sometimes called slime eels and usually feed on small invertebrates and dead organisms.

Neither of these fish is important to sportfishing, other than the damage that lampreys can cause to some game fish. In some areas, lampreys are used for food or harvested as a source of light oil. Hagfish are sought by commercial fishermen because their tough skin can be used to make leatherlike items that are marketed as being made of "eel skin."

Cartilaginous Fish—Sharks, Rays, and Chimeras

These graceful fish can vary considerably in their appearance, but have common aspects that distinguish them from the other classes of fish. The main differences are that their skeletons are composed of a tough but elastic tissue called cartilage rather than real bone; they also lack swimbladders. Many members of this class of fish live on or very near the ocean bottom, probably due to their lack of swimbladders. Cartilaginous fish usually have mouths located on the underside of the body and eyes on top, with several gill slits on each side of the head.

About 850 species of sharks and rays are presently known. Most sharks are long-lived; some species of dogfish can live for eighty years. Females may not become sexually mature until they are thirty years old, and then produce only a few live young. With the increasing harvest of sharks (often just for their fins), the future survival of some species may be precarious.

Many sharks are perceived as dangerous to humans but in actuality most are harmless; shark attacks on humans are rare. There are many more elephant attacks on humans, for example. It is estimated that for each known shark attack on a human, about one million sharks are killed by humans. On the other hand, sharks are among the most successful predators in the ocean.

Rays are distinctive-looking, flattened fish. Some have very small tails, or in a place of a tail they have a whiplike spine that can be poisonous. Most rays are bottom-feeders. An exception is the large and graceful manta ray, which filters its food from sea water. A few rays have electric organs that they can use to stun prey and keep predators away; some can produce up to 200 volts, a level that can be harmful to humans.

Chimeras are relatively rare—only thirty species are known, and they are mainly found in moderately deep water, living and feeding on the bottom. They are commonly called ratfish because of their long tails.

Bony Fish
This class of fish is the largest. Its members are found in all parts of the ocean and in most freshwater environments. Most popular game fish species—bass, tuna, bluefish, bonefish, billfish, and trout—belong to this class. Bony fish are distinguished by their bony (calcified) skeleton, a single gill slit on each side of the head, and a mouth generally at the front of the head. Most have a gas-filled swimbladder, which they use to help maintain their buoyancy in the water. (The term "teleosts" is sometimes used for living bony fishes.) Eels, of which 600 species are known (most live in marine waters), also belong to the bony-fish category. Eels are valued as food in many parts of the world, although not so much in the United States; however, they are superb bait for big striped bass.

WARM- AND COLD-BLOODED FISH
Most bony fish and sharks are cold-blooded, which means that their internal body temperature is the same as that of the surrounding water. The high heat capacity of water makes it hard for fish to have a temperature higher than the surrounding water; also, fish easily lose heat through their skin and gills. There are a few exceptions to being cold-blooded, these include white sharks, tunas, swordfish, and marlin, which are somewhat warm-blooded and can maintain an internal temperature in parts of their body that is higher than the temperature of the surrounding water. In most instances it is just the brain, eyes, or a few other parts of the body that are being kept warm. Some bluefin tuna may have an internal temperature as high as 90 degrees Fahrenheit, regardless of the temperature

of the surrounding water. Other active fish, such as mackerel, bonito, and yellowtail, have internal temperatures just slightly (about 2 degrees) higher than the surrounding water.

The advantage of having a warmer internal temperature is that it allows the animal to maintain a higher metabolism. With a higher metabolism, these fish can convert food into energy quicker and over a wider range of water temperatures than cold-blooded species. Warmer muscles contract faster than cold muscles, which in turn allows a fish to swim faster to search for prey, or to avoid being eaten. A decrease in internal temperature will reduce the fish's metabolism and lead to slower movement. This may, in part, explain the reduction in the fighting and swimming ability of some fish as the water temperature decreases with the changing seasons. Many species of fish prefer waters of a specific temperature range and will leave a region and move elsewhere if the temperature gets out of that range.

Appendix 6

Adaptation

Animals that live in the ocean must adapt to their environment. Those fish living in shallow, estuarine, or coastal waters must be able to survive the variations in temperature and salinity that often occur in these environments. Despite the more arduous physical conditions in the nearshore region, this part of the ocean offers several ecological advantages to fish, namely abundant food, oxygen, and light. Plant growth is usually high in this environment, so organic matter (food) is usually abundant.

In the open ocean, most of the physical and chemical characteristics of sea water are relatively stable, or at least are slow to change; therefore, the marine organisms living there don't often face sudden environmental changes. The reasons why animals inhabit one region of the ocean over another are not known. Certainly, factors such as temperature, feeding habits, and availability of food and light are important factors.

Salinity can determine where fish go, but this factor is more significant in coastal and estuarine waters, in which temperature changes are common. Oceanic animals, perhaps because they have adapted to the constancy of salinity, generally cannot tolerate significant salinity changes. Most will die if currents carry them to an area in which the salinity is significantly different from their normal environment.

Water temperature often establishes faunal boundaries in the ocean. Some fish, however, can move freely from one area into another, regardless of the water temperature. For example, the migration patterns of bluefin tuna show that they can range over most of the ocean. Other fish are more restricted and spend their entire lives within a narrow temperature range.

Most fish can acclimate to changing temperatures in their environment. This may explain why some migrating species are occasionally stranded in a certain area. These fish may get by for a while, but they eventually become stressed and do not survive. Older members of a species usually can tolerate temperature variations and extremes better than the younger or immature members of the same species. Offshore fish tend to live within a narrower temperature range than nearshore fish do. In general, rapid and sudden changes in water temperature are dangerous to fish, though they can acclimate to or move away from an area in which a slow change is underway.

Laboratory experiments on fish indicate that they can detect slight water-temperature changes (less than a fraction of a degree), as well as distinguish if the temperature is rising or falling. However, little is known about how fish actually detect temperature changes and what sensors or organs are used to do so. Their skin is certainly involved, and in some species the lateral-line system shows a response to temperature.

Most of the metabolic processes of fish speed up in warm water and slow down in cool water. These processes include oxygen consumption, growth, swimming rates, feeding, and digestion. In general, for each 18-degree-Fahrenheit (10-degree-Celsius) increase in water temperature, there will be a corresponding doubling in the rate of most biological processes of fish. Conversely, a fish will experience a reduction in the rate of most of its metabolic processes with a drop in water temperature. Further, warm water contains less dissolved oxygen than colder water, and this lack of oxygen can subject fish to increased stress; thus, most fish do better in colder-than-usual temperatures than warmer-than-usual temperatures.

References

The following is a list of marine and fishery science books and articles I used or consulted in preparing this book. I have also listed some of the important saltwater fly-fishing books, but I have not included those on specific species. Other sources of information include marine fishing magazines such as: *Saltwater Fly Fishing, Fly Fishing in Salt Water, Salt Water Sportsman,* and *Sport Fishing.* Local magazines, such as *On The Water,* from New England, *The Fisherman,* from the East Coast, *Florida Sportsman,* and others from the West and Gulf Coast provide valuable information. Freshwater-oriented magazines, such as *Fly Fisherman, American Angler, Fly Tyer,* and *Fly Rod and Reel,* often have an article or two on saltwater fly fishing.

Anderson, Al. *To Catch A Tuna.* Mystic, CT: MT Publications, 1990.

Bardach, J. E., J. J. Magnuson, R. C. May, and J. M. Reinhart, editors. *Fish Behavior and Its Use in the Capture and Culture of Fishes.* International Center for Living Aquatic Resources Management, 1980.

Beck, Barry and Cathy. *Fly Fishing the Flats.* Mechanicsburg, PA: Stackpole Books, 1999.

Block, B. B., H. Dewar, T. Williams, E. D. Prince, C. Farwell, and D. Fudge. "Archival Tagging of Atlantic Bluefin Tuna." *Marine Technology Society Journal,* 32, No. 1, 27–46, 1998.

Bone, Q., N. B. Marshall, and J. H. S. Blaxter. *Biology of Fishes,* 2nd edition. London: Chapman and Hall, 1995.

Bowditch, N. *The American Practical Navigator.* Defense Mapping Agency Hydrographic/Topographic Center, Bethesda, MD: 1995.

Combs, Trey. *Bluewater Fly Fishing.* New York: Lyons and Burford, 1995.

Cox, Bob. *Uptide and Boatcasting.* London: Beekay Publishers, 1990.

Duxbury, A. C., and A. B. Duxbury. *An Introduction to the World's Oceans.* Dubuque, IA: Wm. C. Brown Pub., 1989.

Earnhardt, Tom. *Fly Fishing the Tidewaters.* New York: Lyons and Burford, 1995.

Fox, W. T. *At The Sea's Edge.* A Fireside Book, Simon and Schuster, 1983.

Hewitt, P. G., J. Suchoki, and L. A. Hewitt. *Conceptual Physical Science.* New York: HarperCollins, 1994.

Janzow, Fred, and Rudolph Miller. "An Experiment on Visual Discrimination in the Largemouth Bass Micropterus Salmoides." *Proceedings of the Oklahoma Academy of Sciences*, 59, 34–40, 1979.

Johnson, C. Paul. *The Scientific Angler*. New York: Charles Schribner's Sons, 1984.

Johnson, F. G., and R. R. Stickney, editors. *Fisheries*. Dubuque IA: Kendall/Hunt Pub. Co., 1989.

Kageyama, C. J. *What Fish See: Understanding Optics and Color Shifts for Designing Lures and Flies*. Portland, OR: Frank Amato, 1999.

Kreh, Lefty. *Fly Fishing in Salt Water*. New York: Lyons and Burford, 1999.

Lagler, K. F., J. E. Bardach, R. R. Miller, and D. R. M. Passino. *Ichthyology*. New York: John Wiley and Sons, 1977.

Lerman, Matthew. *Marine Biology—Environment, Diversity, and Ecology*. Menlo Park, CA: Benjamin/Cummings Pub Co., 1986.

Levine, J. S., P. S. Lobel, and E. F. MacNichol, Jr. "Visual Communication in Fishes." *Environmental Physiology of Fishes*, edited by M. A. Ali. New York: Plenum Press, 1980, 447–475.

Marshall, N. B. *The Life of Fishes*. London: Weidenfeld and Nicolson, 1965.

Mitchell, Ed. *Fly Rodding the Coast*. Mechanicsburg, PA: Stackpole Books, 1995.

Moyle, P. B., and J. J. Cech Jr. *Fishes and Introduction to Ichthyology*. 3rd edition. Upper Saddle River, NJ: Prentice Hall, 1996.

Nakamura, H. *Tuna Distribution and Migration*. London: Fishing News Books, 1969.

National Oceanic and Atmospheric Administration. *Estuaries of the United States, Vital Statistics of a National Resource Base*, 1990.

National Oceanic and Atmospheric Administration. *Coastal Wetlands of the Continental United States*, edited by M. C. Watzin and J. G. Gosselink, 1992.

Pinet, P. R. *Oceanography: An Introduction to the Planet Oceanus*. St. Paul MN: West Publishing Co., 1992.

Pitcher, T. J. editor. *The Behavior of Teleost Fish*. London: Chapman and Hall, 1993.

Preble, David. *Fly Fishing Offshore: Cape Cod to Cape Hatteras*. Point Pleasant, NJ: The Fisherman Library Corp., 1998.

Raymond, Steve. *The Estuary Flyfisher*. Portland, OR: Frank Amato, 1996.

Roberts, Jr., G. V. *A Fly Fisher's Guide To Saltwater Naturals And Their Imitations*. Camden, ME: Ragged Mountain Press, 1994.

Ross, David A. *Introduction to Oceanography*. New York: HarperCollins, 1995.

Royce, W. F. *Fishery Development.* New York: Academic Press, 1987.

Royce, W. F. *Introduction to the Practice of Fishery Science.* Academic Press, 1996.

Sosin, Mark, and J. Clark. *Through the Fish's Eye.* New York: Harper and Row, 1973.

Swisher, Doug, and Carl Richards. *Backcountry Fly Fishing in Salt Water.* New York: Lyons and Burford, 1995.

Tabory, Lou. *Inshore Fly Fishing.* New York: Lyons and Burford, 1992.

Webber, H. H. and H. V. Thurman. *Marine Biology.* 2nd edition. New York: HarperCollins, 1991.

Zupanc, G. K. H. *Fish and Their Behavior.* Melle, Germany: Tetra-Verlag, 1988.

Figure Credits

Several figures were adapted from my 1995 book *Introduction to Oceanography*. Jack Cook of the graphics department at Woods Hole Oceanographic Institution redrafted many of these figures. Other figures or photographs were either kindly given to me for use by those indicated below, adapted from other figures, or created for this book. I would like to acknowledge the following:

Chapter 2 Figure 2-1, from the Falmouth Enterprise; Figure 2-5, adapted from the U.S. Naval Oceanographic Office; Figure 2-8, from the U.S. Department of Commerce.

Chapter 3 Figure 3-2, from Larry Largay based on a drawing from the author; Figure 3-4, adapted from the National Oceanic and Atmospheric Administration; Figure 3-8, adapted from U.S. National Ocean Service; Figure 3-9, from Dr. Ivan Valiela; Figure 3-10, from Dr. David Duane; Figure 3-12, adapted from Prof. Matthew Lerman, 1986.

Chapter 4 Figure 4-1, from Capt. Tony Biski; Figure 4-6, from Dr. David Aubrey.

Chapter 6 Figure 6-4, adapted from Prof. Matthew Lerman, 1986; Figure 6-9, data from Marine Recreational Fisheries of Massachusetts.

Chapter 8 Figure 8-3, from Dr. Larry Pratt.

Chapter 10 Figure 10-3, from Ellen Wild; Figure 10-9, from Richard Pittenger.

Chapter 11 Figure 11-1, adapted from Capt. Al Anderson, 1990.

Index